SIX AGES OF EUROPEAN HISTORY

From A.D. 476 to 1878

IN SIX VOLUMES

General Editor: A. H. JOHNSON, M.A.

FELLOW OF ALL SOULS COLLEGE, OXFORD

VOLUME VI

THE REMAKING OF MODERN EUROPE
1789-1878

THE REMAKING OF MODERN EUROPE

FROM THE OUTBREAK OF THE FRENCH REVOLUTION TO THE TREATY OF BERLIN

1789-1878

BY

SIR J. A. R. MARRIOTT

M.A., M.P.

HONORARY FELLOW, FORMERLY FELLOW OF
WORCESTER COLLEGE, OXFORD

WITH TEN MAPS

EIGHTEENTH EDITION

METHUEN & CO. LTD.
36 ESSEX STREET W.C.
LONDON

First Published	-	-	-	January 14th 1909
Second Edition	-	-	-	December	1909
Third Edition	-	-	-	November	1910
Fourth Edition	-	-	-	September	1911
Fifth Edition	-	-	-	May	1913
Sixth Edition	-	-	-	September	1914
Seventh Edition	-	-	-	October	1914
Eighth Edition	-	-	-	March	1915
Ninth Edition	-	-	-	November	1915
Tenth Edition	-	-	-	April	1918
Eleventh Edition	-	-	-	September	1919
Twelfth Edition	-	-	-	October	1920
Thirteenth Edition		.	.	April	1922
Fourteenth Edition		.	.	January	1923
Fifteenth Edition		.	.	February	1924
Sixteenth Edition		.	.	October	1925
Seventeenth Edition		-	-	October	1926
Eighteenth Edition		-	-		1927

PRINTED IN GREAT BRITAIN

TO

E. D. C. M.

PREFACE

THIS little book is intended primarily for students who are beginning the study of foreign history at Schools and Universities. Such students generally have an examination in view, but this is not a cram book. My hope is that it may be found suggestive and stimulating, but not satisfying. That it will serve the less well, on that account, as a text-book for examinations I do not believe, since the best examiners do all in their power to discourage "cram". But it will fail of its main purpose if it does not stimulate a desire for bigger and better books and ampler information.

Any one who has been set down to write the history of a crowded period in a given number of words will judge leniently its many imperfections. Such a task involves a perpetual choice between obscurity and incompleteness. As lucidity seems to me the one essential quality in an introductory sketch I have not hesitated to prefer it to every other consideration. How far I have attained even to this virtue my readers alone can judge. There are glaring omissions, especially in the second part of the book (1815-1878); but within the allotted limits of space I could do no more than suggest the great outstanding achievements of the period. It is my hope some day to fill in the sketch here presented.

I have made free use of the works of my predecessors in the same field, but I hope that I have not, without acknowledgment, appropriated their ideas or phrases. No one, however, who has been for many years teaching a particular subject can be at all certain that his most cherished ideas and most original phrases are really his own. On this point many have suffered cruel disillusionment. For any unwitting and unacknowledged appropriation I crave pardon.

The maps have been designed to subserve an historical rather than a geographical purpose—to emphasise the main lessons which it is the purpose of the text to enforce. I am grateful to Mr. Darbishire for the patience and skill with which he has interpreted my wishes in the matter. For the index I am indebted to the assistance of my wife.

My thanks are due to the Editor of the series for constant advice; but that is no uncommon or recent debt. Not a few teachers of history in Oxford have incurred a heavy debt to him, and mine is among the heaviest. I am grateful also to my friend, Mr. C. R. L. Fletcher, of Magdalen College, for reading the proofs of the early part (1789-1815), and to the Rev. A. B. Beaven, who performed a similar service for the later. Neither of these eminent scholars is responsible for any errors which may appear, but both have saved me from many which do not.

J. A. R. M

WORCESTER COLLEGE
OXFORD
December, 1908

NOTE TO SECOND EDITION

I HAVE to thank my critics and also several correspondents for pointing out slips, and for various suggestions. I have corrected the former and carefully considered the latter. Where they have not been adopted it has generally been from lack of space.

J. A. R. M.

November, 1909

NOTE TO THIRD EDITION

A FEW new " Authorities " have been added, and one or two notes.

J. A. R. M.

October, 1910

NOTE TO FOURTH EDITION

I HAVE corrected a few inconsistencies of spelling and description, detected for the most part by the vigilance of Mr. C. T. Knaus of the Grammar School, Bradford, to whom I wish to express my cordial thanks.

J. A. R. M.

April, 1911

NOTE TO FIFTH EDITION

A NEW edition is called for just at the moment when the polities of Eastern Europe are in a state of solution, and I have thought it better, therefore, to make no change, for the present, in the text of Chapters XIII. and XV. I have added a few recent works to the list contained in Appendix II.

J. A. R. M.

November, 1912

NOTE TO SEVENTEENTH EDITION

I HAVE thought it better to make practically no change in the text of this book ; but, with a view to amplifying and bringing up to date statements in the text, I have added notes to pp. 152, 172, and 241, in which I have ventured to refer students to the information pertinent thereto contained in my more recent works.

J. A. R. M.

June, 1926

CONTENTS

PAGE

CHAPTER I.

INTRODUCTORY - - - - - - - - - 1

CHAPTER II.

THE FRENCH REVOLUTION (1789-1793) - - - - 10

CHAPTER III.

THE CONSTITUENT ASSEMBLY—THE MAKING OF THE CONSTITUTION 21

CHAPTER IV.

EUROPE AND THE REVOLUTION - - - - - - - 32

CHAPTER V.

ENGLAND AND FRANCE—THE REIGN OF TERROR - - - - 40

CHAPTER VI.

THE ADVENT OF NAPOLEON BONAPARTE. THE REACTION IN FRANCE (1794-1802) - - - - - - - - 52

CHAPTER VII.

THE CONSULATE AND THE EMPIRE—ENGLAND AND NAPOLEON - 70

CHAPTER VIII.

TILSIT AND THE CONTINENTAL SYSTEM - - - - 83

CHAPTER IX.

THE NATIONALIST REACTION—THE PENINSULA—GERMANY - - 90

CHAPTER X.

THE MOSCOW CAMPAIGN AND THE WAR OF LIBERATION (1812-1814) 103

PAGE

CHAPTER XI.
THE CONGRESS OF VIENNA AND THE SETTLEMENT OF 1815—THE
HUNDRED DAYS AND WATERLOO - - - - - - 119

CHAPTER XII.
RESTORATION AND REACTION—THE HOLY ALLIANCE - - - 132

CHAPTER XIII.
THE GREEK WAR OF INDEPENDENCE AND THE EASTERN QUESTION 145

CHAPTER XIV.
FRANCE AND HER REVOLUTIONS (1830-1852) - - - - 153

CHAPTER XV.
THE CRIMEAN WAR AND AFTER (1852-1878) - - - - 165

CHAPTER XVI.
REACTION AND REVOLUTION IN ITALY (1815-1849) - - - 173

CHAPTER XVII.
THE UNIFICATION OF ITALY (1859-1871) - - - - - 185

CHAPTER XVIII.
GERMANY (1815-1851)—REACTION, REVOLUTION AND REACTION - 193

CHAPTER XIX.
THE PRUSSIANISATION OF GERMANY (1860-1870) - - - 207

CHAPTER XX.
THE SECOND EMPIRE AND THE FRANCO-GERMAN WAR - - 216

CHAPTER XXI.
AFTERWORD - - - - - - - - - - - 231

APPENDIX I. - - - - - - - - - - 243

APPENDIX II. - - - - - - - - - - 249

INDEX - - - - - - - - - - - 253

CHRONOLOGICAL TABLE OF CONTENTS

		PAGE
1789.	Causes of the French Revolution	14
	Outbreak of French Revolution	10
	Meeting of States-general (May 5)	10
	Tiers état declare themselves National Assembly (June 17)	12
	Oath of the Tennis Court (June 20)	12
	Fall of Bastille (July 14)	12
	Abolition of feudalism (Aug. 4)	21
	Declaration of Rights of Man (Aug.)	22
	Mirabeau	23
	"March of the Maenads" (Oct. 5 and 6)	24
1790.	The new Constitution	25
	Burke's *Reflections*	42
1791.	Death of Mirabeau (April 2)	27
	Flight to Varennes (June 20)	27
	Republican *Fête* (July 17)	28
	The Legislative Assembly (Oct. 1)	29
	The Non-jurors	30
	The *Émigrés*	31
	Declaration of Pilnitz (Aug.)	33
1792.	Death of Emperor Leopold (Mar. 1)	34
	The Girondist Ministry	34
	Louis XVI. declares war on Austria (April 20)	34
	French reverses	34
	Attack on the Tuileries (June 20)	35
	Prussia declares war on France (July 25)	35
	Brunswick's manifesto	35
	The Tenth of August	35
	Advance of the allies	36
	The September massacres	37
	Danton and the National Defence	37
	Valmy (Sept. 20)	37

		PAGE
1792.	French victories -	37
	The National Convention (Sept. 21)	38
	Abolition of the Monarchy (Sept. 21) -	38
	Propagandist decrees (Nov. and Dec.)	40
1793.	Execution of Louis XVI. (Jan. 21) -	38
	Second Partition of Poland (Jan.)	54
	France declares war on England and Holland (Feb. 1)	44
	France declares war on Spain (Mar.) -	44
	Success of the allies (Feb.-Aug.)	46
	Defeat of Dumouriez at Neerwinden (Mar. 18) -	46
	Rising in La Vendée -	46
	Fall of Girondists (June 2) -	46
	Committee of Public Safety (appointed Jan., reorganised July) -	46
	Carnot reorganises French army (Sept.) -	46
	Reign of Terror in France (June-July, 1794)	47
	French victories (Oct.-Dec.)	46, 47
	Execution of Queen Marie Antoinette (Oct. 16) -	48
	Execution of leading Girondists (Oct. 31) -	48
1794.	Fall of Hébertists (Mar. 24), Dantonists (April 5)	49, 50
	The Triumvirate -	50
	Howe's naval victory (June 1) -	53
	Jourdan's victory at Fleurus (June 26)	54
	Thermidorian reaction (July)	50
	Death of Robespierre (July 28) -	51
	French victories -	53
	Belgium incorporated in France -	54
1795.	Conquest of Holland by France -	54
	The Batavian Republic	54
	Third Partition of Poland -	54
	Break up of First Coalition	54
	Peace with Tuscany and Naples -	54
	Treaties of Basle (April and July)	54
	Suppression of risings in La Vendée and Brittany -	55
	Directorial Constitution (Nov.) -	55
	13th Vendémiaire (Oct. 4) -	56
	Napoleon Bonaparte -	57
	English occupation of Cape Colony -	63
	English conquests in East and West Indies	63
1796.	Napoleon Bonaparte's Italian campaign (Lodi, May 10; Arcola, Nov. 15) -	58

PAGE

1796. Check to French in Southern Germany - - - - 59
English conquest of French and Dutch Colonies - - 63
Hoche's expedition to Bantry Bay (Dec.) - - - 63
Failure of Pitt's peace negotiations (March and Dec.) - 64

1797. Battle of Rivoli (Jan. 14) - - - - - - 60
Treaty of Tolentino (Feb.) - - - - - - 59
Siege of Mantua (June, 1796-Feb. 2), its surrender - - 60
English victory off Cape St. Vincent (Feb. 14) - - 63
Reorganisation of Italy : Cispadane, Cisalpine and
    Ligurian Republics (May) - - - - - 60
Troubles in England - - - - - - - 63
Pitt's peace negotiatins (July) - - - - - 64
Coup d'état of 18th Fructidor (Sept. 4) - - - 61
English victory at Camperdown (Oct. 11) - - - 63
Treaty of Campo-Formio (Oct. 17) - - - - 62
Cisalpine Republic - - - - - - - 60

1798. Roman Republic (Feb. 15) - - - - - 64
Helvetian Republic (April 12) - - - - - 64
Napoleon's Egyptian expedition (May, 1798-Oct., 1799) - 64
Malta seized (June 11) - - - - - - 64
Capture of Alexandria (July 2) - - - - - 64
Battle of the Pyramids (July 23) - - - - 64
Nelson's victory at the Nile (Aug. 1) - - - 64
The Second Coalition (England, Russia, Naples, Turkey,
    Portugal, Austria) (Nov. and Dec.) - - - 65

1799. Parthenopean Republic (Jan.) - - - - - 66
Napoleon in Syria (Feb.) - - - - - - 65
Siege of Acre (Mar.-May) - - - - - - 65
Victories of allies - - - - - - - 66
Archduke Charles on Upper Rhine and in Switzerland
    (Mar.-Sept.) - - - - - - - 66
Kray and Suvarroff in Italy (Mar.-Aug.) - - - 66
Napoleon's victory at Aboukir (July 24) - - - 65
His return to France (Oct.) - - - - - 65
Coup d'état of 18th Brumaire (Nov. 9) - - - 65
Establishment of Consulate (Dec.) - - - - 71
Russia retires from Coalition - - - - - 68

1800. Marengo Campaign - - - - - - - 67
Moreau in South Germany - - - - - 67
Napoleon wins Marengo (June 14) - - - - 67
Reconquest of Italy - - - - - - - 67

b

PAGE

1800. Moreau wins Hohenlinden (Dec. 3) - - - - - 67
       Armed neutrality *v.* England (Dec.) - - - - - 68
1801. Treaty of Lunéville (Feb. 9) - - - - - - 67
       Resignation of Pitt (Mar.) - - - - - - - 69
       English victories at Alexandria (Mar.) - - - 68
       Nelson's victory at Copenhagen (April 2) - - - 68
1802. Napoleon President of the Italian Republic (Jan.) - - 76
       Treaty of Amiens (Mar. 25) - - - - - 68
       Concordat confirmed (April) - - - - - - 74
       Napoleon First Consul for life (Aug.) - - - - 72
       Piedmont and Parma annexed to France (Sept. and Oct.) - 76
1803. French aggressions during Peace - - - - 76
       Renewal of war between England and France (May) - - 76
       French occupation of Hanover (June) - - - 77
       English capture St. Lucia and Tobago (June), Guiana
       (Sept.) - - - - - - - - - - 77
1804. Issue of *Code Napoléon* - - - - - - 75
       Murder of Duc d'Enghien (Mar. 21) - - - - 73
       Pitt returns to office (May) - - - - - 77
       Napoleon proclaimed Hereditary Emperor (May 18) - - 72
       Francis II. proclaimed Hereditary Emperor of Austria
       (Aug. 11) - - - - - - - - - 81
       Napoleon crowned by Pius VII. at Paris (Dec. 2) - - 74
1805. Napoleon King of Italy (Mar.) - - - - - 77
       Third Coalition (England, Russia, Austria, Sweden) - - 77
       The Boulogne Army - - - - - - - 78
       Napoleon's scheme for invasion of England - - - 78
       Calder defeats Villeneuve off Cape Finisterre (July 22) - 79
       Napoleon's march to the Danube - - - - - 80
       Mack's capitulation at Ulm (Oct. 20) - - - - 80
       Trafalgar (Oct. 21) - - - - - - - 79
       Austerlitz (Dec. 2) - - - - - - - 80
       Treaties of Schönbrunn (Dec. 15), and Pressburg (26) - 80
1806. England retakes Cape Colony - - - - - - 130
       Death of Pitt (Jan. 23) - - - - - - 82
       Prussia forced to accept Hanover - - - - 84
       England declares war on Prussia (April) - - - 84
       Kingdom of Naples bestowed on Joseph Bonaparte (Feb.) - 81
       Kingdom of Holland bestowed on Louis Bonaparte (June) - 81
       Confederation of the Rhine (July) - - - - 81
       H. R. E. dissolved (Aug. 6) - - - - - - 81

		PAGE
1806.	Prussia declares war on France (Oct. 1)	85
	Jena and Auerstadt (Oct. 14)	85
	Napoleon in Berlin	85
	The Continental System : 1st Berlin Decree (Nov. 21)	85
	Napoleon in Warsaw	87
1807.	England issues *Orders in Council* (Jan.-Nov.)	86
	Battle of Eylau (Feb. 8)	87
	French victory at Friedland (June 14)	87
	Treaties of Tilsit (July 7 and 9)	87
	Distribution of crowns	81
	Bombardment of Copenhagen	88
	Reforms in Prussia	107
	Junot in Portugal, Treaty of Fontainebleau (Oct. 27)	89
	Transportation of House of Braganza to Brazil	89
1808.	Napoleon's interference in Spain	90
	Joseph Bonaparte appointed King of Spain (June)	91
	Joachim Murat King of Naples	91
	Spanish Juntas	92
	Capitulation of Baylen (July 19)	92
	Sir Arthur Wellesley in Portugal	92
	Battle of Vimiero (Aug. 21)	92
	Convention of Cintra (Aug. 30)	93
	Napoleon's victories in Spain (Nov. and Dec.)	93
1809.	Moore's retreat and death	93
	Austria declares war on France (April 15)	95
	Napoleon's advance on Vienna (April)	95
	Battle of Aspern-Essling (May 21-22)	95
	Risings in North Germany	95
	Wellesley in the Peninsula	93
	Napoleon's victory at Wagram (July 6)	96
	Armistice of Znaim (July 12)	96
	Wellesley's victory at Talavera (July 27-28)	93
	British expedition to Walcheren (July to Sept.)	96
	Treaty of Vienna (Oct. 10)	96
1810.	French victories in the Peninsula	99
	Napoleon marries the Archduchess Marie Louise (April)	98
	Holland annexed to France (July)	98
	Wellington's victory at Busaco (Sept. 27)	99
1811.	Masséna retreats from Torres Vedras	99
	Wellington invades Spain	99
	Victories at Fuentes d'Onoro, Almeida and Albuera (May)	99

PAGE

1812.   English victories in Peninsula - - - - - - 100
        Ciudad Rodrigo (Jan.), Badajoz (April) - - - - 100
        Treaty of Abo (April) - - - - - - - 106
        Napoleon declares war on Russia (April 12) - - - 110
        Treaty of Bucharest (May 28) - - - - - - 146
        Napoleon crosses Niemen (June 24) - - - - - 110
        Wellington's victory at Salamanca (July 22) - - - 100
        Wellington in Madrid - - - - - - - - 100
        Battle of Borodino (Sept. 7) - - - - - - 110
        Napoleon in Moscow (Sept.-Oct.) - - - - - 111
        Retreat from Moscow (Oct.-Nov.) - - - - - 111
        Convention of Tauroggen (Dec. 30) - - - - 112
1813.   Prussia concludes Treaty of Kalisch with Russia (Feb. 28) 112
        War of German Liberation - - - - - - - 113
        Prussia declares war on France - - - - - - 113
        Napoleon's victories in Germany (May) - - - - 113
        Armistice of Pläswitz (June 4) - - - - - - 113
        Wellington wins Battle of Vittoria (June 21) - - - 100
        Austria concludes Treaty of Reichenbach (June 27) - - 113
        Austria declares war on France (Aug. 12) - - - 113
        Battle of Dresden (Aug. 26-27) - - - - - - 114
        Treaty of Töplitz (Sept. 19) - - - - - - 120
        Treaty of Ried (Oct. 8) - - - - - - - 120
        Battle of Leipzic (Oct. 16-19) - - - - - - 114
        Wellington in the Pyrenees - - - - - - 100
        Allies enter France (Dec. 31) - - - - - - 115
1814.   Murat joins the allies (Jan. 5) - - - - - - 120
        Congress of Châtillon (Feb. and Mar.) - - - - 116
        Treaty of Chaumont (Mar. 1) - - - - - - 116
        Allies enter Paris (Mar. 31) - - - - - - 116
        Napoleon abdicates (April 6) - - - - - - 116
        Louis XVIII. enters Paris (May 3) - - - - - 117
        Ferdinand VII. enters Madrid (May 14) - - - - 117
        Pius VII. enters Rome (May 24) - - - - - 117
        Victor Emmanuel enters Turin - - - - - - 117
        First Treaty of Paris signed (May 30) - - - - 117
        Charter issued by Louis XVIII. (June 4) - - - - 117
        Norway united to Sweden (Aug.) - - - - - 130
        Congress of Vienna opens (Nov. 1) - - - - - 119
        England and U.S.A. conclude Treaty of Ghent (Dec. 24) - 130
1815.   Divisions at Vienna (Jan.) - - - - - - - 121

PAGE

1815. Napoleon escapes from Elba (Feb. 26) and lands in France
          (Mar. 1) - - - - - - - - - - 121
       Napoleon enters Paris (Mar. 20) - - - - - - 122
       Reign of the *Hundred Days* (Mar. 20-June 29) - - - 122
       Austrian campaign against Murat (April and May) - - 125
       Congress of Vienna—*Final Act* (June 10) - - - 126
       Napoleon crosses Sambre (June 15) - - - - 123
       Napoleon defeats Prussians at Ligny (June 16) - - 123
       Battle of Quatre Bras (June 16) - - - - - 123
       Battle of Waterloo (June 18) - - - - - - 124
       Napoleon abdicates in favour of his son (June 22) - - 124
       Allies enter Paris (July 7) - - - - - - 124
       Louis XVIII. restored (July 9) - - - - - 125
       Napoleon surrenders to H.M.S. *Bellerophon* (July 15) - 124
       Napoleon banished to St. Helena (Aug. 8) - - - 125
       The *Holy Alliance* signed (Sept. 26) - - - - 132
       Ministry of Duc de Richelieu in France (Sept.) - - 134
       Second Treaty of Paris signed (Nov. 20) - - - 125
       Quadruple Treaty (Nov. 20) - - - - - - 132
1816. Reaction in Germany and Spain - - - - - 138
       Accession of John VI. of Portugal and Brazil (Mar.) - 139
1818. Congress of Aix-la-Chapelle - - - - - - 134
       Evacuation of French fortresses (Nov. 30) - - - 134
       Abolition of commercial restrictions in Prussia - - 199
1819. Karlsbad Decrees - - - - - - - - 197
       Beginnings of German Zollverein - - - - - 198
       Ministry of Decazes in France - - - - - 135
1820. Revolution in Spain (Feb.) - - - - - - 138
       Assassination of Duc de Berri (Feb. 13) - - - 135
       Richelieu succeeds Decazes as Prime Minister (Feb. 20) - 135
       Reactionary measures in France - - - - - 135
       Ferdinand VII. compelled to accept Constitution of 1812
          (Mar.) - - - - - - - - - 138
       Revolution in Naples (July) - - - - - 140, 174
       Revolution in Portugal (Aug.) - - - - - 139
       Congress of Troppau (Oct.) ; transferred to Laibach (Dec.) 140
1821. War of Greek Independence begins - - - - 148
       Ferdinand of Naples restored by Austria (Mar.) - - 141
       Rising in Piedmont (Mar.) - - - - - - 176
       Victor Emmanuel I. abdicates in favour of Charles Felix
          (Mar.) - - - - - - - - - 176

PAGE

1821. Austrian victory at Novara (April) - - - - - 176
Richelieu succeeded by Villèle (Dec.) - - - - - 135
John VI. accepts new Constitution in Portugal - - - 139
1822. Brazil declares Independence. Dom Pedro Emperor - 139
Canning succeeds Castlereagh as Foreign Secretary (Aug.) 142
Congress of Verona (Oct.) - - - - - - - 141
1823. French intervention in Spain - - - - - - 142
Canning appoints Consuls in Spanish Colonies - - - 143
Reaction in Portugal - - - - - - - - 143
Monroe doctrine proclaimed in U.S.A. - - - - 143
1824. Death of Louis XVIII.—Charles X. succeeds (Sept. 16) - 135
Coup d'état of Dom Miguel - - - - - - 144
Occupation of Crete by Ibrahim Pasha - - - - 150
1825. Independence of Spanish Colonies recognised by Canning 143
Independence of Brazil recognised by Portugal - - 144
Devastation of the Morea by Ibrahim - - - - - 150
Death of Alexander I. of Russia—Accession of Nicholas
(Dec. 1) - - - - - - - - - - 150
1826. Anglo-Russian Agreement - - - - - - - 150
Fall of Missolonghi (April) - - - - - - - 150
1827. Ibrahim takes Athens (June) - - - - - - 150
Treaty of London (July) - - - - - - - 150
Death of Canning (Aug. 8) - - - - - - - 151
Battle of Navarino (Oct. 20) - - - - - - 150
1828. Martignac succeeds Villèle (Jan.) - - - - - 135
Russia declares war on Turkey - - - - - - 151
1829. Russian victories in Turkey - - - - - - 151
Polignac Prime Minister of France (Aug.) - - - - 135
Treaty of Adrianople (Sept.) - - - - - - 151
1830. French Revolution (July) - - - - - - - 136
Accession of Louis Philippe - - - - - - 137
Insurrection in Belgium - - - - - - - 154
Risings in Germany - - - - - - - - 197
Risings in Italy - - - - - - - - - 177
1831. Death of Charles Felix of Sardinia—Accession of Charles
Albert (April 2) - - - - - - - - 178
Leopold of Saxe-Coburg chosen King of the Belgians - 154
1832. Belgian Independence - - - - - - - 154
Ancona occupied by France - - - - - - 177
Otto of Bavaria elected King of Greece - - - - 151
1833. Reaction in Germany - - - - - - - - 198

		PAGE
1833.	Conquest of Syria by Mehemet Ali	156
	Treaty of Unkiar Skelessi (July)	156
	League of Münchengrätz (Sept.)	198
1839.	Renewed war between Turkey and Mehemet Ali	156
1840.	Treaty of London	157
	Palmerston and the Eastern Question	156
	Mehemet Ali withdraws from Syria	156
	Accession of Frederick William IV. of Prussia (June 7)	200
1846.	The Swiss Sonderbund	157
	Election of Pio Nono (June 16)	179
	The Spanish marriages (Oct. 10)	158
1847.	United Diet in Berlin	200
	War of the Sonderbund	157
1848.	Revolution in Paris (Feb.)	160
	Abdication of Louis Philippe	160
	Second French Republic	161
	Revolutions in Germany, Hungary and Bohemia	201, 202
	Republics established at Milan and Venice	180
	Constitutions in Italy	180
	War between Austria and Sardinia	181
	Victory of Radetsky at Custozza (July 24)	181
	Constituent Assembly at Berlin	204
	German Parliament at Frankfort	204
	Austrian victory in Bohemia	203
	Reaction in Vienna	204
	Abdication of Ferdinand I. of Austria	203
	Accession of Francis Joseph (Dec. 2)	203
	Louis Napoleon elected President of French Republic (Dec. 11)	162
1849.	Republic proclaimed at Rome (Feb.)	181
	Austria defeats Sardinia at Novara (Mar. 23)	181
	Charles Albert abdicates in favour of Victor Emanuel	181
	Revolt of Hungary (April)	203
	Frederick William IV. refuses Imperial Crown of Germany (April)	205
	Failure of federal movement in Germany	205
	Suppression of Hungarian rising	203
	French occupation of Rome	181
	Re-establishment of Papal Government	182
	End of Venetian Republic (Aug.)	181
1851.	*Coup d'état* of Louis Napoleon in France (Dec.)	163

PAGE

1851. Restoration of German Bund - - - - - - 206
1852. Modification of French Constitution - - - - - 163
Cavour Prime Minister of Sardinia - - - - 183
Napoleon becomes Emperor of the French (Dec. 1) - - 163
1853. Marriage of Napoleon III. (Jan. 29) - - - - 164
Outbreak of war between Russia and Turkey - - 167
Massacre of Sinope (Nov. 30) - - - - - 167
1854. Crimean War - - - - - - - - 167
1855. Intervention of Sardinia in the Crimea - - - 167, 183
Death of Czar Nicholas - - - - - - 168
Accession of Alexander II. (Mar. 2) - - - - 168
Fall of Sebastopol (Sept.) - - - - - - 168
Surrender of Kars (Nov.) - - - - - - 168
1856. The Peace of Paris (Mar.) - - - - - - 168
1858. Prince William Regent of Prussia - - - - 207
Napoleon III. meets Cavour at Plombières - - 184
1859. War of Italian Liberation - - - - - - 186
French alliance with Sardinia - - - - - 186
Ferdinand II. succeeded by Francis II. in Two Sicilies
    (May 22) - - - - - - - - 187
Victories of Magenta and Solferino (June) - - - 186
Truce of Villafranca (July 11) - - - - - 186
Union of Northern and Central Italy under Sardinia - 186
1860. Savoy and Nice annexed to France - - - - 187
Garibaldi's Conquest of Sicily and Naples - - 187
Battle of Castel Fidardo (Sept. 18) - - - - 188
Victor Emanuel in Naples (Nov.) - - - - 188
1861. William I. becomes King of Prussia (Jan.) - - 207
Kingdom of Italy - - - - - - - 189
Italian Parliament at Turin (Feb. 1) - - - - 188
Death of Cavour (June 6) - - - - - 189
1862. French Expedition to Mexico - - - - - 219
Garibaldi defeated at Aspromonte (Aug. 29) - - 189
Bismarck becomes Prussian Minister (Sept.) - - 208
Expulsion of King Otto from Greece (Oct.) - - 152
1863. Death of Frederick VII. of Denmark—Accession of
    Christian IX. (Nov. 15) - - - - - 210
Reopening of Schleswig-Holstein question - - 210
Prince George of Denmark becomes King of Greece - 152
1864. Cession of Ionian Isles to Greece - - - - 152
Archduke Maximilian becomes Emperor of Mexico - 219

		PAGE
1864.	Schleswig-Holstein occupied by Austria and Prussia -	210
1865.	Convention of Gastein—War between Prussia and Austria temporarily averted (Aug.) -	211
	Meeting of Napoleon III. and Bismarck at Biarritz -	220
	French troops begin to withdraw from Rome -	190
	Italian capital transferred to Florence -	190
1866.	Bismarck's Treaty with Italy -	211
	Seven Weeks' War -	212
	Battle of Langensalza (June 27) -	212
	Prussian victory at Sadowa (Königgrätz) (July 3) -	212
	Austrian victories against Italy -	190
	Treaty of Prague (Aug. 23) -	212
	Annexation of Hanover, etc., to Prussia -	213
	Cession of Venetia to Italy -	190
1867.	North German Confederation -	213
	Defeat and execution of Emperor Maximilian (June) -	220
	Napoleon's failure to get Luxemburg -	221
	Austrian-Hungarian Ausgleich (Feb.) -	214
	Garibaldi defeated by French troops at Mentana (Nov. 3)	190
1868.	Deposition of Isabella of Spain (Sept.) -	222
1869.	Opening of Suez Canal (Nov. 17) -	237
	Vatican Council -	192
1870.	Hohenzollern candidature in Spain -	222
	Outbreak of Franco-German War -	223
	Prussian victories at Worth, Gravelotte, etc. (Aug.) -	224
	Capitulation of Napoleon III. at Sédan (Sept 2.) -	224
	Overthrow of Second Empire in France (Sept. 4) -	224
	Third Republic -	224
	Siege of Paris -	225
	Campaign on the Loire -	225
	French troops withdrawn from Rome -	191
	Annexation of Papal States to Kingdom of Italy -	191
1871.	William I. of Prussia proclaimed German Emperor (Jan 18)	229
	Rome becomes capital of Italian Kingdom -	191
	Neutrality of Black Sea abrogated -	170
	Surrender of Paris (Jan. 28) -	226
	National Assembly at Bordeaux -	226
	Treaty of Frankfort (May 10) -	226
	Paris Commune (Mar.-May) -	226
	Thiers President of French Republic (Aug.) -	227
	Federal Empire established in Germany -	229

		PAGE
1873.	Death of Napoleon III. (Jan. 9) - - - - - - 227
	MacMahon succeeds Thiers as President (May 1) - - 227
1875.	Revision of French Constitution - - - - - 228
	Insurrection in Bosnia and Herzegovina - - - - 169
1875.	Andrassy Note - - - - - - - - - 170
1876.	Berlin Memorandum - - - - - - - - 170
	Servia and Montenegro declare war upon Turkey - - 170
	Bulgarian atrocities - - - - - - - - 170
1877.	Russo-Turkish War - - - - - - - - 170
1878.	Treaty of San Stefano (Mar.) - - - - - 171
	Intervention of England - - - - - - 171
	Treaty of Berlin (July) - - - - - - - 171

LIST OF MAPS

	PAGE
EUROPE (1789-1908)	3
FRANCO-GERMAN FRONTIER. CAMPAIGNS OF 1793, 1799, 1814, 1815, 1871	45
CENTRAL EUROPE IN 1810	97
THE CAMPAIGN OF TRAFALGAR	101
MAP TO ILLUSTRATE THE PENINSULAR WAR	101
RUSSIA'S WESTERN ADVANCE	147
ITALY (1789-1871)	175
THE GERMAN EMPIRE (1789-1871)	195
THE GROWTH OF PRUSSIA (1786-1867)	209
THE BRITISH EMPIRE (1789-1908)	233

THE
REMAKING OF MODERN EUROPE

1789-1878

CHAPTER I

INTRODUCTORY

THE period of European History between 1789 and 1878 divides naturally into two unequal portions. The dividing line must be drawn at the Battle of Waterloo and the resettlement of Europe at the close of the Great War (1815). The contrast between these two divisions is striking, and suggests a radical difference in the method of treatment. From 1789 to 1815 the gaze of the spectator is concentrated upon France. He is looking upon the successive scenes of a drama—or melodrama—with a unified and coherent plot. He watches a series of political experiments tried upon the Parisian stage: a futile attempt at limited monarchy; a democratic republic; a consulate in the hands of a successful soldier, and finally an Empire based upon military prestige. He sees Europe growing more and more uneasy at the development of events in France, and at length taking up arms in order to lay the horrible spectre of revolution. He sees the assault unexpectedly repulsed by the enthusiasm of the French republicans, and France in her turn assuming the offensive and flinging herself with the ardour of

1

a crusade upon the established Governments of Europe. He sees power pass, as Burke predicted that it must, to the successful soldier, who makes himself master first of the legions and ultimately of the state. He sees Napoleon Bonaparte, not content with the Empire of France, attempting, and with all but complete success, to impose his yoke upon the whole of continental Europe, and he sees his design frustrated by the tenacity, the wealth and the sea power of Great Britain. One scene unfolds itself after another, and each contributes to the systematic development of an impressive drama.

In the second half of the period—from 1815 to 1878—it is different. There is indeed a principle of immense significance underlying the mass of apparently miscellaneous and unrelated events. But at first sight it is difficult to discern it. The attention of the bewildered spectator is drawn now to France, now to Germany, now to Italy, now to Russia, now to the Balkan peninsula and now to the Iberian, now to the far East and now to the far West.

Nevertheless, there is a principle at work which gives unity to the historical manifestations of the nineteenth century. It is to be found in the complex and elusive idea of *Nationality*. But the operation of this force is far from uniform. Sometimes it is disruptive—tending to break up a seeming unity into fragments, as in the provinces formerly subject to the Sultan of Turkey, and in the countries held together by the Austrian Emperor. More often it has tended to unification; to weld into a single whole artificially divided provinces or states, as in Germany and Italy.

I propose, therefore, in the first half of the period (1789-1815) to concentrate attention upon France, and to treat

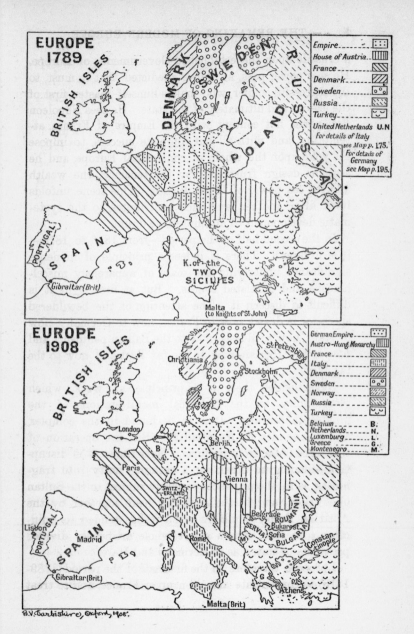

EUROPE 1789

Empire	⠿
House of Austria	⫽
France	⫽
Denmark	⫽
Sweden	○○
Russia	⩘⩘
Turkey	⌣⌣
United Netherlands	U.N

for details of Italy see Map p. 175.
for details of Germany see Map p. 195.

BRITISH ISLES

DENMARK

SWEDEN

RUSSIA

POLAND

PORTUGAL

SPAIN

Gibraltar (Brit)

K. of the TWO SICILIES

Malta (to Knights of St John)

EUROPE 1908

German Empire	⠿
Austro-Hung. Monarchy	⫼
France	⫽
Italy	⫼
Denmark	⫽
Sweden	○○
Norway	⫽
Russia	⩘⩘
Turkey	⌣⌣
Belgium	B.
Netherlands	N.
Luxemburg	L.
Greece	G.
Montenegro	M.

BRITISH ISLES

St. Petersburg

Christiania

Stockholm

London

Berlin

Paris

SWITZ-ERLAND

Vienna

ROUMANIA

Belgrade

Bukarest

SERVIA

Sofia

BULGARIA

Constantinople

Lisbon

SPAIN

Madrid

Rome

PORTUGAL

Gibraltar (Brit)

Athens

Malta (Brit)

B.V. Darbishire, Oxford, 1908.

the history of the other states of Europe as subordinate to the development of events in France. In the second half (1815-1878) I shall adopt a topical rather than a strictly chronological treatment, and shall group the leading facts round the great outstanding developments of the century, such as the unification of Germany and Italy, the Eastern Question, and the Constitutional revolutions in France. This method may involve a certain amount of repetition, but in no other way is it possible to impress upon the student the really characteristic and permanently significant achievements of this epoch.

In this connection the study of political geography is all-important. Before any attempt is made to master the details of the period under review, the student must clearly grasp the main changes in the map of Europe as effected between 1789 and 1878. Intermediate changes may for the moment be ignored, but no effort should be spared to apprehend the nett results of diplomacy and war upon the political boundaries of the leading states.

If we compare the map of Europe [1] at the beginning and end of this period the following among other changes will arrest attention :—

I. Germany

The Holy Roman Empire has disappeared, and a German Empire has come into being. Germany, instead of containing several hundred principalities and city states, bound together by the slenderest of political ties, is now a Federal Empire consisting of Prussia and twenty-four other sovereign states, and the Imperial-land Alsace-Lorraine. From the new Germany the various states ruled by the Austrian Emperor are excluded, and within it Prussia has both extended and consolidated her terri-

[1] See p. 3 *supra*

tories, having absorbed, in addition to the great Rhine
province, Schleswig-Holstein, Lauenburg, Hanover, Hesse,
Nassau, and Frankfort-on-Main.[1]

II. Austria-Hungary

To the South of Germany a new power has arisen and
taken a place in the European polity. Even before the
Holy Roman Empire was dissolved (1806) the Emperor had
assumed the new title of Emperor of Austria (1804). Under
this style the house of Habsburg-Lorraine still successfully
holds together a compact but heterogeneous collection of
states of which the more important are Austria, Hungary,
and Bohemia. The Austrian Netherlands have passed out
of their keeping and have been transformed—after a
brief and unsatisfactory union (1815-1830) with Holland
—into the new kingdom of Belgium. Their Italian provinces have similarly gone to the new kingdom of Italy.

III. Poland

On the Eastern frontier of Germany another significant
change must be noted. That frontier is now coterminous
with that of Russia. The ancient kingdom of Poland,
already dismembered by the first partition of 1772, has
been completely effaced. Portions have fallen to the share
of Austria and Prussia, but the greater part has been
swallowed—though incompletely digested—by Russia.[2]

IV. Russia

The first strides of Russia—Westward and Southward
—were taken in the eighteenth century, but her further
advance between 1789 and 1878 is still sufficiently remarkable. Reference has already been made to the
absorption of a great part of Poland (1793, 1795 and
1815). Finland was snatched from Sweden in 1809; the

[1] See maps, pp. 195 and 209.   [2] See map, p. 146.

dominion of Russia over the Eastern shore of the Baltic
was thus completed. On the Black Sea she had already
obtained a strong grip by the Treaty of Kainardji (1774);
but her frontier to the south-west was further advanced
to the Dniester by the Treaty of Jassy (1792) and to the
Pruth by the Treaty of Bucharest (1812). Of even vaster
extent are her acquisitions to the east of the Black Sea and
to the east of the Caspian, bringing her into immediate
contact with Persia, Afghanistan and the Empire of China.
Of all the changes in the political map there are few more
significant than those which record the steady expansion
of the Russian Empire.

V: The Balkan Peninsula

Hardly less conspicuous than the advance of Russia has
been the shrinkage in the dominions of the Turk. Russia's
expansion in Europe, and still more in Asia, has been
largely at the expense of Turkey. But apart from this the
Sultan's authority has been seriously curtailed. The kingdoms of Greece, Roumania and Servia have been carved out
of his European territory; the Principality of Bulgaria
is independent in all but name; England is in occupation
and virtual possession of Egypt and Cyprus; Austria has
practically incorporated Bosnia and Herzegovina.

VI. Italy

In 1789 Italy was in truth nothing more than a
"geographical expression," divided up into ten separate
states. Central Italy still lay in the grip of the Papacy;
Naples and Sicily (the "Two Sicilies") were ruled by
Spanish Bourbons; Tuscany and most of the smaller
Duchies were in the hands of Habsburgs; Lombardy
was united with Austria; Sardinia and Piedmont were
governed by the Dukes of Savoy, with the title of King

[1] See map, p. 146.

of Sardinia. The republics of Venice and Genoa alone survived to recall the Italy of the Middle Ages, an Italy which though divided was independent. Between 1789 and 1871 the changes in Italian government were kaleidoscopic ; but from 1848 onwards they all tended towards the realisation of independence and unity. By 1871 Italy was at last rid of the foreigner, and her ten states had become united, with Rome for the capital, under the House of Savoy. But the cradle of that House had passed with Nice to France.[1]

VII. France and the Iberian Peninsula

France has undergone less rectification of frontier than most of the great European states. She has gained Nice and Savoy from Italy, and lost Alsace-Lorraine to Germany. Spain and Portugal show no change as regards the map of Europe.

VIII. Scandinavia

Passing to Northern Europe we observe notable changes in the Baltic lands. The cession of Finland by Sweden to Russia has been already mentioned. Sweden was compensated by the acquisition of Norway,[2] snatched from Denmark in 1815, and Denmark itself has suffered further loss by the cession of Schleswig-Holstein to Prussia (1866).

IX. Holland and Belgium

In the Low Countries we have to note the formation of a new kingdom. The Southern Netherlands were in 1789 still in the unwilling custody of Austria. Absorbed for many years into France they were gladly ceded by Austria in 1815 and combined with Holland to form the kingdom of the Netherlands. But the union was brief

---

[1] See map, p. 175.   [2] Declared independent in 1905.

and disastrous, and in 1830 the new kingdom of Belgium was brought into being chiefly through the good offices of England and France.

X. The British Empire

A map of Europe avails but little to indicate the change which in the course of a century has transformed the British Kingdom into a world-Empire. In 1789 the chance of such a transformation seemed remote; the sun of England appeared to have set. Britain had lately lost thirteen colonies in North America, and Canada, though under British rule, could not yet be counted as a British Colony. Advantage had recently been taken of Captain Cook's discoveries to despatch a ship-load of convicts to Botany Bay (1788), but neither in Australia nor in New Zealand had colonisation begun. Cape Colony and Ceylon were still ruled by the Dutch East India Company. Warren Hastings had saved India from the fate of North America, but the expansion of British rule on the great scale was still to come under Lord Wellesley, Lord Hastings and Lord Dalhousie. The story of British expansion during the century under review must be read mainly on the maps of Asia, Africa, Australia and North America. But the map of Europe shows notable additions to the safeguarding of the great Mediterranean highway by the acquisition of Malta and Cyprus, not to speak of the occupation of Egypt.

This summary statement of the chief geographical changes may suffice to indicate the nature of the task before a student of this period. It may also suggest its absorbing interest. But more important even than the number and extent of these territorial readjustments is the question of their political significance. Do the changes seem to obey any given law? Do they point any political moral? Have they, in the main, contributed to the better government, to the material prosperity and the social well-being of the peoples immediately concerned? It has been reckoned that "one-fifth of the population of Europe may now be called to fight *against* flags *under* which the grandfathers of men not yet old might have been called on to fight, and this without reckoning anything for the separation of Austria from Germany, or for transfers from one German or Italian flag to another".[1] This is in itself a fact of immense significance. But the more important question still remains to be answered. Have the changes been due merely to the ambition of rulers and the whims of diplomatists, or have they tended to the fulfilment of a healthy political law and to the increased happiness of the masses of the people whose allegiance has been transferred?

It is the main purpose of the following pages to describe the changes, thus summarised, and to attempt an answer to the question proposed.

[1] Professor Westlake: ap. *Lectures on the History of the Nineteenth Century*. (Cambridge Press.)

CHAPTER II

THE FRENCH REVOLUTION (1789-1793)

Les révolutions qui arrivent dans les plus grands états ne sont
point un effet du hazard, ni du caprice des peuples.—SULLY.

The *States-general*

DURING the winter of 1788-89 France was plunged
into unwonted excitement. Louis XVI. (1774-
1793), amiable and well intentioned, but utterly lacking
in strength of character or clearness of vision, had yielded
to a demand for the summoning of the *States-general*.
This general assembly of the French Estates—the Nobles,
the Clergy and the *Tiers état* or Commons—was almost
coeval in antiquity with the English Parliament, and in
structure was not unlike the original form of that body.
But in the subsequent development of the two bodies there
was no similarity. The *States-general* was entirely dependent on the will of the sovereign, who summoned or
neglected to summon it as he chose ; it never acquired any
real control over legislation or administration, and above
all never kept the power of the purse. During the last
three centuries it had met at long intervals, and since 1614
it had never met at all. It is easy, therefore, to imagine
the excitement caused throughout France by the an-
nouncement that the *States-general* was to meet in May,
1789. There was considerable uncertainty as to proper
forms and methods of election, and few people could have
had any clear conception as to what the *States-general*

10

when elected would do; but the possibilities were as imposing as they were vague, and all men felt dimly that a new era was opening for France. It is estimated that in the winter of 1788-89 about 40,000 political meetings were held, while pamphlets poured in their thousands from the press, and this in a country which had not witnessed a general election for nearly two hundred years.

What were the hopes which inspired the electors? What were the grievances which they intended to redress? These questions we are fortunately able to answer with precision owing to the survival of the *Cahiers*—memoranda of instructions and grievances drawn up by each order for the guidance of their representatives. These *Cahiers* prove that all classes—privileged and unprivileged alike—looked for radical reform. All classes demanded the establishment of constitutional government, and looked to regular meetings of the *States-general* to secure it. The readjustment of taxation, the abolition of privileges and exemptions, the removal of feudal burdens were demanded by the *Tiers état*, and were not resisted —at any rate on paper—by Nobles or Clergy. Securities were to be obtained for personal liberty, offices were to be open to all classes, and all men were to be equal before the law. The *Cahiers* prove, in short, that even before the *States-general* met privilege was doomed, and that no resistance would be offered by any section of the people to far-reaching reforms.

The *States-general* was opened by the King on 5th May, 1789. It consisted of 1,136 deputies, of whom 270 represented the Nobles, 291 the Clergy and 575 the *Tiers état*. By royal decree "double representation" had been given to the Commons, and consequently their deputies outnumbered those of the two other Orders combined.

But the significance of the concession depended entirely upon the decision of another question hitherto undecided. How were the deputies to vote? By orders, in three separate Houses? Or as a single assembly—*par tête?* If in a single House, the Nobles and Clergy would be swamped by the double representation of the *Tiers état* and all real power would be vested in the latter. For six weeks this question was hotly debated and no business was done, but on 17th June the Commons cut the Gordian knot by declaring themselves the National Assembly of France, and invited the other Orders to join them. Three days later (20th June) the Commons, finding themselves excluded by the King's orders from their Hall of Assembly, adjourned forthwith to a neighbouring tennis-court and there registered a solemn oath not to separate until they had given to France a Constitution. Had the King at this critical moment possessed sufficient strength of mind to ignore the advice of courtiers and declare boldly for the Commons, the whole subsequent history of France might have been different. But the King, while announcing a large programme of reform (23rd June), refused to sanction the bold usurpation of the Commons or to recognise the "National Assembly". The latter stuck to their point; the lower Clergy (*curés*) joined them, and together they defied the orders of the King. "Tell your master," cried Mirabeau to the grand master of the ceremonies, "that we are here by the power of the people, and we shall not go hence save at the bayonet's point." The Nobles and the high Ecclesiastics were persuaded by the King to give way, and to join the Commons. The first great victory had been won.

Fall of the Bastille   The King, once more listening to the advice of his Queen and courtiers, now decided to mass troops on Paris, and to dismiss Necker [1] from his councils. Necker, though a successful financier, was a timid, uninspired and narrow-minded statesman, but his dismissal was rightly regarded as a sop to the reactionaries, and caused much excitement in Paris. The concentration of troops caused more. Riots broke out; national guards were enrolled, arms were distributed, and on 14th July the mob, having made themselves masters of the capital, attacked, and after five hours of fighting captured, the Bastille. This old fortress prison held at the time less than a dozen prisoners, but it symbolised all the judicial tyrannies and abominations of the old régime. Its capture was hailed, therefore, with enthusiasm as a blow struck for personal freedom. The King on hearing the news exclaimed: "Why, this is a revolt!" "No, Sire," rejoined the Duc de Liancourt, "it is a revolution!"

It is necessary, at this point, to pause and ask why in the summer of 1789 revolution thus blazed out in France? Revolutions rarely come suddenly, and never by chance. An accidental spark may fire the train, but the train itself must have been long and carefully laid. The causes of the Revolution in France cannot be really understood except by a perusal of its history for the last two hundred years. But here it must suffice to summarise them. *Causes of the French Revolution*

The first point to realise is that for centuries all political power in France had been concentrated in the hands of the Crown: that all limiting and competing authorities had been ruthlessly swept aside. For this concentration there were excellent historical reasons. It was the monarchy which had made France. It was the monarchy which had resisted the efforts of a self-seeking feudal aristocracy which, in its own interests, would gaily have *The Crown*

[1] See Vol. V. of this Series.

dismembered France. It was the monarchy which had withstood the hardly less mischievous tendencies of the political Huguenots. It was the monarchy of Louis XIV. (1643-1715) which, entering upon a heritage bequeathed to it by the patient labours of a long series of great kings, and still greater ministers, had raised France to a dazzling pinnacle of prestige among the powers of Europe. But in the eighteenth century the monarchy had ceased to be efficient. From India and North America France had been expelled by the arms of Englishmen: in Europe its military prestige had been shattered in a series of disastrous and expensive wars. At home things were no better. The personal vices of Louis XV. (1715-1774) were not redeemed by political capacity, and the administration drifted into confusion and bankruptcy. But the Nemesis which waits on autocracy overtook the French monarchy not when things were at their worst under the vicious and incompetent Louis XV., but when reform was being seriously undertaken by the patriotic and well-meaning Louis XVI. (1774-1793). Paradoxical as it may seem it is generally so. The contrast between increasing material prosperity on the one hand and social and fiscal inequalities on the other, was, as Tocqueville has luminously shown, one of the main reasons why revolution broke out in France.[1]

The Nobles   But the Revolution of 1789 was directed not primarily, if at all, against the monarchy, but against the privileged orders: the Nobility and the Clergy. And here again we are confronted by paradox. There was not more of feudal privilege in France than in other continental countries, but less. So long as feudalism was intact, it was immune. Richelieu, early in the seventeenth century,

---

[1] See Tocqueville. *France before* 1789, bk ii., c. i.

had destroyed the political powers of the French nobility :
but the loss of their political functions served to render
only more hateful the survival of social and fiscal
privileges. " Against whom are the Germans fighting ?"
Ranke was asked in 1870. " Against Louis XIV."
was his prompt reply. If Louis XIV. was responsible
for the Franco-German war, Richelieu was largely responsible for the Revolution of 1789.[1] Feudalism as a
political institution had long since disappeared in France;
as a social institution the fabric was intact. The Nobles
still enjoyed virtual immunity from direct taxation, and
escaped too lightly from indirect; they could still compel the peasants to grind their corn at the lord's mill, to
press their grapes in his wine-press, to pay innumerable
dues and tolls, and to submit to social customs some of
which were degrading and all of which were obsolete.
Such privileges were tolerable so long as the Nobles
governed and defended the country, and they were less
felt so long as the peasants were tenants and serfs. But
before the Revolution the Nobles had ceased not only to
be governors but in great measure to be landlords. Serfdom had practically disappeared; the peasant had become the owner of the soil he tilled ; the noble had become
a mere non-resident rent-charger, and the mutual relations
of the two classes had in consequence become intolerable.

The great Ecclesiastics were even more unpopular than The Church
the Nobles. Drawn largely from the same social class
they enjoyed the same social privileges, and their clerical
privileges in addition. And just as Richelieu had undermined the position of the nobles, so Voltaire and the
other great writers of the eighteenth century had under-

[1] Tocqueville's luminous work *L'Ancien Régime* is largely a
commentary on this text.

mined the prestige of the Church. The curés or parish priests for the most part retained the affection of their flocks by their devotion to duty, and by the fact that they shared the poverty and hardships of the peasant class from which they were drawn. And with the *Tiers état* they joined hands when the day of revolution came. Not against them, but against the vast wealth and luxurious lives of the princes of the Church was the satire of Voltaire and the fury of the revolutionary mob directed.

Added to the political and social causes making for revolution in France there were economic and fiscal reasons tending to the same end.

The fiscal system

It is difficult for an Englishman, accustomed for many generations to see the rich bearing the main burden of taxation, to realise the extent to which in France this burden was borne by the poor. It has been estimated that in the eighteenth century a French peasant could count on less than one-fifth of his income for his personal enjoyment and support. Eighty-two per cent. went in taxes, tithe and feudal dues. From direct taxes, as we have seen, the Nobles and Clergy were all but exempt, as were the official classes. Places were, indeed, eagerly sought largely in order to secure this privilege. Of indirect taxation the same classes bore less than their share. The real burden fell upon the poor. Small wonder that France was in chronic bankruptcy, and that every capable financier who came into power demanded—Turgot most loudly of all—that there should be an end of these mischievous exemptions. Unfortunately, the rôle of constitutional opposition was assumed, in the præ-revolutionary era, by the great judicial corporations or *Parlements*. These "nobles of the robe" were themselves highly privileged, and the last principle which they were prepared to accept was that of equality of taxation. Rather than surrender one iota of privilege in this respect they preferred to compel the Crown to summon a meeting of the *States-general*. Never did a privileged order show itself more selfishly short-sighted.

But bad as was the taxative system of the old régime, the commercial system was worse. An unjust and ineffective system of taxation prevents the government from utilising for national purposes the wealth of its citizens. But a bad commercial system prevents the creation of wealth. French trade in the eighteenth century was still wrapped in the swaddling clothes appropriate to infancy. Production was hampered by the survival of "guilds" and corporations, and exchange was rendered as cumbrous and difficult as possible by a multitude of internal custom barriers, and by stacks of antiquated regulations. English travellers well qualified to judge —like Adam Smith and Arthur Young—point to France as a veritable "museum of economic errors". Turgot (Controller-general, 1774-76) did all in his power to reform these abuses. He did much to equalise the burdens of taxation; he restored national credit; he reformed fiscal abuses; he broke down barriers on internal commerce; he suppressed guilds and emancipated industry; he abolished the *corvée* and reformed the *octroi*. But what he was allowed to accomplish was not a tithe of what he proposed, and his project of establishing a uniform tax on land from which none should be exempt was indignantly rejected by the privileged classes. His projected reforms meant the curtailment of privilege; the privileged classes were too strong for this intrepid and enlightened reformer, and he was dismissed. His successor Necker did something, but not enough, and the

Commercial system

2

trade of France was still struggling to emancipate itself from mediæval shackles when the Revolution broke out. Economic reform, therefore, not less than social and political, was imperatively required.

The Philo- sophers

There remains to be noted a curious feature of the situation. In France there existed side by side gross practical abuses and exceptionally enlightened theories. Nowhere was public opinion better informed or more critical. But the mischief was that the critics had no chance of giving effect to their theories in practical administration. Adam Smith learnt his Free Trade principles in France, partly from the French Physiocrats, partly from an examination, at close quarters, of the *reductio ad absurdum* of Protection. He taught Pitt the principles which the latter carried into practical effect at the Exchequer. Turgot was just as apt a pupil of Quesnay as was Pitt of Adam Smith. But while Pitt was the master of the House of Commons, Turgot was the servant of the King. None the less the work of the French theorists, of Quesnay and the Economists, of Diderot and the Encyclopædists, of Voltaire and Montesquieu, and above all Rousseau, must be reckoned as among the most potent of the forces which prepared the way for the Revolution. Napoleon declared that if Rousseau had never lived there would have been no Revolution, and it is true that without Rousseau the Revolution would have followed a very different course. His *Contrat Social*, published in 1762, exercised, and continues to exercise, a profound influence upon political thought. It is the gospel of modern Democracy. All government, according to its maxims, rests upon the consent of the governed. How, he asked, can the individual citizen, while securing the advantages of political society

" obey only himself and remain as free as before " ? He can do so only by entering into the fundamental contract from which emerges the sovereignty of the people. That sovereignty is, accordingly, illimitable, irresponsible, inalienable and indivisible. Voltaire described Rousseau's doctrines as a " code of anarchy," but the influence of his teaching was immediate and profound. Into a soil prepared by social grievances, by political abuses, and by mischievous economic restraints, Rousseau flung broadcast the seed of philosophical speculation. To masses of men who were at once credulous, oppressed, and inexperienced he preached a new social gospel.

Thus was the train of revolution laid. Three sparks ignited the powder.

The first was the revolt of the English Colonies in North America (1765-1783). In that revolution France saw a welcome opportunity of paying off old scores against England, and of putting her own philosophical theories into practice at a neighbour's expense. No doubt France fired a big gun against England, but the recoil was terrific. The American war was the last financial straw, and France sank into bankruptcy from which she did not emerge until the Revolution. Moreover, the success of the rebels encouraged revolutionary doctrines at home. The autocracy was seriously alarmed, and pushed on the work of reform with feverish haste. The last years of the old régime were crowded with reforms projected and effected. But again and again reform found itself broken on the wheel of privilege, and slowly people began to realise that before reform could be effectual privilege must be dislodged, and that privilege would not be dislodged by any existing political machinery.   New and stronger weapons would have to be forged.

The second spark was applied by the Parliament of Paris, which, though the home and incarnation of Privilege, startled the world at this moment by demanding that the *States-general* should be convoked.   The *States-general*, when it met, got rid of much besides the Parliament of Paris.

Finally: during the winter of 1788-89 France was devastated by famine and its trade was dislocated by an economic crisis of unprecedented severity.   It must never be forgotten that the elections to the first *States-general* elected since 1614 took place at a moment when thousands of Frenchmen were starving, and that when it met Paris was thronged by workless and destitute crowds.   But for this fact the French Revolution might never have assumed its lawless and bloodthirsty character.

CHAPTER III

THE CONSTITUENT ASSEMBLY

THE MAKING OF THE CONSTITUTION

Making the Constitution which is a new term they have adopted, as if a Constitution was a pudding to be made from a receipt.—ARTHUR YOUNG.

THE capture of the Bastille marked the beginning of mob rule in Paris. The example of Paris was soon followed by the Provinces. Inflammatory speeches were addressed from thousands of platforms to starving peasants and workless artisans. In the garrison towns fortresses were stormed by the mob and the troops fraternised with the people; in the country, monasteries were sacked and châteaux were burnt. Everywhere the Government showed itself impotent to maintain order or to protect life or property. In a few weeks the old régime, and all for which it stood, had collapsed from end to end of France.

The National Assembly at Versailles, worked up to a pitch of hysterical excitement by the reports which daily arrived from the Provinces, proceeded to a "St. Bartholemew of Property". On 4th August ("the extreme unction day of Feudalism" in Carlyle's phrase) the Assembly adopted a frenzied series of resolutions designed to get rid of the last relics of the feudal system.

The "St. Bartholemew of Property'

21

All men were to be henceforth equal before the law; offices and preferments were to be open to all; justice was to be administered gratuitously; serfdom, forced labour (the *corvée*), all customary services, all exclusive sporting rights were to cease; guilds and corporations were to be dissolved, and labour was henceforth to be "free"; tithes, annates and pluralities were abolished. One night's work thus sufficed to complete the destruction of a social system under which Frenchmen had lived for centuries.

The Rights of Man

Meanwhile there was imperative need for the Assembly to embark on the work of reconstruction. The old Government had collapsed; nothing had been devised to replace it, and France was drifting into anarchy. But precious weeks were consumed in the composition of a Declaration of the "natural, inalienable and sacred rights of man in order that this Declaration, being constantly before all members of the social body shall remind them continually of their rights and duties". Among these rights were "liberty, property, security and resistance to oppression"; freedom from unlawful arrest; freedom of conscience; and security of property. This famous document was published on 27th August, 1789.

Making the Constitution

This done the Assembly proceeded to "make" a new Constitution, "as if," says Arthur Young, "a Constitution was a pudding to be made from a receipt". Two points were decided in September: (1) that the legislature should consist of a single elected chamber, and (2) that upon the legislative proposals of this single chamber the King should have merely a suspensive veto. Against the narrow pedantry of these decisions one strong voice was raised in vain but emphatic protest. It was that of the Count of Mirabeau, the one man who in these constitutional debates displayed any statesmanlike knowledge and grasp.

Honoré Gabriel Riqueti, Comte de Mirabeau,[1] is beyond comparison the most notable figure in the early history of the French Revolution. Born in 1748 he ought to have been in the prime of manhood when elected to the *States-general*, but violent excesses of every kind had not merely undermined a robust constitution but had inspired general mistrust of his character. Rejected as a deputy by his own Order he was elected by the *Tiers état* both at Marseilles and at Aix, and as deputy for Aix he took his seat in 1789. Regarded with suspicion and received with insults his splendid eloquence and ripe political judgment quickly impressed the Assembly. His courage and resource in the crisis of 23rd June established his pre-eminence among a crowd of inexperienced medio-crities, and from that day until his death he mostly domi-nated the Constituent Assembly.

What was Mirabeau's political creed? At what did he aim? For the philosophic abstractions of Lafayette and the windy rhetoric of the Rights of Man Mirabeau had nothing but contempt, while the work of 4th August was to him a "mere orgy". But with the Ancien Régime he had no sympathy, and his supreme desire was to convince the King that the breach with the past was irreparable and to reconcile him to the new order. Not that he desired any weakening of the executive authority. On the contrary, a strong executive was to his mind the first necessity of government, but its strength must be de-rived from the willing assent of the people and from har-monious co-operation with the people's representatives in the Assembly. In fine, Mirabeau desired to see in France

[1] For biography *cf.* P. F. Willert: *Mirabeau.* (Foreign States-men Series.)

a Constitutional Monarchy of the English type, with which he had become familiar and which he fervently admired. Even to Mirabeau, however, the Assembly on this subject refused to listen. But the leadership of the Revolution was soon to pass from the Assembly.

March of the Maenads, 5th and 6th October

Early in October the news reached Paris that the Court at Versailles was contemplating a counter-revolution. The King, it was rumoured, was to withdraw to Metz, and Paris was to be overawed by faithful troops. A military banquet at Versailles gave substance to the rumours. A huge mob, headed by a band of frenzied women, marched out from Paris to Versailles on 5th October, attacked the Palace, and on the 6th carried the King and the royal family back with them to Paris virtually as prisoners. The National Assembly followed the King, and thus the control of the revolutionary movement passed into the hands of radical clubs and the populace of Paris.

The new Constitution

In Paris the work of Constitution-making was resumed in grim earnest by the Assembly. Local government was entirely reorganised: the old Provinces were abolished, and France was symmetrically mapped out into eighty-three Departments. The Departments were subdivided into Districts, Cantons, and Communes or Municipalities. The last numbered 44,000. In every department, district and commune there was an elected council with its executive officers. The electoral franchise was conferred upon all " active " citizens, *i.e.*, all citizens over twenty-five years of age who paid in direct taxes a sum equal to three days' labour. Office was open to all who paid direct taxes to the amount of a silver mark. The administration of justice was thoroughly overhauled. The Parlements and other courts were swept away, with many of the abuses attendant upon them—arbitrary imprisonment, for example, and excessive punishments. A criminal court was established in every department, and in these trial by jury was introduced; a civil court in every district; and besides these numberless courts of summary jurisdiction under *juges de paix*. At Paris there was to be a court of appeal. Unfortunately, a judicial system otherwise admirable was vitiated by the mania for election which pervaded the whole body of reforms effected by the Assembly. Firmness and impartiality could not be expected from judges who held office—and for short terms only—by popular election. Military reforms were carried out with equal thoroughness. The number of highly paid officers was reduced; the pay of the private was improved and all ranks were made eligible for promotion. Privilege of every kind was, of course, doomed. Hereditary titles of nobility were suppressed, while at the other end of the scale the slaves of St. Domingo were summarily emancipated. But not even revolutionary fervour could sustain the burden of government without money, and money was difficult to come by. Necker had come to the end of his tether in regard to loans, and his income tax of 5s. in the £ proved a failure. Under these circumstances greedy eyes were turned to the property of the Church. The curés were ill paid, but the wealth of the high Ecclesiastics and the religious houses was enormous. Tithes were abolished (to the sole advantage of the landowners) on 4th August 1789. In 1790 the religious houses were suppressed and all Church property throughout France was appropriated by the State. To meet immediate necessities *assignats* or promissory notes were issued upon the security of the Church property. The Church itself became a State-department, and a "civil constitution" was imposed upon the Clergy. Here again everything was sacrificed to mathematical symmetry and the mania for election. Every department was to have a bishop, every district a curé, in each case elected by their flock, and the papal veto on such elections was done away with. At the same time gross inequalities of income were redressed. The scheme was not without merits, and though hotly resisted by the Clergy and unsanctioned by the Pope, might have formed the basis of a settlement but for an act of egregious and gratuitous folly. The Assembly insisted that every clergyman should take an oath of allegiance to the new system. At least half refused, the Church of France was rent in twain, and the new Government converted possible adherents into implacable opponents.

It remained to define the relations of the single-chamber legislature to the executive. Partly in deference to the theories of Montesquieu, partly in acceptance of American as against English precedent, most of all from ineradicable suspicion of the Crown and the Court, the Assembly resolved that no executive minister or holder of office under the Crown should be a member of the legislature. Mirabeau, in accordance with his known principles, strove earnestly to avert this divorce, but in vain; and his failure removed the last hope of reconciliation between the Crown and the National Assembly, the last hope that constitutional reform might be effected without destructive revolution.

Foiled in the Assembly Mirabeau did all that in him lay by a series of memoranda [1] characterised by remarkable shrewdness and insight to guide the steps of the King and to save the monarchy. His first plan was the formation

---

[1] Cf. Mirabeau : Correspondance avec le Comte de la Marck. (Paris, 1851.)

of a "Responsible" ministry which should command the confidence both of the Crown and of the Extreme Left. But the materials for such a ministry did not exist. Quick to recognise his failure, Mirabeau's next plan was to induce the King to unite France against Paris. The advice was at once sagacious and bold, but the execution of the scheme needed organising genius of the first order. Where could the Court find agents fit for the task? Mirabeau himself was not fully trusted by the Court, and the golden opportunity which he and he alone might have seized was lost.

But despite his failure Mirabeau's political ascendancy seemed to be never more unquestioned than in the last months of his tempestuous career. In December he was elected President of the Jacobin Club, and on 30th January, President of the Assembly. On 2nd April, 1791, he died. Carlyle confidently affirms that "had Mirabeau lived, the history of France and of the world had been different". It is far from certain; but no one can question the accuracy of Mirabeau's own prediction: "When I am gone they will know what the value of me was. The miseries I have held back will burst from all sides on France. I carry in my heart the death-dirge of the French monarchy: they will fight over its corpse." The one real statesman in France was dead: whether even he could have saved the monarchy and averted the deluge that followed it is impossible to say. It is certain that no one else could.

From this moment the King seems to have realised the hopelessness of his position. On 18th April 1791 he attempted to leave Paris for St. Cloud, but was stopped and turned back by the mob. His one hope now was to get away from the capital. On 20th June the royal family

Flight to Varennes

left Paris secretly for Metz, but the affair was shamefully bungled, they were stopped at Varennes and brought back—virtually prisoners—to the capital.

It is at this moment that the project of a Republic comes distinctly into view. Robespierre [1] and Danton [2] demanded the deposition of the King, but the proposal commanded only thirty votes in the Assembly, and it was decided to suspend the King provisionally until the Constituent Assembly should have completed its labours. The extremists resented this decision and organised a republican demonstration for 17th July. Bailly, the Mayor of Paris, and Lafayette as commander of the National Guard attempted to carry out the orders of the Assembly and maintain order. The mob refused to disperse; the soldiers fired, and twelve people were killed and many wounded. This unfortunate collision, commonly known as the "Massacre of the Champ de Mars," widened the breach between the Assembly and the Parisian mob. But the work of the Constituent Assembly was now complete: on 21st September the new Constitution received the assent of the King; Louis swore to maintain it and was reinstated in office. On 30th September, 1791, the Assembly was dissolved.

The work of the Constituent Assembly has been severely criticised and not without warrant. The members were, of course, utterly lacking in experience of affairs; they were the slaves of certain philosophical theories, and were inspired by a mania for the principle of popular election; they declined to listen to the sagacious advice of the one statesman among them, and they fell into innumerable pitfalls. But there is no reason to

[1] *Cf.* Belloc's *Life* or Morley's Essay, ap. *Miscellanies*, Vol. I.
[2] *Cf. Life* by Beesly or Belloc.

question their honesty or patriotism, or to doubt that they were inspired by a genuine desire to secure for France a new Constitution modelled upon the most approved principles of political science. Moreover, practically all their civil as apart from their political creations have stood the test of time. It was their misfortune rather than their fault that they were men of theory engaged upon the hopeless task of devising popular institutions for a nation which had had no training in the supremely difficult art of self-government.

The new Assembly known as the *Legislative*, met on 1st October, 1791. It consisted of a single chamber of 745 members entirely new to political life. For by an act of self-abnegating folly the *Constituent* had concluded its labours by passing a decree that none of its members should be eligible for election to the new chamoer. Once again, therefore, the destinies of France were committed to men, mostly young lawyers, who were full of theories but devoid of experience.

The Legislative Assembly

Parties quickly defined themselves in the new chamber. The Right consisted of the Constitutionalists—better known as the *Feuillants*, a name derived from their club which met in the Convent of the Feuillants. They posed as the defenders of the Constitution of 1791 and maintained friendly relations with the Court. They rested on the support of Lafayette, the National Guard and the middle classes. The King's best policy would have been to give them his confidence, and to support as far as possible their policy. The Left was divided into two factions, both of them frankly republican, the Girondins and the Jacobins. The latter, numerically the weaker, derived much strength from the support of Paris and particularly of the clubs. At the Jacobin Club Robespierre was supreme; Danton and Camille Desmoulins swayed the destinies of the Cordeliers, while the lusty brewer Santerre exploited the canaille of the Paris faubourgs in the interest of the extreme republican party. Within the chamber the most distinguished, and at first the most influential of the many groups into which the Left was divided was that of the Girondins.

The Girondins

This famous group derived its name from the fact that its leaders came from the department of the Gironde. Among them were such men as Vergniaud, their most brilliant orator, Brissot, the editor of the *Patriote*, with some knowledge of foreign affairs, Condorcet, the philosopher, Guadet and Gensonné. Madame Roland represented the party outside the Assembly. Their ardent republicanism was based on classical models; they were highly gifted, full of fiery eloquence, and totally devoid of experience. They soon became (as Von Sybel says) " the darlings of all those zealous patriots for whom the Cordeliers were too dirty, and the Feuillants too lukewarm ".

The new chamber was confronted by a score of difficulties; among the most pressing were those presented by the position of the Non-juring Clergy and of the Nobles who had fled from France.

The Nonjurors and the *Émigrés*

Many of the Clergy had, as we have seen, refused to take the oath imposed by the Constituent Assembly, but supported by their flocks they still continued to perform their duties. Consequently in November, 1791, a Decree was passed ordering the expulsion of all priests who refused the oath, but the King interposed his veto and the Decree never became law. A similar fate attended a second Decree (27th May, 1792) authorising the departments to banish all Non-jurors. The confusion, therefore, was unrelieved, and the only result was further to alienate the Clergy and such of the people as remained devoted to them.

Still more difficult was the problem presented by the position of the *Émigrés*. From the early days of the Revolution a steady stream of French nobles had poured over the German frontier. The conduct of these men was despicable. By sticking to their posts they might have done something to stem the tide of revolution, or by frankly accepting the new situation they might have guided a movement which they could no longer control. Instead of this, they fled shrieking into Germany to implore the help of foreigners to arrest the progress of revolution. Their conduct at this crisis must be held largely responsible for the outbreak of war, for the excesses of the reign of terror, and for the murder of the King. At Coblentz they established a miniature Court over which the King's brothers, the Count of Provence (afterwards Louis XVIII.) and the Count of Artois (afterwards Charles X.) presided. They organised also a regular army. The Assembly was seriously alarmed. A Decree was passed with the King's assent requiring the Count of Provence to return to France within two months; a second was proposed declaring that all *Émigrés* still in arms on the 1st January, 1792, should be punishable with death as traitors to France and their property be confiscate to the State. The King vetoed this Decree though he urged the *Émigrés* to return.

Meanwhile the *Émigrés* continued their appeals to the German Powers to arrest by force of arms a movement which threatened not France only but every constituted Government in Europe.

The response to this appeal opens a new chapter in the history of the Revolution.

CHAPTER IV

EUROPE AND THE REVOLUTION

> No Monarchy, limited or unlimited, nor any of the old Republics, can possibly be safe as long as this strange, nameless, wild enthusiastic thing is established in the centre of Europe. . . . It is with an armed doctrine that we are at war.—BURKE.

The war of 1792 IS it possible that under any circumstances the Revolutionary movement started in 1789 could have been confined to France? The question thus stated has been variously answered. We can only point to the fact that the conflagration lighted in Paris quickly engulphed the whole of Europe in the vortex of flames.

For this development there were many reasons. (i) The doctrines proclaimed by the National Assembly and adopted by the Legislative Assembly which followed were, if true at all, of universal validity. They asserted the rights not of Frenchmen or Germans, but of man as man. Hence there was no reason why their acceptance should be confined within political frontiers. (ii) The Girondins who rapidly mounted to supreme power in the autumn of 1791 were bent on war partly "to make all tyrants tremble on their thrones of clay," partly as the best hope of consummating the Revolution at home. From the first, therefore, they did everything in their power to provoke a breach between France and her neighbours. (iii) On no side of France were there

32

barriers strong enough to resist the tide of revolutionary sentiment. Most of the Governments of Central Europe were hopelessly decadent. Germany presented a sorry spectacle of weakness and disunion. Its two leading powers, Austria and Prussia, were deadly rivals; its political constitution had for centuries been entirely ineffective; the Holy Roman Empire had long since ceased to be "either Holy, Roman, or an Empire," while in few of the hundreds of states ruled by sovereign princes was there any stirring of a healthy national life. Worst of all, perhaps, were the ecclesiastical states on the Rhine and its tributaries. And while the Governments were rotten, the people were ready to welcome the principles proclaimed in France. Particularly was this the case in the Austrian Netherlands, in the Rhine electorates and (in less degree) in the United Provinces.

No sovereign could be indifferent to the events taking place in France, or deaf to the appeals of the emigrant nobles, least of all the Emperor Leopold. As Head of the Holy Roman Empire, and still more as a ruler of the Austrian Netherlands, he was peculiarly exposed to the revolutionary infection; as brother of the Queen Marie Antoinette he had good reason to fear for the safety of his relatives. But Leopold was a calm and sagacious statesman, and clearly realised that nothing would be more likely to inflame passions in France than foreign intervention.

In August, 1791, the Emperor and the King of Prussia (Frederick William II.) met at Pilnitz. They rejected the appeal of the *Émigrés* for immediate intervention, and refused to let them use their asylum in Germany for making armed preparations against France. At the same time the two monarchs unfortunately issued the

Declaration of Pilnitz

3

Declaration of Pilnitz. This famous document maintained that the position of the King of France was a matter of concern to all European sovereigns. It demanded that the Princes of the Empire should be reinstated in their feudal rights in Alsace, and it expressed the intention of the German monarchs, if other nations concurred, to attain their objects by force of arms. The Emperor was aware that England would not concur, but he foolishly imagined that the empty threat launched from Pilnitz would suffice to bring the extremists in Paris to reason.

It had precisely the opposite effect. It played into the hands of the Girondins and lashed into fury the extreme republicans who, like Robespierre, were against war. Unfortunately Leopold died in 1792 (1st March), and in the same month Louis formed a Girondin ministry, the portfolio of the interior being given to the husband of Madame Roland, and that of foreign affairs to the able but unscrupulous Dumouriez. At the latter's bidding the King announced to the Assembly amid immense enthusiasm that he had declared war on Austria (20th April, 1792).

The declaration was immediately followed by an attack upon the Austrian Netherlands, but the French troops fled in panic, and murdered their own generals. This initial fiasco confirmed the prevailing notion that the war would be over in a few weeks, that the disciplined Germans would sweep aside the armed mob opposed to them, that the allies would march straight on Paris, rescue the French royal family and restore tranquillity to France.

Mob Rule in Paris   Such anticipations were absurdly wide of the mark. The failure of French arms served only to inflame the passions of the mob against the King and still more against the Queen. The Court party was denounced as the "Austrian Committee"; the King's Body Guard guaranteed by the Constitution was dismissed; the dregs of the populace were armed with pikes, and insults were daily offered to the Queen. On 20th June a mob of armed ruffians burst into the palace of the Tuileries, and for four hours surged round the King. The lives of the King and Queen were saved only by their own calm and dignified courage. This outrage roused the Constitutionalists in defence of the Crown and produced a decided though transient reaction. Lafayette left his troops on the frontier and hurried back to Paris to defend the King. But the Jacobins flouted his demands, the King mistrusted his goodwill, and things rapidly went from bad to worse.

On 11th July, after a speech of fiery eloquence from Vergniaud, the Assembly declared that the country was in danger; on 25th July Prussia formally declared war, and a few days later the Prussian commander, the Duke of Brunswick, issued from Coblentz a manifesto to the French people. He summoned all authorities in France to submit to their lawful sovereign, declared that the whole French nation would be held individually responsible for any resistance offered to the allied armies, and threatened Paris with demolition if any outrage were committed upon the King or royal family. This foolish and insolent manifesto sealed the fate of the French monarchy. The reply to it was the insurrection of the 10th of August. *[Brunswick's Manifesto]*

Early in June the King had vetoed a Decree for the assembling of a force of 20,000 fédérés or provincial volunteers in Paris, and on the 13th had dismissed his Girondist ministers. Despite the veto a force of fédérés marched from Marseilles and at the end of July arrived in Paris singing the new national hymn—the "Marseillaise" *[The tenth of August]*

—and determined to "strike down the tyrant". Meanwhile (9th August) the popular leaders set up a new *Commune* (or municipal government) and on the same night sounded the tocsin of insurrection throughout Paris. Mandat, the brave commander of the National Guard, was murdered; the Tuileries were invaded; the Swiss Guard was massacred, and the King, with his family, took refuge in the Assembly. There on the 10th of August a remnant of terror-stricken deputies decreed the suspension of the monarchy. The King was sent as a prisoner to the Temple; a camp was formed under the walls of Paris; the Girondist ministers were restored; Danton—the real author of the 10th of August — became the Minister of Justice, and a National Convention, to be elected by universal manhood suffrage, was summoned to meet immediately.

Advance of the Allies   On 19th August the allied army crossed the Rhine, on the 20th Longwy was invested; on the 24th it capitulated and on the 30th the invaders reached Verdun. Lafayette refusing to recognise the new authority in Paris was declared a traitor, took refuge with the allies, and was succeeded by Dumouriez. The best chance of the allies would have been a bold and rapid advance on Paris. Brunswick, their commander, was a fine strategist of the old school, but the situation demanded more than strategy. Brunswick would risk nothing, advanced with caution and slowly pushed Dumouriez back. The golden opportunity was lost.

The September Massacres   Meanwhile, terrible scenes were enacted within the walls of Paris. The advance of the allies created a panic; the entire control fell into the hands of the Commune; Danton became virtual dictator. His policy was simple. With the allies advancing on Paris; with more than half

France sympathising with the objects they were coming to achieve, the one path of safety for the republican minority was to strike terror into the hearts of their opponents.

"In my opinion," said Danton, "the way to stop the enemy is to make the Royalists fear." The surrender of Verdun (2nd September) opened the road to Paris, and on the same day massacres began in prisons already crowded with Royalists. For five long days the prisoners were handed over to the tender mercies of a band of cut-throats. There was no discrimination of rank, sex or age. Men, women and children, bishops and priests, nobles and magistrates,—all who were suspected of Royalist leanings were foully murdered with the added mockery of judicial forms. The number of victims is variously estimated from 2,000 to 10,000. Marat invited the provinces to follow the brilliant example of Paris.

In fairness it must be added that in the midst of the massacres Danton threw himself with splendid energy into the task of organising the National Defence. The cannonade of Valmy (20th September) checked Brunswick and saved the capital. With Valmy the tide turned; on the 6th of November Dumouriez won a brilliant victory on the Belgian frontier at Jemappes; Mons, Brussels and Antwerp surrendered in turn; the French armies were welcomed by the populace as friends, and the Austrian Netherlands were in the hands of the French Republic. Similar success attended the army of Custine on the Rhine: Mainz, Speier, Worms, Frankfort and Coblentz opened their gates to the French (October). Not less enthusiastic was their welcome on the Southern frontiers. General Montesquieu occupied Savoy, and General

Anselme Nice. Thus before the winter of 1792-93 closed in, the armies of the Republic were in possession of Belgium, Savoy and Nice, and had got a firm grip on the middle Rhine.

The National Convention Meanwhile, in the capital, the pace of revolution was ever quickening. The Legislative Assembly had dissolved itself and had summoned a National Convention to frame a new Constitution for France. The Convention was opened on 21st September, and resolved by acclamation that "royalty was abolished in France," and that Year I. of the Republic should date from that day. A decree of perpetual banishment was passed against the *Émigrés*, and it was resolved to bring the King to trial before the Convention.

Execution of the King The trial opened on 11th December. The Girondins attempted to interpose delays, and suggested that the King's fate should be decided by a vote of the whole nation. But the mob became impatient; on 14th January, 1793, they surrounded the Convention with cries of "Death to the tyrant," and two days later Louis XVI. was by a narrow majority sentenced to death. On 21st January the sentence was executed. Thus died upon the scaffold, with calm courage and unruffled dignity, one of the kindliest, most unselfish and best-intentioned of French kings. Unfortunately he was as weak as he was good. A really strong king might have dissociated himself from the privileged orders and led the movement along the path of ordered reform. But Louis XVI. was incapable of initiative, and not wise enough to profit by the advice of the one counsellor who might have supplied his deficiency. Personally well meaning he fell upon evil days and had not sufficient force of character to "ride the whirlwind" or "direct the storm". His execution was both a crime and a blunder. "Louis must die," said Robespierre, "because the country must live." The dilemma was imaginary; and posterity has endorsed with rare unanimity the dictum of Charles James Fox—"a most revolting act of cruelty and injustice."

CHAPTER V

ENGLAND AND FRANCE

THE REIGN OF TERROR

I detest the French Revolution in the act, in the spirit, in the consequence, and most of all in the example.—BURKE.

He pitied the plumage, but forgot the dying bird.—TOM PAINE ON BURKE.

The Propagandist Decrees

THE execution of Louis XVI. sent a thrill of horror through Europe, but it could not in itself justify foreign intervention. The Revolution, however, was changing its character. Intoxicated by success the republicans, in the autumn of 1792, had challenged the existing order in Europe at large. They had already declared the navigation of the Scheldt open, and issued two propagandist Decrees calling upon all peoples to rise in revolt against their rulers. The importance of the Decree of 15th December, 1792, justifies quotation :—

"The French nation will treat as enemies the people who, refusing or renouncing liberty and equality, are desirous of preserving their prince and privileged castes, or of entering into communication with them. The nation promises and engages never to lay down its arms until the sovereignty and liberty of the people on whose territory the French armies shall have entered, shall be established. It is evident that a people so enamoured of

40

its chains, and so obstinately attached to its state of brutishness as to refuse the restoration of its rights, is the accomplice not only of its own despots, but even of all its crowned usurpers, who divide the domain of the earth and of men. Such a servile people is the declared enemy of the French Republic."

Such conduct rendered the maintenance of neutrality difficult if not impossible. England was particularly embarrassed by the opening of the Scheldt, in conjunction with the French occupation of Belgium. Always sensitive in regard to Antwerp she had specifically guaranteed in the interests of Holland the closing of the Scheldt,[1] and the action of the Convention consequently compelled serious notice.

So far the Government of England had shown no hostility to the Revolutionary movement. Some people took the cynical view of Lord Chesterfield, that if France were kept well occupied at home "the rest of Europe would be quiet". Others welcomed its early stages as likely to procure for France the advantages—long enjoyed in England—of a limited monarchy. Some were flattered to trace in its progress the influence of English writers, more particularly Locke. A few, like Charles James Fox, were excited to enthusiasm even by its more violent episodes.

Unquestionably the first effect of the Revolution was to encourage the political societies and clubs which had come into existence during the American war. Among these the "Revolution Society" obtained some notoriety —after the manner of unimportant busybodies—by sending an address of congratulation to the National Assembly (November, 1789). To this society was addressed the

England and the Revolution

---

[1] *I.e.*, that no goods should be brought up the river except in Dutch ships, or on payment of dues to the Dutch. Treaty of Westphalia, 1648, and several times since.

sermon which Burke took as the text of his *Reflections* upon the French Revolution, a fact which has secured to Dr. Price, the preacher, a spurious immortality.

Burke made from the first no secret of the anxiety and abhorrence with which he regarded the course of events in France, and in November, 1790, he published his *Reflections*. In this famous treatise his first care was to repudiate the suggestion that France was merely improving upon the example set by England in 1688, and to emphasise the contrast between the cautious and conservative advance of England and the abstract and unhistorical radicalism of France. To give any idea of the exuberant wealth of historical illustration, or the profound wisdom of the political reflections by the aid of which Burke enforced his main thesis, would here be impossible. But attention must be drawn to his remarkable prediction. The new system of government set up by the National Assembly would, he prophesied, quickly lead to the destruction of the monarchy; the fall of the monarchy would result in anarchy, from which France could only be rescued by a military despotism. But Burke's first concern was not for France but for his own country, and his treatise has, therefore, been truly described as "a polemic against Jacobinism, particularly English Jacobinism". In both respects it produced an extraordinarily powerful effect. Thirty thousand copies were quickly sold in England and a very large number in France and elsewhere. Nor was the success undeserved; for few similar treatises have so effectively combined the character of a political pamphlet designed to produce an immediate effect, and that of a permanent contribution to political thought.

Not that Burke's influence was wholly salutary. From

the outset he held that the only cure for the highly
contagious disease raging in France was the armed
intervention of the Powers. "This evil in the heart of
Europe must be extirpated from that centre, or no part of
the circumference can be free from the mischief which
radiates from it, and which will spread, circle beyond
circle, in spite of all the little defensive precautions which
can be employed against it." Most people will now agree
that Burke was inaccurate in his diagnosis and unfortunate in his prescription.

But despite Burke's advice, Pitt held steadily on the Pitt and
the Revolu
path of rigid neutrality. There are few charges against tion
any public man more demonstrably false than that which
makes Pitt responsible for the outbreak of war between
Europe and France. But the force of iteration is remarkable, and libel dies hard. To have introduced a
Peace Budget in 1792, and to have reduced both army
and navy, may argue lack of prescience, but at least it
proves the sincerity of his aversion to war. Even after
the Continental war had broken out Pitt clung to the
hope that Great Britain might not only maintain neutrality, but might intervene as arbitrator between the
combatants. Such hopes, though generous, were vain, and
as the summer of 1792 deepened into autumn, Pitt's
struggles for peace, though never relaxed, grew sensibly
less and less effective.

On both sides of the channel passions were rising which
no statesman could control. The republicans in Paris
had challenged all existing Governments, good and bad
alike; they had shown their indifference to existing
obligations; they had proclaimed, in their Decrees, a
Revolutionary crusade; finally, on the 21st of January,
1793, they sent their sovereign to the scaffold. The

execution of Louis XVI., however inconsequently, roused the war temper of the English people. Chauvelin, who had for some time unofficially represented the French Government in London, was sent home, and on the 1st of February, 1793, the Convention declared war upon England and Holland, and a month later upon Spain.

The War of 1793

Between 1793 and 1801 the war between England and France continued without break. Other Powers came in and fell out; coalitions were formed and dissolved; treaties of peace were concluded, and wars were again declared, but all the while the old rivals held doggedly on. Even the treaty concluded at Amiens (1802) represented nothing more than a temporary truce; no real peace was made until after the final overthrow of Napoleon in 1815. But not until the beginning of the Peninsular War (1808) did England play any considerable or continuous part in the military operations on the Continent. This was Pitt's deliberate policy, and it has been abundantly vindicated by the greatest of modern strategists: "It was economically wiser, for the purpose of the coalitions," writes Captain Mahan,[1] "that [Great Britain] should be controlling the sea, supporting the commerce of the world, making money and managing the finances, while other states, whose industries were exposed to the blast of war, and who had not the same commercial aptitudes, did the fighting on land." That in Pitt's conduct of the war there were serious mistakes in detail must be conceded: but he set before himself a definite aim, and he pursued it with dogged tenacity and, on the whole, with conspicuous success.

The adhesion of England, Holland and Spain combined with the distracted condition of France to secure to the

[1] *Influence of Sea Power upon the French Revolution and Empire.*

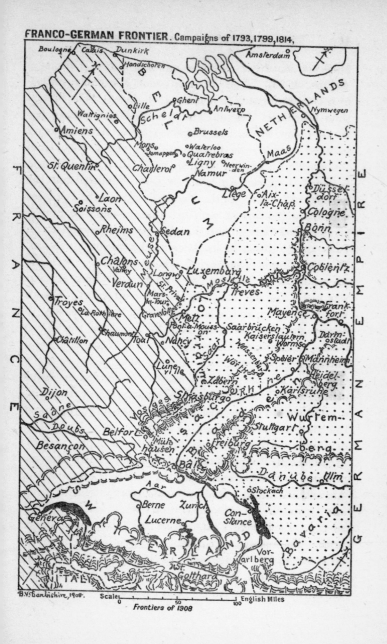

FRANCO-GERMAN FRONTIER. Campaigns of 1793, 1799, 1814.

Boulogne Calais Dunkirk Amsterdam

Hondschooten

B

Lille Ghent Antwerp Nymwegen

Wattignies Scheldt

Amiens Brussels NETHERLANDS

Mons Waterloo Maas

St. Quentin Jemappes Quatrebras

Charleroi Ligny Neerwinden

Namur

Laon Liège Aix-la-Chap. Düsseldorf

Soissons Cologne

Rheims Sedan Bonn

Châlons Valmy Luxemburg Coblentz

Longwy Moselle

Verdun St. Privat Treves

Mars-la-Tour Frankfort

Troyes Gravelotte Metz Mayence

La Rothière Pont-à-Mousson Saarbrücken Darmstadt

Chaumont Toul Nancy Kaiserslautern Worms

Châtillon Oscar Weissenburg Speier Mannheim

Lunéville Wörth Heidelberg

Zabern Karlsruhe

Dijon RHINE Wurtem-

Saône Strasburg Stuttgart berg

Doubs Belfort Freiburg

Besançon Mühlhausen Bâle Danube Ulm

Stockach

Aar Berne Zurich Constance

Geneva Lucerne Bavaria

SWITZERLAND Vorarlberg

ITALY Gotthard

FRANCE GERMAN EMPIRE

B.V.Darbishire, 1908. Scale English Miles

0 50 100

Frontiers of 1908

allies six months of unbroken military success (February-August, 1793).   The Austrians won a notable victory over Dumouriez at Neerwinden (18th March). The French then evacuated Belgium, and the Austrians crossed the frontier and threatened Paris.   Another Austrian army invaded Alsace ; the Prussians drove the French from the middle Rhine; the English, under the Duke of York, besieged Dunkirk ; Admiral Hood was admitted into the harbour of Toulon, and the Spaniards crossed the Pyrenees and conquered Roussillon.   But these reverses to French arms served only to increase the pace of revolution in Paris and to invest its leaders with the halo of patriotism. The desertion of Dumouriez, who took refuge with the Austrians after Neerwinden, and the outbreak of civil war in La Vendée tended in the same direction.   France was in danger, and at all hazards it was necessary to restore unity to her councils.   On 2nd June thirty-two leading Girondists, including Brissot, Vergniaud and Pétion, were arrested, and thus the struggle between the Girondists and the Jacobins was finally decided in favour of the extremer and more vigorous party.   An extraordinary tribunal to judge, without appeal, conspirators against the State had been established in March ; the "Committee of Public Safety," formed originally in April and re-organised in July, was invested with practically supreme powers; while Carnot, admitted to the Committee in August, demanded a *levée en masse*, reorganised the army and inspired its administration with his own fiery energy.   By the early autumn he had 750,000 men under arms.   The results were quickly discernible.   The royalist rising in La Vendée and the South was crushed ; the siege of Dunkirk was raised ; the English were defeated at Hondschoote (September) and the Austrians at Wattignies (October). Thus Neerwinden was avenged and all danger on the North-eastern frontier was averted. Simultaneously Alsace was cleared; the allies were forced back across the Rhine; and before the end of the year the great arsenal of Toulon was recaptured from the English. On every side the armies of Carnot were triumphant.

It is futile to deny that the French victories on the borders were due to the triumph of the Jacobins in the heart of France. The Girondins, with their virtuous declamation and their doctrinaire republicanism form an interesting phase in the development of the Revolution. But they were unequal to the stern realities of war, and military reverses sealed their political doom. The spirit of the new administration was well expressed by Robespierre: "Tyrants beset us without our borders; the friends of tyranny conspire within. In such a crisis the principle of our policy must be this : To govern the people by Reason and the enemies of the people by Terror. Terror is only justice more prompt, more vigorous, more inexorable, and therefore Virtue's child." *The Jacobin triumph and the Reign of Terror*

Every interest was to be subordinated to that of the public safety. The "young men shall go to war; the married men shall forge arms and transport supplies; the wives shall make tents and clothes and serve in the hospitals; the children shall tear old linen into lint; the aged shall resort to the public places to excite the courage of the warriors and hatred against kings." We may detest or deride the cause which evoked this enthusiasm; but the enthusiasm was genuine and not unheroic. Nothing must be permitted to stand in the way. Commercial maxims must be set at naught, and the ordinary guarantees for personal liberty must be suspended. By the "law of the maximum," maximum prices were fixed for provisions, manufactured goods and even raw materials. By the "law of the suspects" the Revolutionary committees—not in Paris only but throughout France—were authorised to imprison all members of noble families, all relatives of *Émigrés*, and all who by word or act or writing showed sympathy with the fallen monarchy or the *Ancien Régime*. The prisons were, before long, crammed to overflowing, and the congestion was relieved only by the daily procession to the Place de la Révolution where the guillotine was doing its ghastly work. "The guillotine, we find, gets always a quicker motion as other things are quickening. The guillotine, by its speed of going, will give index of the general velocity of the Republic. The clanking of its huge axe rising and falling there in horrid systole diastole. . . . Heaven knows there were terrors and horrors enough : yet that was not all the phenomenon : nay, more properly that was not the phenomenon at all, but rather was the *shadow* of it, the negative part of it." There is truth in Carlyle's statement, though the expression is fantastic and rhetorical, and despite our natural and righteous detestation of the 'Terror" and its agents, we must recognise the vigour of those who organised it.

Meanwhile terrible scenes were daily enacted in Paris. On the 16th of October the Queen, Marie Antoinette, went to the scaffold with a dignity and courage not unworthy of the daughter of the great Hungarian Queen, Maria Theresa. The pathos of her death and the brutality of her murderers have thrown a halo of romance around a woman whose influence was almost uniformly mischievous. Marie Antoinette was followed to the scaffold by the twenty-two leaders of the Gironde—among them Vergniaud, Brissot and Madame Roland; by Philippe

Egalité,[1] and by Bailly the first Mayor of Paris under the new municipality, and first President of the States-general itself. The "Terror" thus imposed on Paris was carried out with even greater violence in the provinces. "To be safe," said Hébert, "you must kill everybody." A systematic attempt was made to carry out the prescription. The Vendéan revolt was stamped out in blood, the inhabitants of Toulon and Lyons were practically exterminated, and whole provinces were handed over to military execution in the hope of wiping out a population which could not be coerced into submission.

Thus was the supremacy of the Jacobins established. Before long, however, divisions began to manifest themselves in the ranks of the extreme party. A section led by Danton and inspired by the *Vieux Cordelier* of Camille Desmoulins desired to stay the hand of vengeance and re-establish a Government at once stable and comparatively merciful. At the opposite pole were the followers of Hébert, himself the advocate of unsparing terror and revolting atheism. It was the Hébertists who, having forced the Convention to abolish the Catholic religion and substitute for it the worship of Reason, celebrated (10th November) the Feast of Reason in the Cathedral of Notre Dame.

To the Hébertists Robespierre and his followers offered uncompromising opposition. "If God did not exist," said Robespierre, "it would be necessary to invent Him." Atheism he denounced as aristocratic. By an alliance with the Dantonists Robespierre crushed the Hébertists, and in March, 1794, Hébert himself, Chaumette and

[1] Louis Philippe, Duke of Orleans, great-grandson of the Regent Orleans, and father of Louis Philippe who became King of the French in 1830. See p. 137.

4

Anarcharsis Clootz were sent to the guillotine. Having thus disposed of the extreme Left, Robespierre next turned upon the Moderates, and in April Danton, Camille Desmoulins and many of their followers shared the fate of the Hébertists. So Danton, the hero of Carlyle's famous epic, passes out of the story.

The Trium-virate

The triumvirate of Robespierre, Couthon and St. Just was now supreme. In May, 1794, the Convention, at the instance of Robespierre, resolved to recognise the existence of a Supreme Being, and in June Robespierre himself presided over a blasphemous festival designed in honour of the deity of his own creation. Two days after this festival Couthon proposed to the Convention the famous Law of the 22nd Prairial (10th June)—a law designed to increase the murderous efficiency of the Revolutionary Tribunal by abolishing all formal proof of guilt.

" Of all laws ever passed in the world, this," says Lord Morley, " is the most nakedly iniquitous." Prisoners were henceforth tried in batches without counsel to defend them, and were deprived even of the privilege of calling witnesses for the defence. The Tribunal was, however, undeniably effective. Within six weeks the number of its victims exceeded 1,400 ; but the end was now in sight ; the tyranny of Robespierre and the triumvirate had become intolerable. Had Robespierre himself possessed an atom of practical ability his ascendency might have been considerably prolonged ; but of decisive action he was incapable.

The Re-volution of Thermidor

Thus things hurried on to a crisis. No party and no individual knew who would be the next victims, and all determined to strike at the arch-terrorist. On the 9th of Thermidor the blow was struck. Robespierre,

Couthon and St. Just were arrested, and though the Commune of Paris stood by them the Convention managed to assert itself, and Robespierre and his comrades at last shared the fate of thousands of their victims.

Robespierre is a curious and interesting study: he proclaimed himself to be the champion of morality and a " living martyr to the Republic, at once the victim and the enemy of crime ". It was a pose, but an unconscious one. Fertile in phrases and a genuine sentimentalist, Robespierre probably deceived himself even more than he deceived others. With his death we reach a turning-point in the Revolution, the close of the Terror and the beginning of the reaction. Why France endured for so long (April, 1793-July, 1794) a system under which thousands [1] of innocent victims were sent to the scaffold in the name of Liberty remains one of the enigmas of history. The Terror was the work of a contemptible and not wholly compact minority, and its overthrow was welcomed by the vast majority of the citizens of France.

"Oui, il y a un Dieu," said a Parisian artisan, as he gazed upon the prostrate body of Robespierre. The sentiment was re-echoed throughout France.

[1] Taine puts it at 17,000, but this is probably an exaggeration. It is estimated that between April, 1793, and July, 1794, 2,625 persons were sentenced to death by the Revolutionary Tribunal at Paris alone.

CHAPTER VI

THE ADVENT OF NAPOLEON BONAPARTE. THE REACTION IN FRANCE (1794-1802)

Constitutional Government is a chimera at the conclusion of a Revolution such as that of France. It is not under shelter of legal authority that parties whose passions have been so violently excited can arrange themselves and repose; a more vigorous power is required to restrain them, to fuse their still burning elements, and protect them against foreign violence. That power is the Empire of the sword.—THIERS.

The Reaction

THE "Revolution of Thermidor" marks the beginning of reaction. Nearly all parties were now anxious to put an end to the Terror, and to re-establish a settled Government. The Revolutionary Tribunal was suspended; the Law of the 22nd Prairial was annulled; the suspects were gradually released; the agents of the Terror were brought to that justice which they had so hideously burlesqued; the decree proscribing the priests and nobles was revoked; the seventy-three excluded Girondist deputies were recalled to the Convention, and, in December, 1794, the Jacobin Club was closed. Finally, with a laudable anxiety to restore a healthy tone to commerce and finance, the *Law of the maximum* was repealed, and the system of requisitions for the supply of the army was gradually abandoned (December). These measures, though eminently wise and just, served for the moment only to intensify the financial crisis. By the end of 1794 as-

52

signats (or paper money) to the nominal value of 7,000 million francs were in circulation, and within twelve months this huge amount was more than doubled. The value of this paper currency fell with corresponding rapidity. In December, 1794, the assignats were worth 22 per cent. only of their face value; in May, 1795, they had fallen to 7 per cent., and by the end of the year to 1 per cent. With the fall in the value of the currency prices rose to starvation height; an assignat of 100 francs would scarcely purchase a plate of soup, and distress, both in Paris and the provinces, became intense. In the spring of 1795 the remnant of the Jacobin party rallied sufficiently to make political capital out of distress and to inflame the starving populace to a couple of revolts (12th Germinal and 1st Prairial). But after several days of street fighting these insurrections were suppressed, and the Convention took advantage of its victory finally to extinguish the power of the Terrorists. The National Guard was reorganised, the populace was disarmed; sixty deputies of the "Mountain" or Jacobin party were proscribed, and many of the leading agents of the late administration were guillotined or exiled to Cayenne.

The triumph of the Moderates was accentuated by the extraordinary success which in the main had attended the arms of France. The victory of the allies during the spring and summer of 1793 was a mere flash in the pan. Before the end of that year France, as we have seen, was rapidly regaining the ground she had lost, and in 1794 was able to resume the offensive. England indeed maintained her position at sea and inflicted a decisive defeat upon the French fleet on the 1st of June. But Howe's famous victory was counter-balanced by that of Jourdan

French
Victories

at Fleurus (26th June); the English and Austrians were driven back on Holland, the Prussians had to give way on the middle Rhine, and by the end of 1794 Belgium was once more in the hands of France. " Eight pitched battles won, 116 towns and 230 forts taken, 90,000 prisoners and 3,800 guns captured." Such was the French record for 1794. From Belgium the French advanced into Holland, and early in 1795 they proclaimed there, to the undisguised satisfaction of the inhabitants, the Batavian Republic. As a consequence England virtually withdrew from all part in the continental struggle and concentrated her efforts upon the maritime and colonial contest. On the Italian and Spanish frontiers French arms were no less successful. Political forces were also working in their favour, and the European coalition was rapidly going to pieces. From the first Prussia had been more interested in the development of events in Poland than in France. In conjunction with Russia she had effected the Second Partition of Poland in 1793, and in 1795 the two Powers admitted Austria to a share in the final dismemberment of that unhappy country.

Treaties of Basle, 1795 — In the same year the war of the First Coalition came to an end. The Grand Duke of Tuscany made peace early in 1795, and during the summer a series of treaties was concluded at Basle. Prussia (5th April, 1795) agreed to surrender her provinces to the west of the Rhine, and for ten years took no further part in the war; France granted peace, on Prussia's intercession, to the Northern States of the Empire, and by a secret Treaty (5th August) agreed to compensate Prussia, in return for the Rhine frontier, with territory to the east of that river. Spain purchased peace by the cession of part of St. Domingo, and England, Austria and Sardinia were thus left alone to confront France.

Meanwhile, encouraged by the progress of the anti-Jacobin reaction, the Royalist *Émigrés* attempted to reinforce the efforts of the Vendéans in the West. In June, 1795, they made a descent upon Quiberon Bay, but their forces were routed by Hoche, and the attempt served only to demonstrate the military incapacity of the *Émigrés* and the attachment of the French people to the Republic. Before the end of the year Hoche by a combination of sternness and clemency at last succeeded in bringing the risings in La Vendée and Brittany to an end. Royalist Risings in the West

Victorious over its enemies abroad and at home, and relieved of one source of embarrassment by the death of the young Louis XVII.[1] (8th June, 1795), the Republic now made a determined effort to secure for itself a stable government. The effort issued in the establishment of the government of the Directory. A brief experience had taught France the practical inconvenience of a single-chamber legislature. Under the new constitution, therefore, the legislative authority was vested in two Councils— the Council of Cinq-Cent and the Council of Ancients. The former had the sole right to initiate legislation. The latter possessed only the right of veto. One-third of each Council was to retire every year, though it was subsequently decreed that of the first Councils two-thirds should be selected from the members of the outgoing Convention. This "perpetuation" decree was passed partly to avoid the opposite blunder of 1791, and partly to exclude Royalists from the new Councils. But though not indefensible the provision was taken to betray a lack of confidence in the electorate, and it gave the new constitution a bad start. The Constitution of the Year III

[1] Nominally succeeded his father, Louis XVI., as a lad of eight in 1793.

The executive power was confided to a Directory of five members, selected by the Council of Ancients from a list of ten presented by the Cinq-Cents. One Director was to retire annually, but otherwise the Directors, removable by impeachment, were not responsible either to the legislature or to the people. This, in fact, was the cardinal defect of the Constitution of the Year III. : neither directly nor through the Legislature could the country impress its will upon the executive. The supreme importance of securing harmonious co-operation between law-makers and executive administrators was a lesson which Frenchmen were slow to learn. But nothing did more to wreck successive constitutions than the neglect of this truth. The Directorial Constitution was no exception to the rule.

13th Vendémiaire

Its first peril was, however, successfully encountered in the insurrection of 13th Vendémiaire (5th October, 1795). The insurgents, led by a combination of reactionaries and extreme democrats, were inflamed by the " perpetuation decree " of the Convention. The latter decided on stern measures of repression, and entrusted the execution of them to Barras and a young Corsican gunner who had been favourably mentioned in despatches from Toulon— Napoleon Bonaparte. Bonaparte carried out his orders with characteristic thoroughness. The " whiff of grapeshot " dispersed the insurgents ; and the Convention, triumphant over all its foes, declared its long session (since September, 1792) closed.

Napoleon Bonaparte

The first batch of Directors included, besides three nonentities, Barras and Carnot, but the appearance of the "strong man " upon the stage of Parisian politics opens a new act in the drama of the Revolution. By his aid the Convention had triumphed ; on his strong arm the

Directory was to lean; in him the Revolution was to find both consummation and contradiction. For Napoleon Bonaparte was at once the embodiment of the principles of the Revolution and the representative of the reaction against them.

Born at Ajaccio in Corsica (1769) Bonaparte was educated at the military schools of Brienne and Paris. He appears to have had some thoughts of entering the service of the English East India Company, where "gunners were better appreciated than in France," but remaining in Corsica he resisted the separatist movement in the island, and when the Corsicans, led by Paoli, declared their independence of France (1793), Bonaparte took refuge in Marseilles. In France he posed as a Jacobin, attached himself to the party of Robespierre, and in August, 1793, found himself virtually in command of the artillery in the force raised for the siege of Toulon. In that siege he greatly distinguished himself, and in 1794 he was appointed general of artillery in the army of Italy. The fall of Robespierre (July, 1794) endangered for the moment the position he had won, and he was suspended from his command; but his talents were too great to be ignored, and before the end of the year a post was found for him at the war office. His signal service to the Republic in the insurrection of 13th Vendémiaire was rewarded by his appointment to the command of the army of Italy. He had been employed at the war office to draw a plan for an Italian campaign, and Carnot's eagle eye discerned in the draftsman the soldier best fitted to execute his own plan. That his appointment to this important command coincided with his marriage to Josephine Beauharnais (March, 1796) is true; but it was due less to the social influence which he then for the first time enjoyed, than to the recognition of sheer military capacity.   Before the end of March he left Paris to take up his command.

That command marks the real beginning of Bonaparte's political career, and a turning-point in the history of the war.

The Italian Campaign At the end of the eighteenth century Italy had reached the nadir of impotence and degradation. For centuries she had served as the cockpit of contending dynasties, and had suffered the domination now of Habsburg now of Bourbon. In 1796 Italy was divided into ten states. The Milanese (Lombardy) was the only one actually united with a foreign Empire (Austria), but Tuscany was an appanage of the Austrian House, and several of the smaller Duchies were under its influence. One Spanish Bourbon was on the throne of the Two Sicilies and another was Duke of Parma and Piacenza. Venice and Genoa still retained their republican independence, but without any of their ancient vigour; while central Italy lay benumbed under the hand of the Papacy. Piedmont, ruled by the King of Sardinia, alone among the Italian states showed any sign of vigorous political life, and even Piedmont failed when the hour of trial came.

Such was the Italy into which, in the spring of 1796, Bonaparte marched, proclaiming himself the champion of Italian freedom and the destined restorer of Italian nationality.

His plan of campaign against Austria involved a threefold advance on Vienna. Jourdan, in command of the army which had lately conquered the Netherlands, was to advance into Germany by the valley of the Main; Moreau was to cross the Rhine at Strasburg and advance by the Danube; Napoleon himself was to attack in north Italy and take the Austrians in flank. The scheme though brilliant in conception demanded great nicety of execution, and, except where Napoleon himself commanded, it broke down. Jourdan and Moreau found themselves opposed by the Archduke Charles, a strategist of the first order, at the head of 100,000 troops. Jourdan crossed the Rhine at Cologne and at Düsseldorf, and penetrated into the Palatinate, but defeated by the Archduke at Amberg (24th August) and Würzburg (3rd September) was glad to regain French territory without further disaster. Moreau made a dash into Bavaria and got as far as Munich, but the defeat of his colleague left him to face alone the army of the victorious Archduke. No course was open to him but to fall back on the Rhine, and by a series of masterly rear-guard actions he regained Strasburg in December.

Far different was the issue of the Italian campaign under Napoleon. His first business was to drive in a wedge between the Austrians and their Sardinian allies. This done he compelled the King of Sardinia to sue for an armistice before the campaign was a fortnight old. Peace was concluded on 15th May, by which Sardinia ceded Savoy and Nice to France and allowed Bonaparte to occupy the strong fortresses of Tortona, Valenza and Coni.

Having crushed the Piedmontese Bonaparte now turned upon the Austrians, forced a passage over the bridge of Lodi (10th May), and entered Milan on the 16th. All Lombardy, with the exception of Mantua, was now at his feet. Alarmed by the brilliant success of French arms other Italian Powers hastened to come to terms with the victorious general. The Dukes of Parma and Modena concluded armistices with the French in May; the Pope and the King of Naples in June. By the definitive Peace of Tolentino (19th February, 1797) the Pope was compelled to renounce all claim to Avignon and to cede Bologna and Ferrara to France. Meanwhile Bonaparte had already begun the reorganisation of Italy. Before the end of 1796 Austrian Lombardy was erected into the Transpadane Republic, and Bologna, Ferrara, Modena and Reggio combined to form a Cispadane Republic.

But Mantua was still untaken. Incomparably the most important strategical point in North Italy, this great fortress resisted all the efforts of Bonaparte from June, 1796, to February, 1797. Again and again the Austrians attempted to relieve it, but Wurmser was defeated at Brescia and at Castiglione in August; Alvinzi was routed after three days' fighting at Arcola (15th-19th November), and again at Rivoli (14th January), and on 2nd February Mantua surrendered. Bonaparte was now free to advance on Vienna : but in April preliminaries of peace were signed at Leoben, and after six months of negotiation a definitive peace was concluded between France and Austria at Campo-Formio (17th October, 1797).

During those six months Bonaparte had not been idle. In May he picked a quarrel with Venice, and having deposed the ruling oligarchy, in the sacred name of "Liberty" he occupied the city itself, and the Venetian islands off the Greek coast (Corfu, Cephalonia, etc.). In June he reorganised northern and central Italy into the Cisalpine Republic, consisting of the Transpadane and Cispadane Republics, Austrian Lombardy, Romagna and the Legations, to which were subsequently added the Valtelline, the western portion of Venetia and other strips of territory. In the same month (4th June) Genoa was converted into the Ligurian Republic in strict dependence upon France. Nor was Bonaparte neglectful of political developments at home. The Directory had not succeeded in tranquillising France; Pichegru, strongly suspected of royalism, had become President of the Cinq-Cent, and Barthélemy, an avowed royalist, had succeeded Letourneur as Director. The Councils themselves had by the new elections been strongly reinforced by royalists, and Barras and his republican colleagues in dire alarm sent for the conqueror of Italy. Bonaparte knew how to wait; the pear was not yet ripe, but he despatched Augereau—a trusted lieutenant—to Paris, and by Augereau's help the *coup d'état* of 18th Fructidor (4th September, 1797) was effected. Fifty-three members of the Councils, including Pichegru, were arrested and sent into exile; Carnot and Barthélemy, threatened with a like fate, managed to escape, and the authority of the republican Directors was temporarily restored. What is the real significance of Fructidor? Ostensibly a defeat for the royalists it put one more nail into the coffin of the Republic. In the long run Bonaparte was the sole gainer. His language had already begun to indicate an increasing independence of his nominal masters. "Do you suppose," he wrote in May, 1797, "that I triumph in Italy for the glory of the lawyers of the Directory, a Carnot or a Barras? Do you suppose that I mean to found a Republic? What an idea? A Republic of thirty millions of people! With our morals, our vices! How is such a thing possible? The nation wants a chief, a chief covered with glory, not theories of government, phrases, ideological essays that the French do not understand. They want some playthings; that will be enough; they will play with them and let themselves be led, always supposing they are cleverly prevented from seeing the goal towards which they are moving." His tone in the peace negotiations with Austria corresponded with these views. He was the

18th Fructidor

independent conqueror not the servant of a tottering Republic, and as such he granted to the Emperor the terms
finally embodied in the Peace of Campo-Formio (17th
October, 1797). By this exceedingly important treaty:—

(1) The Austrian Netherlands were definitely ceded to France;
(2) the Republic of Venice was annihilated and its territories partitioned: Continental Venetia east of the Adige, Istria and Dalmatia
were annexed to Austria; Venetia west of the Adige to the Cisalpine Republic; the Ionian islands to France; (3) Austria recognised the Cisalpine Republic and agreed to indemnify the Duke of
Modena with Breisgau.

Such was the public treaty; the secret terms were even
more significant. By these Austria was to acquiesce in
the attainment of the Rhine frontier by France; the dis-
possessed princes were to be indemnified in Germany, and
Austria was to be compensated with Salzburg and a slice
of Bavaria.

The Treaty of Campo-Formio was at once a triumph
for Bonaparte and a real satisfaction to Austria. Bonaparte had won for France the "scientific frontier" (the
Rhine, the Alps and the Pyrenees), for which Richelieu
and Louis XIV. had sighed and fought in vain; he had
acquired Savoy and Nice; he had established the domination of France in Italy and in Holland; and he had
planted the French flag in the Ionian isles. Austria, on
the other hand, gained much and lost little that she cared
to keep. Despite defeat, her position remained unexpectedly advantageous.

That Bonaparte deliberately spared and even caressed
Austria at Campo-Formio there can be no doubt. He
was already flying at higher game.

The acquisition of the Ionian isles by France is the
key to Bonaparte's policy. They were a stepping-stone

to Egypt, and Egypt, as Bonaparte believed, was the key to the conflict between France and England. "Really to destroy England," he wrote in August, 1797, "we must make ourselves masters of Egypt." What were his chances of success?

The French conquest of Holland in 1795 led England, as we have seen, to concentrate her efforts on the maritime and colonial struggle. After the establishment of the Batavian Republic Holland became to all intents and purposes a dependency of France. England, therefore, promptly declared war upon her, and as a result many of the Dutch colonies fell into British hands. Cape Colony was occupied in 1795 : Malacca, Ceylon and part of the West Indies were conquered in the same year. Spain similarly threw in her lot with France and with similar results. For a maritime Power to enter into alliance at this juncture with France was merely to expose itself and its colonies to the attack of the British navy. Thus Spain's declaration of war was immediately followed by the loss of Trinidad and by the annihilation of her navy at Cape St. Vincent (February, 1797). Holland suffered similarly at Camperdown in October. St. Vincent and St. Lucia, taken by the French in 1795, were recaptured by Abercromby in 1796, and in December of the same year Hoche failed in his attempted descent upon Ireland.

But though England's successes at sea were virtually unbroken, the outlook for her in 1797 was not free from anxiety. Ireland was on the verge of rebellion; there were mutinies in the fleet and no little discontent at home; a financial panic compelled the suspension of cash payments, and Consols fell to 48. Moreover, on the Continent there was no longer a soldier in arms

Napoleon Bonaparte and England

against the French Republic. Pitt, always averse to
the war, was now more than ever anxious to make peace.
Twice in 1796 he had made overtures to the Directory,
and in 1797 negotiations were resumed at Lille. Lord
Malmesbury, to whom they were entrusted, was sincerely
anxious for peace, but his efforts to obtain it were vain,
and Pitt no sooner realised their vanity than he threw
himself with vigour into the task of forming a second
coalition against France.

Hardly was the ink dry on the Treaty of Campo-
Formio before it became clear that Bonaparte regarded it
not as a settlement but as a stepping-stone. Disturbances in Rome led to the occupation of the City
by French troops (February, 1798). The advent of the
French was soon followed by the establishment of the
Roman Republic and the expulsion of the Pope. The
Swiss Federation was the next victim. The Swiss were
now as ever anxious to avoid being involved in the
continental turmoil: but no efforts could avail; early in
1798 Switzerland was conquered, and the Helvetic Republic was established in close dependence upon France.

The Egyp-
tian Ex-
pedition

But Bonaparte himself had bigger things on hand.
Soon after the *coup d'état* of Fructidor he was appointed
to the chief command of the " army of England ". His
immediate objective was Egypt, and on 18th May, 1798,
he set sail at the head of a great expedition from Toulon.
Malta was occupied without resistance from the Knights
(10th June); Bonaparte landed his troops in Egypt (1st
July); took Alexandria (2nd July); fought and won the
battle of the Pyramids (21st July), and occupied Cairo on
the 22nd. Egypt was in his hands. But Nelson and the
English fleet were on his track, and on 1st August they annihilated the French fleet in the battle of the Nile. Nelson's

great victory rendered Bonaparte's position in Egypt exceedingly precarious. Deprived of his fleet, cut off from his base, a lesser man would have deemed it desperate. On 1st September Turkey, encouraged by Nelson's victory, declared war on the French and prepared for the reconquest of Egypt. Bonaparte, therefore, determined to take the offensive in Syria. He took Jaffa by assault, laid siege to Acre (March, 1799) and inflicted a terrible defeat upon the Turks at Mount Tabor (16th April). Acre, thanks to Sir Sidney Smith, proved impregnable, and Bonaparte decided to retreat on Egypt. From Egypt the Turks were determined to dislodge him. On 11th July a second Turkish army despatched from Rhodes disembarked at Aboukir, only to be annihilated by the French and driven headlong into the sea on 25th July. This battle of Aboukir (to be carefully distinguished from Nelson's victory in Aboukir Bay twelve months earlier) established Bonaparte's supremacy in Egypt. But it was a barren victory. News from France convinced him that the moment for striking the effective blow in French politics had come, and that it must be struck in Paris. On 25th August, precisely a month after the victory of Aboukir, he embarked at Alexandria, leaving the command in Egypt to Kléber. The Mediterranean was carefully patrolled by the English fleet, but Bonaparte managed to evade it, landed at Fréjus on 9th October and on the 16th reached Paris. On 9th November he carried out the *coup d'état* of 18th Brumaire, and by a single blow, struck at precisely the right moment, made himself master of France.

During Bonaparte's absence in Egypt events had moved rapidly in Europe. In the winter of 1798-99 a fresh coalition was formed, largely through the efforts of Pitt,

War of the Second Coalition, 1798-1801

5

against France. Great Britain, Russia and Austria were the chief parties, but Turkey, Naples (the Two Sicilies) and Portugal also adhered to it. Prussia alone stood conspicuously aloof. The war opened in Southern Italy where Ferdinand of Naples overthrew the recent Roman Republic and invited the Pope to return to the Vatican. But his triumph was brief. The Directory marched an army into Italy. Charles Emmanuel IV. of Sardinia was expelled from Turin and compelled to take refuge in Sardinia; Ferdinand of Naples was driven to Palermo; the Roman Republic was re-established, and Southern Italy was organised as the Parthenopean Republic (January, 1799).

Campaign of 1799

But the campaign of 1799 was in the main unfortunate for France, though Masséna's grip on Switzerland prevented the allies from turning their victories in the field to much account. Their plan was to attack France (i) by way of the upper Rhine and (ii) in North Italy. On the upper Rhine the Archduke Charles was completely victorious. He defeated Jourdan at Stockach (north of Lake Constance, 25th March, 1799); drove Masséna back in Switzerland, occupied Zürich, and took Mannheim (18th September). Not less decisive were the victories of the Austro-Russian forces in North Italy. Kray's victory on the Adige (Magnano, 5th April), drove the French back on Milan, and Suvaroff's brilliant campaign (April-June) completed their discomfiture. After the great battle of Trebbia (17th-19th June) the French power in Italy seemed to be annihilated. The Roman, Parthenopean and Cisalpine Republics were overthrown; Genoa alone was held by France. But despite reverses in the field France held the key of the strategical position, and both in a military and a political sense the coalition was a rope of sand. Suvaroff, owing to his own insolence and Austrian jealousy, had to retire over the St. Gothard. While he was still in the Pass Masséna inflicted a crushing defeat on the Russians under Korsakoff at Zürich (26th September); the fruits of Suvaroff's great campaign were lost, and Russia withdrew in dudgeon from the war. A Russo-British descent upon Holland (August-September, 1799) had served little purpose except to demonstrate afresh the incapacity of the Duke of York.

The campaign of 1800 opened under very different conditions. The futile Directory had gone, and the resources of France were concentrated under a single dominating intellect. The result was seen at once. Austria was attacked vigorously by the Danube and in North Italy. Bonaparte's campaign in Italy was crowned by the great victory of Marengo (14th June) and Moreau's march into the heart of South Germany by that of Hohenlinden (3rd December). Austria was once more at the mercy of Bonaparte, and in February, 1801, was compelled to sign the Peace of Lunéville. *Campaign of 1800 and Peace of Lunéville (1801)*

By that Treaty the concessions already made at Campo-Formio were confirmed: the Emperor Francis was further compelled to accept the Adige as his boundary in North Italy; to surrender Tuscany to the son of the Bourbon Duke of Parma, an arrangement preliminary to the latter's elevation to the kingdom of Etruria: to recognise the Cisalpine, the Ligurian, the Helvetic and the Batavian Republics, and to acknowledge the right of France to Belgium and the Rhine frontier. *Provisions of Lunéville*

Bonaparte subsequently concluded with Naples a peace by which King Ferdinand agreed to exclude British and Turkish vessels from his harbours, and to surrender to France the *Stato dei Presidii* (*i.e.*, the maritime districts of Tuscany) for the augmentation of a future kingdom of Etruria. By a treaty with Spain the latter ceded Louisiana to France, from whom it was subsequently purchased (1803) by the United States.

Once more Great Britain stood alone confronting France. Bonaparte had had little difficulty in detaching the Czar Paul of Russia from the coalition. More than that, the Czar, instigated by France, had revived against England the Armed Neutrality (December, 1800), consisting of Russia, Prussia, Sweden and Denmark. But this sinister combination was quickly broken up first by Nelson's brilliant victory at Copenhagen (2nd April, 1801), and, secondly, by the assassination of the Czar Paul (March, 1801). Paul's successor Alexander I. was a man of a different mould and temper. Meanwhile Great Britain was determined to allow no remnant of Bonaparte's authority to remain in Egypt. The victory of Sir Ralph Abercromby at Alexandria (March, 1801) practically decided the matter: in September the French agreed to evacuate Egypt, which was forthwith restored to the Porte. There was no longer any immediate obstacle in the way of the conclusion of peace, and on 25th March, 1802, a treaty was signed at Amiens between England on the one side, and France, Spain and the Batavian Republic on the other.

Peace of
Amiens,
1802

France agreed to evacuate the Papal States and Naples, to restore Egypt to the Porte and to acknowledge the independence of the Ionian islands. Great Britain, on the other hand, restored to France and her allies all the conquests made during the war, except Ceylon (captured from Holland in 1795) and Trinidad (taken from Spain in 1797); she agreed that Malta should be restored to the Knights of St. John, and tacitly accepted the continental settlement as defined at Lunéville.

The Treaty of Amiens, the only peace made between

Great Britain and France during the long series of Revolutionary and Napoleonic wars, proved to be a hollow truce.   But Pitt was no longer at the helm in England, and Bonaparte desired a breathing space in which to consolidate his power in France.

CHAPTER VII

THE CONSULATE AND THE EMPIRE

ENGLAND AND NAPOLEON

We have done with the romance of the Revolution ; we must now commence its history.—NAPOLEON.

Steps
towards
the Empire

AT peace not only with Europe but with England Bonaparte had now an opportunity to establish his position in France. He did not neglect it. The way had been cleared by the *coup d'état* of the 18th Brumaire. During the absence of Bonaparte in Egypt, the unpopularity of the Directory had become more and more profound. It began to be whispered that the Directors, conscious of their weakness and jealous of the reputation of the successful soldier, had sent Bonaparte to Egypt to get rid of him. His reappearance in France was timed with perfect precision. He found everything ready for the step which he had long foreseen. On the 15th Brumaire he came to an understanding with the Abbé Siéyès, one of the Directors, and three days later the *coup d'état* was effected. The Directory was dissolved ; the Council of the Cinq-Cents was driven out at the point of the bayonet ; that of the Ancients acquiesced, and executive power was provisionally conferred upon Siéyès, Roger Ducos and Bonaparte. Thus was accomplished the destruction at once of the Directory and of the Republic.   Few Frenchmen regretted them; the *coup d'état* of Brumaire was almost universally approved. Royalists and reactionaries, moderates and republicans all saw in the overthrow of the Directory the possibility of the opening of a new era satisfactory to their several interests, hopeful for their divergent aims.   The royalists regarded it as a step towards the restoration of the Bourbons; the moderate republicans fondly imagined that it might establish "Liberty"—so frequently proclaimed in word, so constantly denied in fact; the masses saw in it—with greater insight—the triumph of the strong man who would restore order in France.   Many hopes were shattered in the months that followed; the harvest of Brumaire was reaped exclusively by Bonaparte.   Thus was the prediction of Burke literally and remarkably fulfilled.   The popular general had arrived who understood "the art of conciliating the soldiery," and possessed "the true spirit of command," and who knew how to draw "the eyes of all men upon himself".

The provisional Government lasted only until the 13th of December.   On that day the new *Constitution of the Year VIII.* was promulgated.   Drafted by the prince of constitution-mongers, the Abbé Siéyès, it seemed the most fantastic scheme ever evolved out of the brain of a doctrinaire.   But perhaps there was method in its madness.

The Consulate Constitution

The scheme, despite lip homage to democratic ideas, virtually extinguished popular representation.   The legislature was to consist of three bodies: (i) a *Senate* of 80 members, nominated for life, and charged with the duty of selecting (from a list of 5,000 sent up by the departments) the members of the two other bodies, and of vetoing any " unconstitutional " measures passed by them;

(ii) a *Tribunate* of 100 members, which could discuss laws, but could not vote on them; and (iii) a *Corps Législatif*, which could vote upon laws without debate. The executive was vested in a Grand Elector and two Consuls, and a Council of State, nominated by the former, the principal function of the Council being to prepare laws to be discussed by the *Tribunate*, and voted on by the *Corps Législatif*. The Grand Elector having nominated the Consuls was to hold a mysterious position without responsibility or real power. Such was the "phantom" constitution of the Abbé Siéyès, the culminating absurdity of the constitutional experiments attempted during the last ten years in France. Napoleon [1] turned it inside out. The legislature was "impotent for mischief," and might be neglected for the moment, but he dealt drastically with the phantom Grand Elector. Siéyès, as Mr. Fyffe says, "might apportion the act of deliberation among debating societies and dumb juries to the full extent of his own ingenuity; but the moment that he applied his disintegrating method to the executive, Bonaparte swept away the flimsy reasoner, and set in the midst of his edifice of shadows the reality of an absolute personal rule". The Grand Elector was transformed into a First Consul with powers which rendered him master of France. To him was to belong the right of nominating all the chief officials who were to be responsible solely to him; of initiating legislation, and of nominating the members of the Senate. In 1802 Napoleon was confirmed in the Consulate for life, with power to nominate a successor, and in 1804 he accepted, or rather assumed, the Imperial Crown. Though the way had been long prepared, two reasons may have precipitated the final transformation of the Consulate into

The
Empire,
1804

[1] After he becomes Ruler of France I write of him as Napoleon instead of Bonaparte.

an hereditary Empire: the renewal of war with England and the detection of a conspiracy against the First Consul. Of this conspiracy, as of the Popish Plot of 1678, it may be said :—

> The wished occasion of the Plot he takes,
> Some circumstances finds, but more he makes.[1]

The prime movers in the plot were Georges Cadoudal, a Breton zealot, and the republican generals Pichegru and Moreau; the English Government was at least privy to it. Napoleon, thanks to Fouché and the French police, had all the threads of the conspiracy in his hands from the first; some were actually spun by him, but he dexterously waited until the arrangements were complete and the leaders within his grasp. His patience and dexterity were amply rewarded. Pichegru and Moreau were suddenly arrested with other leading conspirators in Paris. Pichegru died, probably by a violent death, in prison; Moreau suffered two years' imprisonment and then went into exile in America. But it was desirable that some member of the Bourbon house should be involved in the conspiracy. The Count of Artois could not be enticed from his retirement in England; it was determined, therefore, to make the Duc d'Enghien the victim. This young Bourbon prince was living quietly in Baden, when he was suddenly seized by French troops, marched off to Vincennes, and after the mockery of a court-martial was shot (March, 1804). His innocence was subsequently admitted by Napoleon with cynical frankness. "I had to choose between continuous persecution and one decisive blow, and my decision was not doubtful. I have for ever silenced both royalists and Jacobins. Only the republicans remain—mere dreamers who think that a Republic can be made out of an old monarchy." The dreamers,

[1] Dryden : *Absolom and Achitophel.*

he believed, were few and unimportant. The gorgeous ceremonial in the Cathedral of Notre Dame, and the acclamations which hailed the coronation of the new Charlemagne, appeared to justify his belief.

Reorganisation of French Institutions under Napoleon

Meanwhile the new Dictator had already entered upon the stupendous task of reorganising the institutions of France and of building up afresh the fabric of social order.

In this work Napoleon showed himself at once the heir of the Revolution, and the product of the reaction against it. Of "Liberty" he retained nothing but the husk; but virtual autocracy was combined with a large measure of social and fiscal "equality". The Constitution of the Year VIII. was further emasculated (notably by the modification and ultimate suppression of the *Tribunate*) until all power was concentrated in the hands of Napoleon. As with Central so also with Local institutions. The elective system established in 1790 had issued in hopeless chaos. Local government, therefore, was reorganised on centralised and autocratic lines; the elected Councils were reduced to impotence; the Departments were placed under prefects, the "Arrondisements" under sub-prefects, and the Communes under mayors—in each case appointed by, and responsible to, the central government. Similarly, the levying of taxation was taken out of the hands of local bodies and vested in those of controllers appointed from Paris. The exchequer and the taxpayer alike benefited. The peasant paid less and the Government got more. The establishment of the Bank of France (1800) further tended to restore financial confidence. Social confidence was restored by the repeal of the cruel *Law of Hostages*, and of almost all Laws and Decrees against the emigrant nobility; ecclesiastical tranquillity by the Concordat (1801). Ever since 1790 the Church in France had been rent in twain by the Civil Constitution of the Clergy. This schism was at last healed, and with the goodwill of the Papacy the Church took its place in the ordered autocracy of Napoleon. The Pope undertook to secure the resignation of all the bishops; the vacant sees were then filled impartially from "Constitutionals" and "Nonjurors"; the State was to nominate, the Pope to institute; the bishops in their turn were to renominate and reinstate the curés; the sales of Church property were confirmed, and the clergy became the salaried officials of the State. Such was the famous Concordat of 1801. As with the Church, so with education. Both were to subserve the work of social and political reconstruction. "So long," said Napoleon, "as people are not taught from childhood whether they are to be republicans or monarchists, Catholics or free-thinkers, the State will not form a nation; it will rest on vague bases and be constantly subject to change and disorder." The educational system was reorganised in consonance with this fundamental conception. A single "University of France" was set up under officials appointed by Napoleon, and the University in its turn was to control the whole educational machinery higher, secondary, technical and elementary. The Press was brought under similar control; a strict censorship was established, and recalcitrant journals were suppressed. The Judiciary was rendered hardly less dependent upon the will of the executive. A small committee of experts had been appointed in 1793 to codify the law, and the results of their labours, carried through under the direct supervision of Napoleon, still survive in the famous *Code Napoléon* (1807). Much of the law of Continental Europe is based upon this code to-day. Thus did France exchange liberty for efficiency.[1] With "equality," Napoleon had less quarrel. The institution of the Legion of Honour (1802) proved that he was quick to realise that French democracy has little affection for an undecorated equality; but "equality of opportunity" is the best guarantee of efficiency, and this principle was rigidly respected by Napoleon.

Renewal of War

In the midst of all this activity at home, Napoleon again became involved in war. The truce with England secured by the Treaty of Amiens proved to be of short duration. Napoleon complained that the British Government declined to evacuate Malta. England complained that Napoleon's aggressions in time of peace were hardly less numerous and less lucrative than in time of war. Piedmont had been annexed to France; Napoleon himself had become President of the Italian Republic in 1802 and "mediator" of Switzerland in 1803; the Batavian and the Ligurian Republics had been virtually incorporated in France. The English newspapers attacked Napoleon, and the *Moniteur* published an official report of Colonel Sebastiani's mission in Egypt, which gave great offence to the English Government. The latter consequently demanded (i) that France should evacuate Holland and Switzerland; (ii) that England should retain Malta for at least ten years; and (iii) should acquire Lampedusa—an island off the coast of Tunis. The demands, though not unreasonable in view of Napoleon's conduct, were such

[1] On this, *cf.* Lord Acton, who enforces the great truth proclaimed by De Tocqueville that "the French Revolution, far from reversing the political spirit of the old State, only carried out the same principles with intenser energy. The State which was absolute before became still more absolute, and the organs of the popular will became more efficient agents for the exercise of arbitrary power". (*Historical Essays and Studies*, p. 182.)

as could not be accepted, and, on the 18th May, 1803, England declared war.

From 1803-5 the war was devoid of serious incidents. England struck at the West Indies, capturing Tobago, St. Lucia and Guiana (from the Dutch) in 1803, while Napoleon, in flagrant violation of the Treaty of Basle, occupied Hanover and Naples. Of all the Powers Prussia was most nearly touched, both in honour and material interests, by the occupation of Hanover; but Prussia, under Frederick William III. and Haugwitz, was bent upon the maintenance of neutrality and offered no protest. Even the closing of the Elbe and the Weser to English ships—a notable anticipation of the Continental system— failed to rouse North Germany. Austria and Russia, how- ever, were becoming restless. The treacherous murder of the Duc d'Enghien; Napoleon's assumption of the Imperial Crown (December, 1804), and most of all, per- haps, his assumption of the Crown of Italy (May, 1805), roused the hostility of the Czar and the Emperor. Hence Pitt, who had returned to power in April, 1804, was able in 1805 to form the Third Coalition.

In this, England and Russia were joined by Austria and The Third Coalition Gustavus IV. of Sweden. The avowed objects of the allies were to drive France out of Italy, Hanover, Holland and Switzerland; to restore Piedmont to the King of Sardinia; Naples to its Bourbon king; and to unite Hol- land and Belgium under the House of Orange as a barrier against France. Prussia still adhered to her policy of neutrality, Bavaria, Baden and Würtemberg were on the side of France.

The main interest of the campaign of 1805 centred in The the attempt of Napoleon to achieve the supreme object of Trafalgar Campaign his military ambition—the invasion of England. To this end he mobilised a great army at Boulogne, and constructed a flotilla of flat-bottomed boats to transport it across the Channel. But to the success of his scheme one condition was essential : he must have at least temporary command of the Channel. This was to be obtained by a concentration of the French fleets then in the harbours of Brest, Rochefort and Toulon. The naval scheme was complicated, and had the fatal weakness of being planned not by a sailor, but by a soldier who assumed the same precision of movement in fleets as in armies. Nevertheless, it was only just less successful than ingenious. The English disposition was as follows : the Toulon fleet under Villeneuve was watched by Nelson; that of Rochefort under Missiessy by Collingwood; that of Brest under Gantheaume by Cornwallis. Villeneuve was to slip out of Toulon, pick up some Spanish ships at Cadiz, and draw Nelson after him to the West Indies; Missiessy, having slipped out of Rochefort, was to join Villeneuve at Martinique; and Gantheaume, having eluded Cornwallis, was to make all speed across the Atlantic and effect a junction with the Toulon and Rochefort fleets at Martinique. The combined squadron was then to make all sail for Europe and appear off Boulogne between 10th June and 10th July.

Villeneuve successfully eluded Nelson, and with the fleets of Toulon and Cadiz reached Martinique on 14th May, 1805.[1] Missiessy, who had reached Martinique in February, was by that time on his way back to Europe (Rochefort, 20th May). Nelson, despite a false impression that Egypt was Villeneuve's objective, was soon on his heels, and got to Barbadoes on 4th June. Villeneuve, however, again eluded him in the West Indies,

[1] See map, p. 101.

turned and made for Europe. Nelson learnt the news at
Trinidad (12th June); at once realised the game, and despatched a swift brig—the *Curieux*—to warn the Admiralty at home. The Admiralty got the news on 8th July;
reinforced Cornwallis off Brest, and ordered Sir Robert
Calder to intercept Villeneuve off Cape Finisterre. Calder
engaged Villeneuve off Cape Finisterre on the 22nd of
July. The action itself was indecisive, but Villeneuve
failed to push on to Brest, retired to refit at Vigo, then
slipped into Corunna, and on 15th August decided to
make for Cadiz. Calder's action off Finisterre ruined
Napoleon's plan for the invasion of England. Nelson
meanwhile had got back to Europe on 18th July, and
formed his junction with Cornwallis, off Brest, a month
later (15th August). On 19th October Villeneuve, in obedience to Napoleon's order to bring the fleet round to Toulon,
crept out of Cadiz, and on 21st October Nelson, who had
joined Collingwood off Cadiz on 28th September, inflicted
a crushing defeat upon the combined fleets of France and
Spain at Trafalgar. The results of Nelson's great victory
cannot be exaggerated: not only did it destroy the French
and Spanish fleets; not only did it establish the naval
ascendancy of England; but it compelled Napoleon to
adopt a policy which ultimately proved his ruin. With
England indisputably supreme at sea Napoleon could
strike at her only with economic weapons. Thus the
"Continental system" was the last desperate plunge of
a gambler on the brink of ruin.

But no one could have anticipated such results in 1805. The Cam-
The year closed in gloom for England, in triumph for Austerlitz
Napoleon. The failure of Villeneuve to reach Brest,
the prompt return of Nelson, convinced Napoleon that
invasion was impossible. With extraordinary rapidity
his plan was changed: by 26th August the Boulogne

army was on the march for the upper Rhine, and on 6th October it reached the Danube. The Austrian General Mack found himself surrounded at Ulm before he knew that Napoleon had left Boulogne, and on 20th October was compelled to capitulate. The road to Vienna was now open; on 13th November the Austrian capital was occupied by Murat, and on 2nd December Napoleon himself inflicted a terrible defeat upon the Czar and the Emperor Francis at Austerlitz in Moravia. Austerlitz smashed the Third Coalition, and Prussia, just on the point of tardy intervention, was compelled to accept from Napoleon the humiliating Treaty of Schönbrunn (15th December).

By this Treaty Prussia was compelled to accept Hanover from Napoleon and to exclude English ships from her harbours.

Treaty of Pressburg

Even more disastrous, though less humiliating, were the terms imposed upon Austria in the Treaty of Pressburg (26th December, 1805). Hitherto Austria had been leniently treated; but Napoleon now made up his mind that the power which had formed the backbone of three Continental Coalitions must be crushed.

By the Treaty of Pressburg Austria resigned Venetia, Istria and Dalmatia, to the kingdom of Italy and recognised Napoleon as its king; to Bavaria, raised by Napoleon to the dignity of a kingdom, she ceded the whole of the Tyrol with the Vorarlberg, and several Bishoprics and minor principalities : to Würtemberg (also converted into a kingdom) and to Baden she ceded her outlying provinces in Western Germany.

Reconstitution of Germany

Austria thus lost 3,000,000 subjects and large revenues ; was cut off from Italy, from Switzerland and from the Rhine; and was reduced to the rank of a third-rate Power. The time had now come for the final reconstitution of Germany, long contemplated by Napoleon, and on 19th July, 1806, the Confederation of the Rhine was formally proclaimed under his Protectorate. The Kings of Bavaria and Würtemberg, the Grand Dukes of Baden, Hesse-Darmstadt and Berg, the Archbishop of Mainz, and nine minor princes definitely separated from the German Empire and accepted the protection of Napoleon, whom they pledged themselves to support with an army of 63,000 men. On 1st August, 1806, France formally declared that she no longer recognised the Holy Roman Empire, and on 6th August, 1806, that venerable institution came to a dishonoured end. It had long since ceased to be effective, but it was at least a symbol of German unity, and its dissolution marked the attainment of an end for which France had been struggling for centuries. The work of Richelieu, of Mazarin and of Louis XIV. was thus consummated by Napoleon. Meanwhile, the Emperor Francis II. became (1804) Hereditary Emperor of Austria under the title of Francis I.

The Treaty of Pressburg marks an epoch of immense significance in the history of the Napoleonic Empire. Henceforth Napoleon was in truth a second Charlemagne, a veritable Emperor of the West; and just, as in an earlier period, the French Republic had surrounded itself with client Republics, so the new Charlemagne surrounded himself with dependent kingdoms. The Dukes of Bavaria and Würtemberg were, as we have seen, advanced to kingly rank ; Ferdinand of Naples was declared, by the same fiat, to have forfeited his crown, which was assigned to Joseph Bonaparte; the Batavian Republic was transformed into the kingdom of Holland for another brother, Louis (1806), and a year later a kingdom of Westphalia (1807) was carved out of North

6

Germany at the expense of Prussia, Hanover, Brunswick and Hesse for a third brother, Jerome.

Austerlitz had indeed avenged Trafalgar. It had done more: it had hastened the end of William Pitt. The great English statesman died on 23rd January, 1806. The historians of the last generation, notably Lord Macaulay, were wont to deride Pitt as an incompetent war minister. The juster view is now beginning to prevail that Pitt did more than any other single man, Nelson and Wellington hardly excepted, to save England and to save Europe from the domination of the Corsican adventurer. He died indeed at a moment of gloom, so deep as hardly to be relieved by Nelson's great victory, but his primary task was already implicitly accomplished. Napoleon had made himself master of the Continent, but that was only half his task. He had yet to face the mistress of the sea. Austerlitz might dazzle contemporaries, but Napoleon's ultimate defeat, unless he was prepared to abandon the dearest ambition of his heart, had been already assured by the seamanship of Nelson and the tenacity of Pitt.

CHAPTER VIII

TILSIT AND THE CONTINENTAL SYSTEM

Take special care that the ladies of your establishment drink
Swiss tea ; it is as good as that of China. Let them take care also
that no part of their dress is composed of English merchandise ;
tell that to Madame Junot ; if the wives of my chief officers do not
set the example, whom can I expect to follow it ? It is *a contest of
life or death between France and England ;* I must look for the most
cordial support in all those by whom I am surrounded.—NAPOLEON
TO JUNOT, 23rd November, 1806.

I will no longer tolerate an English ambassador in Europe. I
will declare war against any Power that receives one. . . . The
English no longer respect neutrals at sea ; I will no longer respect
neutrals on land.—NAPOLEON TO PORTUGAL.

AUSTERLITZ smashed the Third Coalition and
knocked Austria out of the game, but it did not
end the war. Russia retired to recruit her forces; Fox,
after Pitt's death, entered upon negotiations with France,
but a new enemy was forthcoming from an unexpected
quarter. Prussia at last turned against Napoleon.

For more than ten years Prussia had been a negligible
quantity in the politics of Western Europe. More responsible than any other Power for the initiation of the
contest against Revolutionary France, Prussia, with her
eyes fixed upon Poland, had retired from the war at an
early stage (1795).[1] Prussia was now suffering the

Policy of
Prussia

[1] See p. 54.

Nemesis which awaits all over-centralised autocracies. The administrative system bequeathed by the great Frederick to his successors had fallen into hopeless chaos and corruption. The mainspring had gone, and the machinery had rusted. Mirabeau had foretold the disaster now so near at hand. " The Prussian monarchy is so constituted that it cannot bear up under any calamity." The army, in particular, was in a miserable state. The officers, still drawn exclusively from the noble caste, were mostly very old, or very ignorant, or both. The rank and file—so far as they were native—were serfs "compelled to defend a country which starved them" (Seeley). There was perhaps some reason for the persistent refusal of Frederick William III. to be drawn from a policy of neutrality. Many efforts had been made to draw him. So late as 1805 Napoleon had vainly offered him Hanover and the Imperial Crown. The efforts of Austria and Russia had been equally fruitless. Neither cajolery, threats nor humiliations seemed potent to affect the stolid neutrality of Frederick William. But when, in October, 1805, Bernadotte marched his army through the Prussian territory of Anspach the insult was bitterly resented at Berlin. Haugwitz was despatched with an ultimatum to Napoleon, who played with him until after Austerlitz, and then dictated the Treaty of Schönbrunn. Napoleon's supreme object was to add to the number of England's enemies. Hence the humiliating and embarrassing gift of Hanover to Prussia. Fox justly described Prussia's conduct in accepting it as " a compound of everything that is contemptible in servility, with everything that is odious in rapacity ". But as far as England was concerned the only result was the seizure of some 400 Prussian ships in English ports, and the

annihilation of Prussia's maritime commerce. Great
was the indignation of Prussia when she learnt (6th
August, 1806) that in negotiation with England Napoleon had offered to restore Hanover. The temper of
the Court, roused to a sense of its degradation by the
patriotic Queen Louisa, found an echo in the popular
indignation excited by the judicial murder of a Nürnberg
bookseller, Palm, who was shot (25th August) by Napoleon
for circulating a patriotic pamphlet, *Germany in her
Deep Humiliation.* On 1st October, 1806, Prussia declared war on France. Her action, hitherto procrastina-
ting, was now foolishly precipitate. Austria lay crushed
under Napoleon's heel; Russia was not ready for a
renewal of the fray; England could give no immediate
help. The whole wrath of Napoleon was concentrated
upon Prussia, and the disastrous defeats of Jena and
Auerstadt (14th October) were the result. The power
of Prussia was annihilated at a single blow, and within
a fortnight Napoleon was master of the whole of
Brandenburg. One after another the great fortresses,
Erfurt, Halle, Spandau opened their gates, and on 27th
October Napoleon entered Berlin in triumph. Saxony,
erected into a kingdom, was drawn into the Rhenish Confederation ; Weimar and four other small Duchies went
with her; Brunswick and Hesse-Cassel were converted
into the kingdom of Westphalia for Jerome Bonaparte.

But Napoleon's eyes were fixed on England, not on
Germany. From Berlin he issued the famous Decree
which inaugurated the *Continental System* (21st November, 1806). " I mean," he said, " to recover with my land
armies the Cape and Surinam." England itself Napoleon
could not reach ; he determined, therefore, to bring her
to her knees by the ruin of her trade. The Berlin Decree

The Continental System

was the first instalment of this policy. It declared the British Isles to be in a state of blockade ; interdicted all trade with England ; ordered all British merchandise to be confiscated wherever found, and all British subjects prisoners of war : and forbade the reception in French or allied ports of any ship coming from Great Britain or her colonies.

The boycott of British trade was further extended by Decrees issued from Warsaw (25th January, 1807), Milan (17th December, 1807) and Fontainebleau (18th October, 1810). The British Government retaliated in a series of *Orders in Council* (January-November, 1807) which declared all ports from which the British flag was excluded to be in a state of blockade ; prohibited any ship from entering a French or allied port ; and declared any ship proceeding to such a port and paying customs there, good prize, unless it had touched at a British port. Between the Decrees launched by Napoleon and the British reprisals there was this essential difference : Great Britain had the power of rendering them effective ; Napoleon had not. Both have been subjected to serious criticism, perhaps in neither case wholly deserved. The situation was without precedent. The struggle was *à outrance*, but the two protagonists had no common element on which to fight. Napoleon was master of the continent : England was mistress of the seas. Neither could directly assail the other. Thus the *Continental System*, however disastrous in its ultimate effects, must be regarded not so much as the gratuitous insolence of overweening pride but as the last throw of a political gambler compelled by the exigencies of the game to risk all or face ruin. In a word, the *Continental System* was forced upon Napoleon by Nelson's last and greatest victory at Trafalgar.

Meanwhile Napoleon, master of Brandenburg, ad- <small>Napoleon</small>
vanced to the Vistula, beyond which the Prussian Court <small>in Poland</small>
had retired. The familiar tactics were repeated. Napo-
leon proclaimed himself the restorer of an annihilated
nationality, and the Poles were summoned to strike a
blow for independence. They flocked in thousands to
Napoleon's standard: but the Russians fought stubbornly
behind the Vistula. At Eylau (8th February, 1807)
Napoleon was checked by the Russians; but at Friedland
(14th June) he won a decisive victory, and the great fortresses of Danzig and Konigsberg fell into his hands. The
Russians and Prussians were driven across the Niemen,
and accepted an armistice which paved the way for the
famous Treaty of Tilsit.

With characteristic rapidity Napoleon had determined <small>Peace of</small>
on a new move. The relations between Russia and Eng- <small>Tilsit, 1807</small>
land were none too good, why not come to terms with
the Czar and so add another to England's enemies? Such
was the object of the historic interview between Napoleon
and Alexander in a floating pavilion moored in the middle
of the Niemen (25th June, 1807). The bargain was soon
struck. Prussia was to be dismembered; England to be
crushed and ruined; Napoleon and Alexander to divide
the world between them. The details were embodied in
the Treaty of Tilsit (with Russia, 7th July):—

By this: Russia recognised the Napoleonic kingdoms of Naples,
Holland and Westphalia; the Confederation of the Rhine; the
Duchy of Warsaw, under Saxony; and Dantzic, as a free city. The
Vistula was to be the western boundary of Russia, and the latter
agreed to mediate between France and England. The treaty with
Prussia (9th July, 1807) deprived the Hohenzollern of all their
provinces west of the Elbe, and of all their acquisitions since 1772
from Poland; imposed upon them a crushing indemnity, and re-

quired them to recognise the Napoleonic kingdoms and to keep their harbours closed against English trade.

Terms more onerous and humiliating have rarely been imposed upon a defeated foe. But even more significant was the secret arrangement between Napoleon and Alexander.

By this : Russia was to cede the Ionian islands to France, and to make common cause with her if England did not come to terms by 1st November. In return she was to get Finland from Sweden ; Moldavia and Wallachia from Turkey ; while Sweden, Denmark and Portugal were to be coerced into war with England.

Such was the basis of the Tilsit conspiracy—a conspiracy designed for the ruin of Great Britain.

England and the Danish Fleet

Fortunately for this country the Foreign Office had lately passed into the hands of Canning. Canning got wind of the secret agreement, and in order to anticipate Napoleon at once despatched an English fleet to Copenhagen. Denmark was required to deposit its fleet with England, under pledge that it should be restored intact on the conclusion of the war. Denmark naturally refused, and England was under the disagreeable necessity of bombarding Copenhagen and taking the fleet by force (September, 1807). Canning's action must be justified by the law of self-preservation. Napoleon had himself declared the impossibility of neutrality; the Danish fleet was a pawn of considerable importance; it had to be borrowed either by England or France, and England could at least offer better security both for principal and interest. Canning's promptitude countermined the Tilsit conspiracy.

Attack on Portugal

Foiled in the Baltic Napoleon turned next to the Iberian Peninsula. In 1801 he had compelled Spain to attack Portugal in order to force the latter to close her ports to English commerce. This step was fatal to the trade of Portugal, and in 1804 she purchased from Napoleon a formal recognition of neutrality. After Tilsit this arrangement no longer suited Napoleon's convenience. Accordingly he determined to revoke the neutrality, to partition Portugal and to seize its fleet. As a preliminary he demanded the adhesion of Portugal to the *Continental System;* the seizure of all English subjects and property within the kingdom, and an immediate declaration of war against England. Portugal hesitated to comply. Hesitation was enough. Junot, at the head of a large army already collected on the Spanish frontier, crossed the Bidassoa on 19th October and advanced against Portugal; the royal family escaped, under the protection of the English fleet, to Brazil; one day later (1st December, 1807) Junot entered Lisbon, and a declaration was issued that "the House of Braganza had ceased to reign". But Napoleon was forestalled. The Portuguese fleet was saved. The attack upon Portugal, insignificant in itself, proved to be the opening of one of the most momentous chapters in European history. Hitherto Napoleon had been at war mainly with Governments, and one Government after another had gone down before him. He was now to come into conflict with a people, and thus to evoke, in antagonism to himself, the potent force of nationality. Tilsit, so commonly regarded as the zenith of Napoleon's career, marks, in reality, the beginning of his decline. To all outward seeming his power was never more dazzling, never more intact. But the seeds of decay had been already sown, and the harvest, though distant, was assured.

CHAPTER IX

THE NATIONALIST REACTION

THE PENINSULA—GERMANY

From Spain the living spark went forth :
The flame hath caught, the flame hath spread !
  It warms, it fires the furthest North.
Behold ! the awakened Moscovite
Meets the tyrant in his might ;
The Brandenburg, at Freedom's call,
Rises more glorious from his fall ;
And Frederic, best and greatest of the name,
Treads in the path of duty and of fame.
See Austria from her painful trance awake !
The breath of God goes forth—the dry bones shake !
Up Germany ! with all thy nations rise !
Land of the virtuous and the wise,
No longer let that free, that mighty mind
Endure its shame !   She rose as from the dead,
She broke her chains upon the oppressor's head.
Glory to God !   Deliverance for Mankind ! [1]
                    SOUTHEY, *Carmen Triumphale*, 1813.

NAPOLEON'S attack on Portugal was only the prelude to a much larger enterprise.   Spain, like
Prussia, had retired from the first coalition in 1795, and for
the last twelve years had acted as a vassal state of France.
Under the influence of his minister Godoy, the feeble
Charles IV. had done little but register the edicts which
issued from Paris.   He declared war, concluded peace

---

[1] I quote these lines for their historical not their literary value.

and again made war, obediently at the bidding of France, and invariably to his own detriment. Still Napoleon was unsatisfied. "Un Bourbon sur le trône d'Espagne, c'est un voisin trop dangereux." After Tilsit, therefore, he determined to expel the feeble dynasty, to make Spain a dependency of France, and to put one of his own brothers on the throne. The domestic quarrels among the Spanish Bourbons and the refractoriness of Portugal gave him his chance. On 27th October, 1807, the Treaty of Fontainebleau was concluded.

By this: Portugal and her colonies were to be partitioned between the King of Etruria, the Spanish minister Godoy, and France. The first was a Spanish prince who was to surrender Tuscany to Napoleon's kingdom of Italy; Charles IV. was to be dowered with half the colonies of Portugal and become "Emperor of the two Americas". Spain was, in return, to join in the attack on Portugal.

That attack, as we have seen, had already begun. Its immediate purpose was frustrated, but it left France virtually in military occupation of Spain. By a series of unblushing intrigues, Napoleon then proceeded to push aside the King, the heir and the minister. Charles IV., Ferdinand, Prince of Asturias, and Godoy, "Prince of the Peace," were lured separately to Bayonne ; there the King and Prince were compelled to execute an abdication of the throne, and a handful of Spanish Grandees were induced to elect to the vacant throne Joseph Bonaparte, who was forthwith crowned at Madrid (July, 1808). Joachim Murat, who had prepared the way for Joseph in Spain, was rewarded by the succession to the throne of Naples.

Meanwhile Joseph's tenure in Madrid was uncertain The and brief. Napoleon might indeed push aside the feeble Spanish Rising

Spanish Bourbons, but it was only to find himself confronted by the Spanish people.   To impose his yoke upon
a people, loosely united among themselves, intensely provincial in sentiment and long inured to guerilla warfare,
proved to be no easy task.   To Napoleon himself the
uprising of a people was a strange phenomenon, as yet
undreamt of in his philosophy.   He was destined to
learn more of it before long.   No sooner was Joseph
nominated to Madrid than Spain blazed forth into angry
resistance.   Committees or *Juntas* were speedily organised
in the different provinces; troops were enrolled; more
than one repulse was inflicted upon the seasoned soldiers
of France, and on 19th July, 1808, Dupont was compelled to capitulate with his whole army, at Baylen.
Joseph fled from Madrid on 1st August, and on the 15th
Palafox successfully defended Saragossa.   The Spanish
rising had opened a new chapter in the history of the
Napoleonic era.   The nationalist reaction had begun.

England
and the
Peninsular
War

England, to whom the Spanish patriots applied for
help, at once realised its significance.   Canning in particular perceived the potentialities of the new force which
with blind fatuity and vulgar insolence Napoleon had
aroused.   His response to the application of the *Junta*
was emphatic and prompt.   "We shall proceed upon the
principle that any nation of Europe which starts up with
a determination to oppose a Power which, whether pro-
fessing insidious peace or declaring open war, is the
common enemy of all nations, becomes instantly our
ally."   On the principle announced by Canning England
acted throughout the remainder of the war.

Sir Arthur
Wellesley

On 1st August Sir Arthur Wellesley landed in Portugal, and three weeks later won a brilliant victory at
Vimiero (21st August).   Unfortunately, however, he was

superseded by Sir Harry Burrard. Burrard in turn was
superseded by Sir Hew Dalrymple, who concluded with
Junot the disastrous Convention of Cintra (30th August,
1808). The French were, indeed, compelled to evacuate
Portugal, but their army stores and spoils were carried to
France in English ships. Wellesley came home, and Sir
John Moore was appointed to the supreme command.
Moore was a fine soldier, but too despondent in temper
for a war of this special kind. Moreover, Napoleon had
himself assumed command in Spain, had defeated the
Spanish forces near Burgos (10th November), had advanced on Madrid, and restored his brother Joseph to the
throne (9th December). Moore, who had been marching
on Burgos " with his hand always on the bridle," determined to retreat on Corunna and was killed at the
moment of a brilliant victory won under the walls of
that town (16th January, 1809). His army returned to
England in miserable plight, but in the spring Wellesley
was appointed to the command. Portugal was quickly
cleared of the French; Wellesley advanced on Madrid
and on 27th, 28th July, 1809, won a great victory at
Talavera. He was obliged for the moment to retreat on
Portugal, but with Talavera his great career in the
Peninsula definitely began. Thenceforward for five long
years he kept alight, through fortune good and bad, the
fire of insurrection, supporting with his organised forces
the guerilla warfare of the Spaniards and Portuguese.

The importance of that insurrection cannot be exaggerated. For the first time England was enabled to
take a leading and continuous part in the military
operations of the Continent; Europe was taught that
Napoleon was not invincible, and he himself acknowledged
that the " Spanish ulcer" drained his military and financial strength ; finally, an immense impulse was given to

the nationalist movement in Germany. Even in the
Habsburg dominions, so long dominated by absolutist
ideas, the thrill of nationalist sentiment was felt.

Austrian
Rising,
1809

Ever since the humiliations heaped upon her at Pressburg, Austria had been waiting for the opportunity of
revenge, and steadily preparing to make it effective.
The Archduke Charles had been appointed generalissimo,
and with the help of Count Stadion had thoroughly reformed the army administration. Incompetent officers
were cashiered; military schools for the training of
officers were opened; regulations were issued for kindly
treatment of the private soldier; journals devoted to the
discussion of technical military problems were published;
all able-bodied men, between the ages of nineteen and
forty-five, were enlisted in the Landwehr, and a reserve
was formed of nearly 250,000 men; finally, an appeal,
inspired by the example of Spain, was issued to the
patriotism of the German folk (6th April, 1809).
"Soldiers! the freedom of Europe has sought refuge
under your colours. Your triumphs will loose her fetters,
your German brethren, still in the ranks of the enemy,
await deliverance by you." The moment for a national
rising in Germany against the yoke of Napoleon seemed
eminently propitious. Three hundred thousand French
troops were shut up in Spain; the Czar was said to be
restless; England was ready to help anywhere and everywhere; North Germany, thanks to the work of Stein,
and Hardenberg,[1] and Scharnhorst, and Von Humboldt,
thanks not less to the patriotic appeals of Schiller (*William
Tell*, 1804) and Fichte (*Addresses to the German Nation*, 1808) was ripe for revolt; the brave peasants of
the Tyrol, incorporated since 1805 in Napoleon's mush-

[1] See p. 107 *infra.*

room kingdom of Bavaria, were eager for a chance to throw off the hateful yoke; everything seemed propitious. But in the event everything was disastrous.

Austria declared war on France on 15th April, 1809. A magnificent army, under the Archduke Charles, entered Bavaria; a second, under the Archduke John, raised the standard of revolt in the Tyrol and marched into Italy; a third, under the Archduke Ferdinand, advanced to Warsaw. The Tyrolese peasants fought with splendid courage, but the regulars were badly led, and Napoleon's strategy once more proved irresistible. In a week's campaign (18th-22nd April, 1809) the Archduke Charles was forced back upon Vienna, and on 13th May the French Emperor was once more in the Austrian capital. But for the next two months Napoleon's position was really critical, and with good generalship, with any approach to co-operation between the Austrian archdukes, a crushing defeat might have been inflicted upon him. As it was, he was severely repulsed, with a loss of 27,000 men, in the great battle of Aspern-Essling, on the Danube below Vienna (21st, 22nd May, 1809). The news of Aspern was received with a thrill throughout Europe. "In Prussia," wrote one, "the enthusiasm is general; the spell is broken; Napoleon is no longer invincible!" Even Frederick William was emboldened to promise that after one more victory he would throw in his lot with Austria. The Duke of Brunswick flung himself upon Saxony and drove the King out of Dresden; Dornberg rose in Hesse; Schill raised the standard of revolt in Prussia; Westphalia prepared to rise against Jerome; England fitted out an expedition for a descent upon North Germany. All the portents were favourable, and it seemed as though the day of German liberation were at hand. But Napoleon was not beaten yet. The six weeks after Aspern were exceedingly critical, but on 5th and 6th July he fought and won the battle of Wagram. Wagram was not a rout like Austerlitz, but it was sufficiently decisive to induce Austria to accept the armistice of Znaim (12th July), and ultimately to acquiesce in the Treaty of Vienna (10th October, 1809). Before the treaty was concluded Napoleon's hands were strengthened by the failure of Wellington to push on after Talavera, and still more by the disastrous issue of a British expedition to the Scheldt. At the end of July a British force of 40,000 men descended upon the Isle of Walcheren, with the object of capturing Antwerp and destroying the French fleet. The idea was a brilliant one, but the execution was disastrously feeble, and in September the army, decimated by disease, returned to England.

The failure of the English diversion enabled Napoleon to impose very severe terms upon Austria :—

Treaty of Vienna or Schön-brun, 10th October, 1809 — Austria had to surrender Western Galicia to the Grand Duchy of Warsaw (King of Saxony) and Eastern Galicia to Russia ; Trieste, Croatia, Carniola, and the greater part of Carinthia (the "Illyrian Provinces") went to Napoleon, and the Tyrol and the Vorarlberg, together with Salzburg and a strip of upper Austria, were restored to Bavaria. Austria lost 4,500,000 subjects ; she had to pay a war indemnity of £3,400,000 ; to reduce her army to 150,000 men, and to promise strict adhesion to the *Continental System*.

Thus at the end of 1809 Napoleon's power was to all appearance not merely unbroken, but actually increasing. He advanced boldly along the path of annexation, and at the same time redoubled his efforts for the ruin and humiliation of the only foe against whom he was as yet entirely impotent.

To this end a few more turns were given to the screw

CENTRAL EUROPE in 1810

Kingdom of Denmark
SWEDEN
Königsberg
Dantzic W. PRUSSIA E.
Pomerania
Hamburg
Bremen
Brandenburg
Grand Duchy
Berlin
Warsaw of
Hanover
Magdeburg
Elbe
Oder
WARSAW
Amsterdam
Cassel
Leipzig
Saxony
Breslau
Silesia
Antwerp
Cologne
Erfurt
Dresden
Boulogne
Calais
Meuse
Frankfort
Prague
Vistula
Paris
Mainz
Rhine
AUSTRIAN
Seine
Strassburg
Ratisbon
Stuttgart
Vienna
Orleans
Bâle
Ulm
Danube
Budapest
Loire
Berne
Munich
Salzburg
EMPIRE
Switzerland
Bavaria
Lyons
Drave
Bordeaux
Turin
Milan
Venice
Save
OTTOMAN
Genoa
Po
San Marino
EMPIRE
Marseilles
Florence
Montenegro
Corsica
Rome
Kingdom
of
Benevento
NAPLES
Vittoria
Naples
Ebro
Saregossa
Barcelona
Kingdom
of
Spain
Kingdom
of
Sardinia
Palermo
K.
of
Sicily

ENGLISH MILES
100 50 0   100

H.V. Bartishire, Oxford, 1908.

Kingdom of Prussia		Kingdom of Sardinia	
Confederation of the Rhine	French Empire	do. of Naples	
Kingdom of Italy		do. of Sicily	

7

Napoleon's Annexations of the *Continental System,* and recalcitrant or even half-hearted vassals were ruthlessly deposed. The Pope Pius VII. refused to shut his ports to English ships. Immediately the Papal States were annexed to the kingdom of Italy (July, 1809), and the Pope—reduced to the rank of a bishop—found himself a prisoner at Savona. In Holland Louis Bonaparte found the yoke of the Continental System intolerable and resigned his crown (1st July, 1810). Holland itself was formally incorporated in France before the end of the year. Shortly afterwards Hamburg and other Hanse Towns, the Duchy of Oldenburg, half the kingdom of Westphalia and part of the Grand Duchy of Berg were similarly incorporated. The annexation of Oldenburg caused friction with Russia, as its Duke was the Czar's brother-in-law. But the claims neither of kinship nor of friendship could be permitted to stand in Napoleon's way. The Continent must at all costs be hermetically sealed against English commerce. " A puncture at any one point must produce a general collapse of the experiment " (Rose). But how long could a puncture be avoided ? How long would Europe endure the strangulation of its commerce and the ruin of its industries ? The next two years would show.

Napoleon's Marriage to Marie Louise   Early in 1810 Napoleon's personal position was sensibly strengthened by an event of far-reaching significance. The new Charlemagne had no heir. His devoted wife Josephine was, therefore, divorced at the end of 1809, and negotiations were opened for a bride from Petersburg or Vienna. On 1st April, 1810, Napoleon was married to the Archduchess Marie Louise of Austria—a niece of Marie Antoinette—and a year later a son was born and announced to the world as King of Rome.

Meanwhile Wellington, notwithstanding the forced

retreat after Talavera, was still holding the French Wellington in the Peninsula marshals at bay, and keeping brilliantly alight the torch of national resistance in Spain and Portugal. Clear for the moment of all other complications Napoleon determined in 1810 to concentrate his efforts upon the Peninsula. By the middle of that year there were no less than 370,000 French troops in Spain. Soult with one great army forced the passes of the Sierra Morena (20th January), captured Seville (31st January), and overran Andalusia; and later in the year Masséna with a still stronger force advanced on Portugal. Wellington had spent the winter in constructing the lines of Torres Vedras behind which he was practically unassailable.

The great fortress of Ciudad Rodrigo surrendered, after a gallant defence, on 10th July, Almeida on 27th August, but at Busaco (27th September) Wellington inflicted a severe defeat upon Masséna and then retired behind the lines of Torres Vedras. Outside them the country had been laid bare; the French troops suffered terrible privations, and in March, 1811, Masséna, having lost 30,000 men, was compelled to retire, impotent to pierce the famous lines. Reinforced from England Wellington was now ready to take the offensive. He defeated Masséna at Fuentes de Onoro (5th May, 1811), and took Almeida, while his colleague Beresford won a brilliant but fruitless victory at Albuera (16th May). The operations of 1811 did not seriously shake the French position in the Peninsula. Badajoz and Ciudad Rodrigo were untaken, Cadiz could not shake off its blockaders; Marmont was encamped on Portuguese soil.

But 1812 was a year of triumph for English arms. Wellington made a brilliant dash on Ciudad Rodrigo (19th January, 1812); stormed Badajoz (6th April); and

routed Marmont at Salamanca (22nd July). In consequence of these victories the siege at Cadiz was raised,
the French evacuated the south of Spain, Joseph fled
from Madrid, and Wellington entered the capital in
triumph (12th August). But he could not hold Madrid
nor take Burgos. The French reoccupied the capital
in November, and Wellington, for the last time, retired
to his winter quarters in Portugal. In 1813 Soult, with
the flower of the Peninsular army, was withdrawn to
Germany. Wellington was now at last ready to make
the decisive movement which was to drive the French
armies out of Spain. Moving rapidly north, and leaning
upon his fleet, he threatened the only great military road
from Madrid to the Pyrenees. The French in haste
abandoned the capital and made for the frontier. But
Wellington moved faster than the French, blocked the
road at Vittoria and then inflicted a crushing defeat
upon Joseph.

Wellington then determined to fight his way across
the Pyrenees into France. Soult was sent back from
Dresden to oppose him, but San Sebastian surrendered
on 30th August, Pampeluna on 31st October, and the
French forces were steadily driven across the Pyrenees.

The great struggle was virtually at an end. Wellington
followed up his successes on French soil in the spring of
1814, but on 6th April, 1814, Napoleon ceased to be
Emperor of the French. The Spanish insurrection had
done its work. Thanks to the dogged patriotism of the
Spanish *Juntas*, thanks to the splendid tenacity and
skill of Wellington, Napoleon had been compelled to keep
a large army in the Peninsula which would have been
invaluable on the Elbe. Though he contemptuously
described the struggle as a " war of priests and monks," he

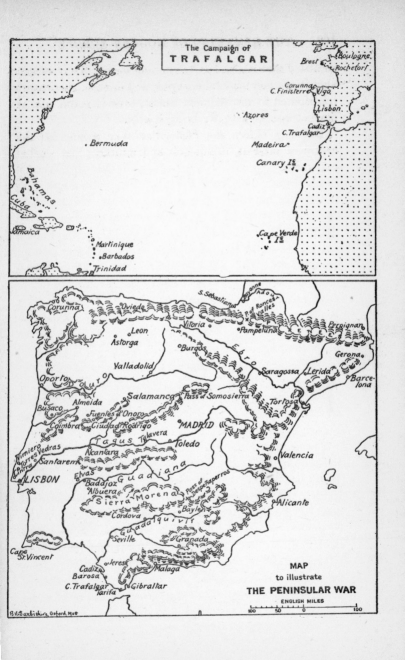

admitted that it acted as " a running sore ". Unquestionably it drained his vital energies, and in no small measure contributed to his ultimate defeat, even if it did not, as Marbot asserts, actually bring it about.

But long before the Peninsular War was ended the centre of interest, diplomatic and military, had shifted eastwards.

CHAPTER X

THE MOSCOW CAMPAIGN AND THE WAR OF LIBERATION
(1812-1814)

> But now, rous'd slowly from her opiate bed,
> Lethargic Europe lifts the heavy head ;
> Feels round her heart the creeping torpor close,
> And starts with horror from her dire repose.

AT Tilsit, as we have seen, Napoleon and the Czar Alexander agreed to divide the world between them. But however dazzling the prospect, the actual share of the junior partner was singularly unsubstantial. The bargain struck at Tilsit was renewed at Erfurt (1808). About to plunge personally into the Spanish war Napoleon thought it desirable to make assurance doubly sure on his eastern frontiers. Accordingly, in October, 1808, the Emperor of the West held high court at Erfurt for a fortnight. There were assembled the Emperor of the East, the four vassal Kings of the Rhenish Confederation, and a crowd of princes and ambassadors. The social festivities were on a magnificent scale, but the diplomatic results did not go much beyond Tilsit. The Czar was to receive Finland and the Danubian principalities, and in return to recognise the Napoleonic dynasty in Spain.

But two years had passed since Erfurt, three since Tilsit, and Finland was still in the hands of Sweden, Moldavia and Wallachia in those of the Sultan. Nor were other causes of alienation between the two Emperors

Breach between France and Russia

103

lacking. The continued encroachments of Napoleon along the north German coast—particularly the annexation of Oldenburg—caused growing uneasiness at Petersburg; his suspicious solicitude on behalf of the Poles caused even more, especially in view of his marriage with the Austrian Archduchess Marie Louise (1st April, 1810). But all these things were trifling compared with the suffering and humiliation brought upon his vassals and allies by the increasing stringency of the *Continental System*. In the earlier stages of that system a considerable number of licenses of exemption had been issued both by England and France. These mitigated to some extent the hardships which the system entailed; but as the struggle became fiercer, even these exemptions ceased, and terrible misery ensued. A severe commercial crisis occurred in England in 1810-11, but our sufferings were as nothing compared with those of France and her dependencies. Factories were brought to a standstill for lack of raw material; the price of necessaries rose to famine standard; credit collapsed; merchants were ruined. One illustration of the commercial dislocation must suffice. It is stated (by Dr. Rose) that " owing to the prohibition of all intercourse with England two parcels of silk sent from Bergamo to London were smuggled, one by way of Smyrna, the other by way of Archangel to their destination : the former took one year, the latter two years, in the wanderings necessitated by Napoleon's Decrees ". If such were the inconveniences to which England was subjected, despite her complete command of the sea, it is easy to imagine what sufferings were endured by Frenchmen, Germans and Russians. The time was fast approaching when they became intolerable.

And Napoleon knew it. "I shall have war with Russia on grounds which lie beyond human possibilities, because they are rooted in the case itself." These were Napoleon's own words to the Austrian minister Metternich in the autumn of 1810. About the same time the Czar had refused, despite the insistence of Napoleon, to confiscate, in Russian harbours, neutral ships carrying colonial produce. From that moment Napoleon bent all his energies to the isolation of the Czar. Approaches were even made to England, only, of course, to be indignantly refused. Abominably as Russia had behaved to her, England was still true to Canning's maxim: to be at war with Napoleon is to be in alliance with England. Napoleon then tried the Turks. But the Sultan remembered Tilsit and Erfurt, and lending a ready ear to the advice of England made opportune peace with Russia at Bucharest (28th May, 1812). Nor was Napoleon more successful with Sweden. Marshal Bernadotte, who had been chosen by the Swedish Estates as Crown Prince in 1810, had long been growing restless under the rigours of his former patron's *Continental System*. In November, 1810, he had been forced, much against his will, into war with England —a war which England, be it said, did not resent. The letter in which Napoleon announced his decision to Bernadotte is characteristic enough to justify quotation: "You tell me that you wish to remain at peace with France, but I say, let me have proofs of this disposition. Foreign commerce is the present *cheval de bataille* of all nations. I can immediately cause you to be attacked by the Danes and Russians; and I will instantly do so if within fifteen days you are not at war with England I have been long enough the dupe of Sweden as well as of Prussia; but the latter Power has at last learned by the catastrophe of Holland that it was necessary to take a decided line. I cannot reckon always on the alliance of Russia. I loved the King of Holland, but nevertheless I confiscated his dominions because he would not obey my will. I did the same with the Swiss. They hesitated to confiscate the English goods; I marched my troops into their dominions, and they soon obeyed. On the fifteenth day from this, war must be declared, or my ambassador has orders to demand his passports. Open war, or a sincere alliance. These are my last words."

But Sweden came to terms with Russia in April, 1812 (Treaty of Abo), and with England in July (Treaty of Örebro). By the latter Swedish ports were opened to English goods; by the former Russia undertook, in return for the co-operation of a Swedish force in North Germany, to secure Norway for Sweden at the conclusion of peace.

Thus Russia was protected on both her outer flanks: by the Swedish alliance on the Baltic, and by the Treaty of Bucharest on her Southern frontier.

But the inner flanks were secured, by treaties with Austria and Prussia, by Napoleon. Austria promised in return for Galicia to provide 30,000 men for defensive purposes; Prussia undertook to give free passage across Prussian territory to the " Grand Army," and to provide 20,000 men for offensive or defensive operations, and 20,000 more for garrison duty. Napoleon in return merely guaranteed the maintenance of the mutilated Prussian kingdom in its *status quo*. This treaty—" a treaty . . . which added the people of Frederick the Great to that inglorious crowd which fought at Napoleon's orders against whatever remained of independence and nationality in Europe" (Fyffe)—was the despair of the patriotic party in Prussia.

For Prussia was no longer the Prussia which had Reforms in Prussia succumbed at Jena and turned the cheek to the smiter at Tilsit. Tilsit marked at once the nadir of humiliation and the beginning of resurrection. Of the group of patriots to whom the revival of Prussia, and ultimately of Germany, was due, by far the greatest was Baron Vom Stein (1757-1831). To this masterful statesman Frederick William entrusted the direction of Prussian affairs three months after Tilsit (4th October, 1807). He was in office for little more than twelve months, but in that short period Prussia was transformed. By the *Edict of Emancipation* (9th October, 1807) all personal servitude was abolished; the rigid caste system was broken down; all callings were thrown open to noble, citizen and peasant alike; free trade in land was established, and land was left free to pass from hand to hand and class to class. Thus the Prussian peasants became personally free, but they were still bound to render fixed rents to their lords. A further measure of reform was due to Hardenberg, who by his agrarian law of 1811 abolished dual ownership and converted peasant copyholders into proprietors. One-third of the holding was surrendered to the lord in commutation of all feudal dues, and the remaining two-thirds was retained by the peasant owners in full and unshackled proprietorship. But the agrarian legislation did not stand alone. By the *Municipal Act* (1808) Stein carried through a large measure for the reform of local self-government. The towns were freed from their dependence upon the feudal lords or the central government, and the administration of their affairs was entrusted to elected Councils. The central government was similarly reformed by the establishment of a responsible ministerial cabinet, and but for the fact that in the very midst of his reforming activity (December, 1808) he was sent into exile at the bidding of Napoleon, there is no doubt that Stein would have crowned the edifice he was erecting by the establishment of a regular parliamentary constitution. An ardent disciple of Turgot and Adam Smith, Stein also did much to emancipate Prussian industry.

Not less important were the measures simultaneously taken for the reorganisation of national defence. This was primarily the work of Stein's colleagues Scharnhorst and Gneisenau. The old system, based upon the caste principle, had demonstrated its futility at Jena. After Erfurt Napoleon ordered that the Prussian army should be reduced to 42,000 men. This was Scharnhorst's opportunity. Henceforth every Prussian citizen was to be trained to the use of arms. The active army was limited to 40,000; but after a short service with the colours the citizen was to pass into the reserve, and in addition there was to be a *Landwehr* for defensive service at home, and a *Landsturm*—or general arming of the population for guerilla warfare.

What Scharnhorst did for national defence Humboldt effected for national education. Thus economically, politically, militarily and educationally Prussia was transformed between 1807 and 1812. Most of all, a new spirit was breathed into the Prussian people, a spirit which, though often repressed and sometimes quiescent, was destined to lead to the ultimate triumph of 1870. "We must," said Stein, "keep alive in the nation the spirit of discontent with their oppression, with our dependence on a foreign nation, insolent and growing daily more frivolous. . . . The war must be waged for the liberation of Germany by Germans."

In 1812 it seemed as though the moment for the war of liberation had come. Stein, now in Russia, and acting as the unofficial adviser of the Czar, was strongly in favour of a definite and open alliance between Prussia and Russia. By such an alliance Prussia had everything to gain and little to lose. But the timid Frederick William III. was still unable to shake off the hypnotic influence of Napoleon, and Hardenberg reluctantly assented to the humiliating terms detailed above.

The preparations for the great Russian campaign were now all but complete. To the whole enterprise there was strong opposition in France. Mollien (the finance minister) insistently urged upon his master the embarrassment which it would cause to French finance. "Because the finances are embarrassed, they need war," was Napoleon's retort. To no counsels of prudence would he listen; to no such counsels could he listen. The Russian campaign has been described as the most gratuitous and causeless of all Napoleon's military enterprises. Those only can regard it as causeless who fail to grasp the essential fact of the situation. *Delenda est Carthago.* Napoleon's one real enemy was England. England could be reached, if at all, only through her commerce. From the rigid rule of the *Continental System* no deviation, therefore, could be permitted. Thus as Seeley has insisted :—

"Russia's partial abandonment of the *Continental System* was not merely a pretext but the real ground of the war. Napoleon had no alternative between fighting for his system and abandoning the only method open to him of carrying on war against England."

War was declared on 12th April, 1812. In May

Napoleon held a great reception at Dresden to encourage his allies, and on 24th June he crossed the Niemen at the head of an army of 680,000 men. This great host was composed of the Imperial Guard and the flower of the French army—perhaps 250,000 men in all; about 150,000 Germans from the Rhenish Confederation; 80,000 Italians under Murat; 60,000 Poles, and a miscellaneous crowd of Dutchmen and Spaniards, Swiss, Portuguese and Illyrians. It was not only the largest but the most curiously cosmopolitan army ever put into the field in modern days. To this were at first opposed some 400,000 Russian troops under the supreme command of Barclay de Tolly.

Napoleon's precise plan of campaign is still matter of controversy.[1] "To reach Smolensko in 1812; to liberate Lithuania; to march on to Moscow in 1813, and then in the ancient capital of the Russians to receive the submission of the Czar." Such, according to Metternich, was Napoleon's plan. But whatever his intentions, Napoleon was drawn on, in part by the coolness of his reception in Poland, still more by the Russian tactics. Barclay retreated towards St. Petersburg, another Russian general Bagration towards Moscow, and no pitched battle was fought. Smolensko, the great fortress which barred the entrance to Russia proper, was abandoned after a brief resistance, and once more the French were lured on to their doom. The population, fanatically hostile, retreated before the French army, devastating their country and burning their towns. On the 7th of September the Russians turned at Borodino, and there the first pitched battle of the campaign was fought; 50,000 Russians and 30,000 Frenchmen fell. A week later Napoleon was in

[1] For a criticism of it cf. Marshal Marmont, ap. Greville: *Memoirs*, ii. 35.

Moscow in command of a capital deserted by the inhabitants and devoted to the flames. For fourteen days the conflagration raged. In Moscow, however, he tarried for two months (15th September-19th October), waiting for the submission that never came. Gradually the position became unendurable; the French force was decimated by disease, but it was impossible to feed even the remnant of it.

On 19th October the retreat began. To avoid the wasted country Napoleon marched southwards, but the battle of Maro-Jaroslavitz (24th October) forced him to fall back on the already devastated route; the retreat, constantly harassed by the Russians under Kutusoff, became a flight after the battle of Krasnoi (15th November), and after the passage of the Beresina (26th-28th November) it became a rout.

The bitter Russian winter intensified the sufferings of the starved army; Napoleon deserted it on 5th December, and made his way to Paris, and on 13th December a ragged remnant of perhaps 100,000 men re-crossed the Niemen and made their way to Leipzic. Not less than half a million men had been sacrificed in this disastrous campaign.

What was its nett result? That it gave the *coup de grace* to Napoleon cannot be affirmed. Within three months he had raised, by incomparable energy, a new army; the loyalty of France was unbroken; the Rhenish Confederation showed no sign of defection; Austria refused to throw in her lot with his enemies; Frederick William of Prussia still hesitated to break with him, and Alexander himself was undecided whether to seize Prussian Poland and revenge himself on Prussia, or to pursue the French into Germany, put himself at the head

Results of retreat from Moscow

of the German Patriots and pose as the liberator of Europe. Luckily for Germany, and luckily for Europe, Stein was still at the Czar's side, and General Yorck was in command of the Prussian auxiliaries. On 30th December Yorck, on his own authority, concluded with Alexander the Convention of Tauroggen, declaring the neutrality of his force. Frederick William repudiated the Convention and ordered the arrest of the general. Yorck was undismayed: "With bleeding heart I burst the bond of obedience, and carry on the war upon my own responsibility. The army desires war with France; the nation desires it; the King himself desires it, but his will is not free. The army must make his will free." It did. Stein and Yorck virtually assumed the reins of government; the King's hand was forced; Prussia threw in her lot with Russia; Alexander's army crossed the Niemen on 13th January, 1813, and on 28th February the Treaty of Kalisch was concluded. This treaty ratified the alliance of Russia and Prussia, and the Czar promised not to lay down arms until Prussia was restored, as regards area and population, to the position she had enjoyed before Tilsit.

It is not too much to say that Stein and Yorck had thus laid the foundations not only of modern Prussia, but of modern Germany. The nation was called to arms against France, and the response, though long delayed, was not uncertain.

The War of German Liberation   The history of the war of German Liberation falls into two periods: (i) from the Prussian declaration of war (17th March, 1813) down to the armistice of Pläswitz (4th June); and (ii) from the adhesion of Austria (12th August, 1813) to the entry of the allies into Paris (31st March, 1814).

During the first period it was a popular war waged on

the principles of Stein for the liberation of Germany by Germans; in the second the adhesion of Austria gave to the war, and still more to the settlement which crowned it, a dynastic not to say a reactionary character. Stein and Yorck inspired the earlier movement, Metternich dominated the latter.

Frederick William III. formally declared war on the French on 17th March, 1813. Napoleon had been busily engaged ever since his return to France in raising a new army of 350,000 men. But he was not yet ready to advance; the French forces, therefore, fell back on Magdeburg, and before the end of April the Cossacks and Prussians had occupied Dresden; but Napoleon was now at hand, and on 2nd May drove the allies from their position at Lützen, forced them back behind the Elbe, and himself occupied Dresden (14th May). A week later an obstinately contested battle was fought at Bautzen on the Spree (20th, 21st May). The allies, though beaten, fell back in perfect order on Silesia, and on 4th June Napoleon proposed a seven weeks' armistice. He wanted time to bring up the army of Italy into Carniola in order to intimidate Austria into neutrality. The armistice was, however, as Napoleon subsequently admitted, a fatal blunder. Austria had no wish to exalt Russia and Prussia at the expense of France, but on Napoleon's refusal of her proffered mediation she concluded with the allies the Treaty of Reichenbach (27th June), by which she agreed to join the allies if Napoleon refused the terms proposed by her. The conditions were that Napoleon should retain the Presidency of the Rheinbund, but should restore the Illyrian provinces to Austria; suppress the Grand Duchy of Warsaw, and surrender the territory taken from Prussia at Tilsit and from North

8

Germany in 1810. As Napoleon foolishly neglected to accept the terms before the specified day, Austria declared war (12th August), and the second period of the War of Liberation began.

Battles of Dresden and Leipzic Napoleon was now at Dresden in command of 440,000 men; opposed to him were three great armies: the Austrians, 250,000 strong under Schwarzenberg in Bohemia; Blücher at the head of 100,000 Russians and Prussians in Silesia; and a similar number of Russians, Prussians and Swedes under the Crown Prince Bernadotte of Sweden in North Germany. Besides these, the allies had 300,000 men in reserve, to say nothing of the forces in the Peninsula under Wellington, who was at this moment fighting his way through the Pyrenees. Napoleon's vast power was beginning to crumble. He defeated, indeed, the grand army of Austria at Dresden (26th, 27th August); but on the same day Blücher won a victory over Macdonald in Silesia; on 23rd August Bülow repulsed the advance of Oudinot upon Berlin, and drove him back upon the Elbe; and on 6th September Ney was routed at Dennewitz. Napoleon's plan of a triple attack was thus entirely frustrated, and after some weeks of fighting the allies took the offensive and crossed the Elbe in the first week of October. There, on the plain of Leipzic, the final issue was joined. To the 300,000 troops of the allies Napoleon could oppose only 170,000, and in the great battle of Leipzic—" the battle of the nations "— (16th-19th October), he opposed them in vain. Leipzic has been described as " the greatest battle in all authentic history, the culmination of all the military effort of the Napoleonic age " (Fyffe). Leipzic smashed the military power of Napoleon; he lost 40,000 men, killed and wounded, 30,000 prisoners and 260 guns. The victors lost, in killed and wounded, 54,000. A fortnight later (2nd November) Napoleon and the remnant of his great army re-crossed the Rhine.

In Germany his power collapsed like a pack of cards. The vassal-princes of the Rhein-bund hastened, with the exception of Saxony, to throw in their lot with the allies; fortress after fortress surrendered: Dantzic, Dresden, Stettin, Lübeck, Torgau and others; King Jerome fled from Westphalia, and the princes, deposed to make room for him, were restored: Holland was liberated, and William of Orange was recalled.

But, among the allies, there were divided counsels. Blücher wanted to push on at once across the Rhine, but the sovereigns, under the influence of Austria, decided (9th November) to offer terms to Napoleon. It is difficult to realise that even after Leipzic Napoleon might have had peace on terms that would have gladdened the heart of Richelieu or Louis XIV. France was to withdraw within her "natural frontiers"—the Rhine, the Alps and the Pyrenees; Belgium, the Rhenish Provinces and Savoy were to be retained, and Napoleon was to keep the Crown. But Napoleon hesitated to accept, and on the 1st December the offer was withdrawn. Austria was still anxious not to push matters to extremities, but at the end of December the allies entered France, 400,000 strong. Blücher marched straight for Paris; the Austrians, under Schwarzenberg, entered France by the gap of Belfort: Bülow came south from Holland. They were to concentrate in Champagne. Napoleon was thus confronted by three armies each larger than his own, but by incomparable strategy and taking advantage of the Seine and its tributaries the Marne and the Aube, and aided not a little by the dilatory and half-hearted tactics

of Austria, he held the allies at bay for nine weeks.
Twice he might have had peace on terms which would
have left him in possession of the throne and the frontiers
of 1791. After Blücher's victory at La Rothière (1st
February), a Congress was opened at Châtillon on the
upper Seine (5th-9th February, 1814). Caulaincourt was
entrusted with full powers on behalf of France, but
hesitated to accept the frontiers of 1791, involving the
loss of Belgium, of the Rhenish Provinces and Savoy.
Then came another week's fighting (10th-14th February),
greatly in favour of Napoleon, and again conferences
at Châtillon (17th February, etc.). Napoleon now
attempted, by private negotiations with the Emperor
Francis, to get the terms which he had failed to accept in
November. But the time had gone by for them. On 1st
March the great Powers—England, Russia, Austria and
Prussia—concluded the Treaty of Chaumont, cementing a
twenty years' alliance, and mutually pledging themselves
against separate negotiations: each Power agreed to
supply 150,000 men, and England promised a subsidy of
five million sterling. Ten days later Blücher won a
great victory at Laon, and Napoleon left open the road
to Paris. Even now Napoleon might have thrown himself on the communications of the allies, but after some
fighting in the suburbs, the capital surrendered on 30th
March, and on the following day the allies entered it in
triumph. Napoleon was formally deposed by the Senate
(2nd April), a provisional Government was set up under
Talleyrand—the most astute of French statesmen; and
on 13th April Napoleon was compelled to accept the
Treaty of Fontainebleau.

Napoleon was compelled to abdicate and to renounce all rights
on France for himself and his family. In return he was to have

Elba in full sovereignty and a pension of two million francs for himself; the Duchies of Parma, Piacenza and Guastalla for the Empress Marie Louise ; and pensions of two and a half millions for members of his family.

The allies had now to decide the fate of France and of Europe. For France various alternatives were suggested. Napoleon himself was impossible; a Regency under the Empress was favoured by the Czar; Bernadotte was proposed as king, and even Eugene Beauharnais, but at length, largely on the advice of Talleyrand, the principle of legitimacy was accepted, and the Bourbons were recalled. Louis XVIII. re-entered Paris after an absence of three and twenty years on 3rd May, and shortly afterwards accepted a Charter which guaranteed a Parliamentary Constitution to France. On 14th May another Bourbon, Ferdinand VII., was restored to Madrid, and on the 24th Pius VII., released from imprisonment, made a solemn re-entry into Rome. About the same time Victor Emmanuel was restored to Turin. *The First Peace of Paris*

Meanwhile the allies were busy arranging terms of peace in Paris, and on 30th May the first Treaty of Paris was signed.

France was treated with extraordinary leniency, not to say generosity. She was restored to the limits of 1792, with the addition of a slice of Savoy and strips of territory on the Eastern frontier and the confirmation of Avignon ; no war indemnity was imposed, and France was not even required to disgorge the art treasures (with the exception of the Vienna library and some trophies from Berlin) stolen from nearly every capital in Europe. France engaged not to fortify any places in the East Indies, or to keep any military force there except for police purposes. England. restored all the French Colonies taken in the war, except Tobago, St. Lucia and the Ile de France (Mauritius). France recognised the independence of Switzerland, the Netherlands, and the various German and Italian States so long controlled by Napoleon. England extorted from France a promise for the abolition of the slave trade, and, in addition to the Colonies mentioned above, retained Malta, and agreed to purchase from Holland Cape Colony, already (1806) acquired by conquest. Other outstanding questions (on some of which private agreement had already been reached by the four leading Powers) were referred to a Congress to meet at Vienna in two months.

A criticism of the settlement thus effected may more fitly be deferred until its completion in 1815.

With Napoleon an exile in Elba ; with the legitimate rulers restored to France, Spain, Holland and Sardinia ; with the Pope once more at the Vatican, the great monarchs and diplomatists might fairly be allowed to take breath before plunging into the discussion of the difficult problems which awaited solution at Vienna.

CHAPTER XI

THE CONGRESS OF VIENNA AND THE SETTLEMENT OF 1815

THE HUNDRED DAYS AND WATERLOO

> We are all glad that the Treaty of Vienna has been torn up; but it ought to be borne in mind that it was in its origin, partly indeed a counter-revolutionary arrangement of the despots, but partly also a military arrangement framed not without necessity to secure Europe against the cruel rapacity of France.—GOLDWIN SMITH.

THE greatest of all European Congresses was formally opened at Vienna on 1st November, 1814. In brilliance of personnel and in magnitude of issues there has been no parallel to it in modern history. Of monarchs there were present no less than six: the Czar Alexander—a curious mixture of shrewdness and mysticism, of ambition and magnanimity; Frederick William III. of Prussia; Francis I., Emperor now only of Austria, and the Kings of Denmark, Bavaria and Würtemberg. German electors, dukes and princes were there in crowds, while among the diplomatists the most influential were Lord Castlereagh and the Duke of Wellington from England; Hardenberg and Humboldt from Prussia; Nesselrode from Russia; Prince Metternich from Austria; and finally Talleyrand, who with great adroitness procured admission to the Congress on the ground that the quarrel of the Powers had been not with France but with

Congress of Vienna

119

Napoleon. All the States of Europe, except Turkey, were represented. The task before the Congress was to rebuild the European States system, demolished by the wars of a quarter of a century. Its work has been severely criticised, nor can it be denied that many blunders were made, that little foresight was shown, that important principles were ignored, and that selfish interests were too much regarded. Two things should, however, be remembered: (i) that though the diplomatists were called on to rebuild, it was on old and encumbered sites; and (ii) that they entered upon their task with their hands bound by several recently concluded treaties. By the Treaty of Abo (1812) Norway had been promised to Sweden; by that of Kalisch (February, 1813) Russia had undertaken that Prussia should be restored to a position equal to that which she occupied before Tilsit; by that of Reichenbach (June, 1813) it had been agreed by Russia, Austria and Prussia that the Grand Duchy of Warsaw should be partitioned among them; by that of Töplitz (September, 1813) Austria had been promised her possessions of 1805, and the independence of the Rhenish confederates had been guaranteed; by that of Ried (October, 1813) the King of Bavaria had received a pledge that he should retain full sovereign rights, and all territory acquired through Napoleon, except the Tyrol and the Austrian districts on the Inn; while Murat had received a promise of Naples (11th January, 1814). Moreover, by secret agreements made in Paris it had already been decided that Holland should acquire Belgium; that Venetia and part of Lombardy should go to Austria, and Genoa to Sardinia. Thus the hands of the diplomatists were far from free.

The most difficult questions still to be decided were the

future of Poland; the position of Saxony; the settlement of the Rhine frontier; and the Constitution of Germany. The Czar was determined to have Poland. *C'est à moi*, he said, laying his hand upon Poland on the outstretched map; and it was difficult to resist his claim. "Avec 600,000 hommes on ne négoçie pas beaucoup," as one observed. But if Poland were to go to Russia, Prussia must get compensation elsewhere. Shall it be in Saxony, or on the Rhine, or both? Is conquered France to be allowed to retain Alsace and Lorraine? Is not this the opportunity for depriving her of ill-gotten gains threatening to Germany? And as to Germany itself: is the old Empire to be restored? Can a new Empire be evolved? Is Austria or Prussia to dominate it? And what of the minor States. How are the pledges of Töplitz and Ried to be redeemed? The mere statement of the problems suggests the difficulties of solution, and it was soon found that the Congress tended to split into two parties: on the one side Russia and Prussia; on the other, Metternich, Castlereagh and the smaller German Princes, while Talleyrand was ever on the watch to utilise the dissensions of the allies for the benefit of France; and Talleyrand did not watch in vain.

The quarrels were at their height, and war between the allies seemed a not remote possibility, when news reached Vienna that caused all thoughts of dissension to be laid aside and the bonds of alliance to be drawn closer than ever.

Tiring of his contracted sovereignty Napoleon had escaped from Elba, and on 1st March, 1815, had landed with about 1,500 men on the coast of France, near Cannes. From Cannes he marched straight on to Paris: towns opened their gates; his old army—marshals and

The Hundred Days

privates alike—flocked to his standard; the Bourbons fled, and on 30th March, amid scenes of frantic enthusiasm, Napoleon entered the capital. Once more the Bourbon monarchy collapsed. The reasons are not far to seek. Louis XVIII. was no bigoted adherent of the old régime, but, easy going and complacent, he allowed power to fall into the hands of his brother, the Count of Artois. The Count was a reactionary fanatic, and surrounded himself with priests and *Émigrés* even more rabid than himself— men who were determined to wipe out every trace of the work of the last twenty-five years. They forgot that in that time a new France had come into being, a France which mocked at Fraternity, which had never known the meaning of Liberty, but which clung passionately to the advantages they had secured under the name of Equality Above all, the restored Bourbons failed to win the affection of the army, and, as Wellington wrote, "the King of France without the army is no king". The accuracy of Wellington's observation was forcibly demonstrated after Napoleon's return.

The manifesto which the ex-Emperor then put forth was conceived with admirable skill. "He had come," he declared, "to save France from the outrages of the returning nobles; to secure to the peasant the possession of his land; to uphold the rights won in 1789, against a minority which sought to re-establish the privileges of caste and the feudal burdens of the last century; France had made trial of the Bourbons; it had done well to do so, but the experiment had failed; the Bourbon monarchy had proved incapable of detaching itself from its worst supports, the priests and nobles; only the dynasty which owed its throne to the Revolution could maintain the social work of the Revolution. . . . He renounced war and conquest . . . he would govern henceforth as a constitutional sovereign and seek to bequeath a constitutional Crown to his son."

France was cajoled; Europe was not. Once more the allies flew to arms; before Napoleon had reached Paris the Treaty of Chaumont was definitely renewed; each of the four great Powers was to furnish 150,000 men and to keep them in the field "until Bonaparte should have been rendered incapable of stirring up further trouble". Most of the minor Powers gave in their adherence and promised assistance against the common scourge.

Waterloo Campaign

For three months Napoleon laboured assiduously to raise and equip his army; by the end of May 200,000 men were ready to take the field, and on 12th June Napoleon himself started for the front. The troops of the allies were posted on a line extending from the Scheldt to the Moselle. Wellington was at Brussels at the head of a miscellaneous force of 105,000 men, of whom 30,000 were British. His line extended from Ghent to Mons. Blücher was at Namur with 117,000 Prussians, their line extending from Charleroi to Liége. Napoleon's plan was to smash in the centre of a thin line, divide his enemies, defeat them in detail and march on Brussels. On 14th June he was at the head of a force of 125,000 men concentrated on a front of thirty-five miles on the western bank of the Sambre; on the 15th he crossed the Belgian frontier, attacked the Prussian right at Charleroi, and by that night was in possession of Charleroi and the bridges over the Sambre. Next morning (16th June) Napoleon himself attacked Blücher at Ligny, and ordered Ney to clear Wellington out of Quatre Bras and then to fall upon Blücher's right flank at Ligny. This was the first crisis of the campaign. Ney found that he had more than enough to do at Quatre Bras and never got near Blücher. On the contrary, Wellington beat him back with losses of about 4,000 men on each side. Meanwhile at Ligny Napoleon defeated Blücher, but by no means decisively. The Prussians lost 20,000, the French 11,000, and after the battle Napoleon lost touch of his enemy. This was the second critical point: for Blücher, instead of retiring on Liége, as Napoleon imagined, wisely made for Wavre in order to keep in touch with his English colleague. Consequently Grouchy, despatched in pursuit of Blücher with 30,000 men, never found him. On the 17th Napoleon, making an unaccountably late start, moved slowly on towards Brussels, and on the 18th found the

Battle of Waterloo

road blocked by Wellington at Waterloo. On that historic field Wellington sustained the attack for five hours (11-4) alone. But his tactics were based on the assumption that Blücher would come to his assistance; about four o'clock the first Prussians came up, but not until six or later was their help effective. By that time the great battle was all but won; the Prussian cavalry turned a defeat into a rout. Napoleon lost 30,000 men and all his guns; Wellington lost 13,000, and the Prussians 6,000. But the great war was ended. The road to Paris was open, and on 7th July the allied army for the second time entered the French capital.

Napoleon fled from Waterloo to Paris; abdicated in favour of his son (22nd June), and made his way to Rochefort with the intent to escape to America. But his old enemies were on the watch; escape was impossible, and on 15th July he surrendered to Admiral Hotham of H.M.S. *Bellerophon*. Brought to the shores of England, but never permitted to touch them, Napoleon was deported to the Island of St. Helena, and there died, a prisoner, in 1821.

While England and Prussia had been disposing of Napoleon in the North, Austria had been dealing with his brother-in-law Murat in South Italy. Murat, despite the guarantee of the allies, threw in his lot with Napoleon, was defeated by the Austrians, fled to France and later to Corsica, and was ultimately captured and shot. His action untied one of the diplomatic knots and rendered easy the restoration of the Bourbons, in the person of King Ferdinand, to the throne of Naples.

By this time the diplomatists in Paris and Vienna were nearing the end of their labours. Louis XVIII. had returned to Paris on 9th July, but France had got to pay for her recent escapade. Still the terms imposed upon her were extraordinarily lenient. *Second Peace of Paris*

By the second Treaty of Paris (20th November, 1815) she was compelled to give up most of Savoy and the other territorial acquisitions of 1814 ; to disgorge the stolen art treasures ; to pay an indemnity of 700 million francs, and to leave eighteen of the fortresses on her northern and eastern frontiers in the occupation of the allies for five years as a pledge of good behaviour.

On one question there was much dispute among the allies. Ought France to be left in possession of Alsace and Lorraine, filched from the German Empire during the last two centuries? The German Powers—Hardenberg with special emphasis—urged that this was the appropriate moment for restitution. " If," said the latter, " we want a durable and safe peace, as we have so often announced and declared, if France herself sincerely wants such a peace with her neighbours, she must give back to her neighbours the line of defence she has taken from them ; to Germany Alsace and the fortifications of the

Netherlands, the Meuse, Mosel and Saar. Not till then will France find herself in her true line of defence with the Vosges and her double line of fortresses from the Meuse to the sea; and not till then will France remain quiet. Let us not lose the moment so favourable to the weal both of Europe and France which now offers of establishing a durable and sure peace. . . . If we let it slip, streams of blood will flow to attain this object, and the cry of the unhappy victims will call us to give an account of our conduct."

Hardenberg's foresight was more than justified by the events of 1870. But 1870 was far ahead. The immediate concern of the allies was peace and stability; with a restless and embittered France there would be neither. "What have you been fighting all these years?" asked Wellington. "Not France, but the spirit of Revolution embodied in a crusade. You want to re-establish a regular government in France under the ancient dynasty. Are you going to associate their restoration with the loss of provinces so precious to France?" Wellington prevailed against Hardenberg, and for half a century Alsace and Lorraine remained French. The argument was nicely balanced: History was on the side of Hardenberg; Policy and local sentiment on that of the Duke. That France had used the provinces for offensive purposes against Germany is true; that the loss of them would have pro-voked an early renewal of the contest is probable.

Meanwhile the Congress at Vienna had not allowed itself to be interrupted by the Hundred Days, and in June, 1815, concluded its labours. The main points of the great settlement which it effected must now be summarised.

The Czar Alexander, as we have seen, came to Vienna

determined to restore the ancient kingdom of the Poles, Results of Congress of Vienna
with himself as king, and his determination bore down
all opposition.   Thus the Grand Duchy of Warsaw
passed in its entirety, except Posen and Thorn, to Russia, (i) Russia
who also acquired Finland from the Swedes.

The Duchy of Posen with Thorn and Danzig went to
Prussia, who further obtained—again in the teeth of (ii) Prussia
prolonged and bitter opposition—the northern half of
Saxony, Swedish Pomerania, and, most important of all,
a huge province on both sides of the Rhine, including the
Duchies of Westphalia, Cleves and Berg, the secularised
Bishop-Electorates of Köln, Trier, Aachen, the Bishopric
of Münster and strips of Limburg and Luxemburg.   Thus
was the promise of Kalisch fulfilled.   Poland had gone to
Russia; Anspach and Bayreuth to Bavaria, Hildesheim
and East Friesland to Hanover.   But Prussia in extent
and population was in a position much better than before
Tilsit, and with far larger possibilities.   1815 was indeed
the turning-point in the fortunes both of Prussia and
Germany.   Prussia was forced, almost against her will,
to find compensation for her losses in the East by acquisitions in the West.   The population she lost was
mostly Slav;   the 2,000,000 subjects she gained were
Germans.   Above all, by the acquisition of the Rhine
Province she was compelled, as the champion of Germany,
to confront France.

But to estimate the full significance of these changes (iii) Austria
they must be considered in connection with the simultaneous changes in the position of Austria.   For the last
two hundred years Austria had been more and more
neglecting German interests and devoting herself to the
consolidation of her dynastic interests in Hungary and
Italy.   In 1815 she gladly surrendered the Netherlands

(Belgium) to Holland to form with the latter a great barrier kingdom under the House of Orange. As compensation she acquired Venetia and Lombardy, and recovered the Illyrian Provinces, Eastern Galicia (from Russia), and from Bavaria the Tyrol, Salzburg and the Vorarlberg. Bavaria in turn was compensated with Bayreuth and Anspach (from Prussia), and the Rhenish Palatinate. Hanover became a kingdom with some small accessions of territory. Baden and Würtemberg remained unchanged.

(iv) The Constitution of Germany

But even more difficult than the adjustment of the territorial claims of the several German Princes was the settlement of the constitutional question for Germany as a whole. On this point there was great diversity of opinion, due on the one side to the inveterate rivalry of Austria and Prussia, and on the other to the anxiety of the lesser Princes to lose none of the sovereign rights conferred on them by Napoleon. Stein, to whom the Liberation of Germany was so largely due, originally favoured the division of Germany into two great Federal States, under Austria and Prussia respectively; but this was strongly resisted by Metternich, who objected not less firmly to a revival of the old Empire. Unless, therefore, Germany was to be split up into numberless independent States, it became clear that some form of federal union would have to be evolved. Prussia hoped to make it really effective, Austria to whittle it down, and Austria was supported by the smaller States, who fear 1 that any union would necessarily curtail their independence. Eventually an exceedingly loose form of confederation was established, under which the thirty-nine Sovereign Princes and Free Cities formed themselves into what was little more than a perpetual League, under the name of the "Germanic Bund". A federal diet was to sit at Frankfort-on-Main under the presidency of Austria. The several States agreed to defend Germany as a whole and its component States against any attack, and mutually to guarantee the territories of all members of the Bund.

It was further agreed that in every State representative institutions should be established. But the federal tie was of the weakest. To the ardent spirits who had made the War of Liberation such an issue was a bitter disappointment. But reactionary as was the attitude of the Sovereign Princes, seeds had been sown among the German peoples, destined to yield a rich harvest in the future. Though all traces of the Napoleonic occupation were carefully erased upon the map, it none the less left an indelible impression upon Germany.

The settlement of Italy presented similar features. (v) Italy There also an attempt was made to erase the handiwork of Napoleon, and with the same temporary success. The Bourbon King Ferdinand once more reigned over the Two Sicilies; the Pope was again master of the States of the Church; Austria, as we have seen, carved out for herself a great Lombardo-Venetian Principality; the ex-Empress Marie Louise was installed in Parma, and Austrian cadets in Modena and Tuscany; while Victor Emmanuel I. was restored to Piedmont and Savoy, with the important addition of Genoa. Once again the dynastic principle seemed to have triumphed over the national, and the outlook for the future was dark. But the Napoleonic unification had nevertheless left permanent results behind.

Switzerland, enlarged by the addition of the Cantons (vi) Switzerland of Valais, Neuchatel and Geneva (twenty-two in all), was guaranteed by the Powers in perpetual neutrality.

In Northern Europe the same principles reappear.

9

(vii)
Northern
Europe

Norway, torn from Denmark, was united to Sweden, which lost Finland to Russia and Western Pomerania to Prussia. Belgium was united to Holland.   Belgians and Dutchmen were opposed in race, creed and historical tradition, and the union was effected purely in the interests of the European equilibrium.

(viii) Great
Britain

One Power remains to be considered.   Great Britain had entered upon the struggle with no selfish aim; she had sustained it with unequalled pertinacity; but in the territorial readjustments at Paris and Vienna she had little interest.   She struggled hard to effect a stable settlement on equitable lines; she was anxious that a due balance of power should be maintained; she used her influence for the abolition of the slave trade, but her acquisitions in Europe were confined to Heligoland and Malta and the protectorate of the Ionian Isles.   Her substantial gains were farther afield.   For ten years she had been undisputed mistress of the sea, and the colonial possessions of France, Holland and Spain were entirely at her mercy, and mostly in her grasp.   At the Peace she retained Trinidad (from Spain), Mauritius, Tobago and St. Lucia (from France), and Ceylon, Demerara and Essequibo (from Holland).   Cape Colony, originally acquired by conquest, was reacquired by purchase from the Dutch. In India also the British dominions were largely extended in the period between 1789 and 1815.   The war with the United States (1812-14), into which we were driven by the fiscal policy of Napoleon, ended in the mutual restoration of conquests and an agreement to abolish the slave trade (Peace of Ghent, 24th December, 1814).

Such were the main features of the great settlement of 1815.   Few of them were permanent: many were quite temporary.   The union of Sweden and Norway lasted ninety years; that of Holland and Belgium, fifteen; the Rhine frontier had to be readjusted in 1870. The settlement ignored the nationality principle which had been evoked by the Napoleonic occupations of Germany and Italy and by the attempted conquest of Spain—a principle destined to dominate European politics during the coming century; it marked a reversion to the outworn ideas of the eighteenth century: to the doctrine of "balance," and the supremacy of dynastic interests; the clock was set back by the re-partition of Italy and the ineffective re-constitution of Germany. All this is true. None the less the Congress of Vienna marks not merely the close of an old epoch but the beginning of a new. The devouring ambition of Russia is conspicuous; an important though unconscious step is taken towards the Prussianisation of Germany; England's true sphere of activity is seen to be ultra-European; the House of Savoy is stimulated by the acquisition of Genoa towards the fulfilment of its Italian mission; the solicitude of England for the fate of the slaves heralds an era of humanitarian legislation; the phantasy of the Holy Alliance is a prelude to the concert of Europe. The diplomatists of Vienna may have been exceptionally selfish and short-sighted, but twenty years of revolution and upheaval had evoked aspirations and intensified forces which no statesman could control.

To trace the operation of those forces and the fulfilment of those aspirations is the purpose of the pages that follow.

CHAPTER XII

RESTORATION AND REACTION

THE HOLY ALLIANCE

It is verbiage.—METTERNICH, on the Holy Alliance.

Government by Congresses FOR twenty-five years Continental Europe had been a prey to revolution; for the next fifteen it was given over to reaction. That reaction has been frequently ascribed to the dominant influence of the Czar Alexander. During the second occupation of Paris the Czar drafted a declaration pledging the allied rulers to regulate their policy, internal and external alike, by the principles of the Christian religion. To this "Holy Alliance" the Emperor of Austria and the King of Prussia formally adhered. Metternich declared it to be "verbiage"; Castlereagh was led to doubt the Czar's sanity; Canning, with more reason, to question his sincerity. But if the Holy Alliance was the dream of a mystic, the Quadruple Treaty (20th November, 1815), concluded between Austria, Russia, Prussia and England, was a substantial diplomatic fact. Based upon the Treaty of Chaumont it provided for a twenty years' alliance, to be cemented and maintained by periodical meetings between the sovereigns or their plenipotentiaries, and thus inaugurated a system of government by Congresses. The admission of France (1818) converted the Quadruple Alliance into the

" Moral Pentarchy of Europe," which endured until it was
broken up after 1822, by the masterful independence of
Canning. Its aims will be disclosed in connection with
the Congresses of Aix-la-Chapelle (1818), Troppau (1820),
Laibach (1821) and Verona (1822).

Until 1818 France was excluded from the Committee The
of the Great Powers; but in the history of the European Restoration in France
reaction it is France which must first claim our attention.
Not because France dominates Europe, as she had done
in the seventeenth and eighteenth centuries, but because
the clearly marked "periods" in French history and its
outstanding "crises" afford the best clue to the bewilder-
ing maze of continental history during the nineteenth
century.

Between 1815 and 1900 France tried five distinct constitutional experiments: (i) 1815-30, the restored Bourbon monarchy under Louis XVIII. (1815-24) and Charles
X. (1824-30), ending in the "July" Revolution; (ii) "constitutional" monarchy under the House of Orleans (1830-
48), ending in the Revolution of 1848; (iii) the second
Republic (1848-52); (iv) the second Napoleonic Empire
(1852-70); and (v) the third Republic (1870). But it
happens that the French Revolutions of 1830, of 1848
and 1870 mark, not for France only but for Europe at
large, epochs of first-rate importance. Lucidity, therefore, compels us to deal first with France.

Louis XVIII. was at the time of his first restoration an Louis
old gentleman of fifty-nine (b. 1755), and so fat and gouty XVIII.
that he could not sit a horse. Endowed with much
more common sense than either of his brothers (Louis
XVI. and the Count of Artois), he realised from the
outset the impossibility of reviving the præ-revolutionary
régime. He talked indeed of "linking again the chain

of tradition which had been broken during a period of nefarious crimes," and 1814 was to him [1] not the first but the nineteenth year of his reign. But he frankly accepted the social work of the Revolution, and issued (4th June, 1814) a *Charter* of an exceedingly liberal character. Under this Constitution there were to be two legislative chambers; a responsible ministry and a tolerably wide franchise; the Napoleonic nobility was to be confirmed in its titles and placed on a social equality with the old noblesse; the Press was to be free, and though the Roman Catholic Church was to be established there was to be complete religious toleration. Finally, the eligibility of all classes for employment under the State was to form part of the public law of France.

The Constitutional Charter

The Charter unquestionably provided a fair basis for a constitutional régime; but unfortunately the first Chamber elected under it proved violently reactionary (*Chambre introuvable*). Marshal Ney was shot; 7,000 Bonapartists were imprisoned, and persecution ensued so fierce as to earn for itself the name of the "White Terror". Talleyrand and Fouché, whose tact and skill had done so much to smooth the path for the restoration, were dismissed (1815) to make room for the Duc de Richelieu, who though an *Émigré* was not an "ultra". In 1818 Richelieu won a distinct diplomatic triumph by inducing the allies at the Congress of Aix-la-Chapelle to admit France to the "Pentarchy" of the five great Powers and to shorten the period of foreign occupation. Aix-la-Chapelle marked in fact the re-admission of France to the polite society of Europe. But a general election resulted in the return of a moderate liberal majority, and

Reaction in France

---

[1] *Cf.* Charles II. of England.

Richelieu had to give place to Decazes, whose programme was " to royalise France and to nationalise the monarchy ". The principle thus enunciated was eminently sound, but unfortunately the murder (1820) of the Duc de Berri, second grandson of the Count of Artois, and heir-pre-sumptive to the Crown, led to another and more prolonged royalist reaction. On the wave of this reaction Richelieu came back to power. But for the " ultras," who were now supreme, Richelieu himself was far too moderate, and he in his turn had to give way to Villèle, the leader of the ultra-royalists and clericalists. Among his own party Villèle won much prestige by his success in restoring by force of arms the despotic Government of Ferdinand VII. in Spain.[1]

The death of Louis XVIII. (1824) and the accession of Charles X. the Count of Artois under the style of Charles X. gave (1824-30) a further impetus to the reactionary movement. The new King had posed, ever since the restoration, as the leader of the extreme Right. Bigoted, ignorant and superstitious, the comrade of the *Émigrés* and the tool of the Jesuits, he plunged headlong down the hill of reaction. The Chamber of Deputies, however, was against him, and for a while checked his course. An appeal to the country (1827) served only to increase the "moderate" majority and to turn out Villèle in favour of Martignac. But Martignac's moderation was in the eyes of the King and his friends nothing less than treason to the monarchy, and in 1829 he was dismissed to make way for Prince Paul de Polignac, Count Labour-donnaie and Bourmont. The last, nominated to the ministry of war, was notorious as a deserter from the Bonapartist cause on the eve of Waterloo; and all three

[1] *Cf.* p. 137.

were known to be reactionaries of the most violent type, whose appointment was taken to signify war to the Charter and the Constitution. The Chambers were quick to realise the danger and to take up the challenge. The lower Chamber was consequently dissolved. The country, deaf to the allurement of a successful military expedition which added Algiers to the dominions of France, returned an increased liberal majority. The King and Polignac were then forced to play their last card.

The Ordinances of St. Cloud Before the Chambers met they issued the famous *Ordinances of St. Cloud* (26th July, 1830). The *Ordinances* were nothing less than a royalist *coup d'état*. The Chambers were again dissolved; a system of double election was devised; the electoral franchise was raised; freedom of the Press was abolished, and a number of "ultras" were nominated to the Council of State. France was momentarily stunned. The Press, led by M. Thiers a young journalist who had lately come to Paris, was the first to recover from the stupor; an emphatic protest was entered against the *Ordinances*, and the nation was called upon to resist the Government. On 27th July Marshal Marmont was entrusted by Polignac with the defence of the capital : barricades hastily erected were quickly demolished, and some citizens were killed or wounded in street combats. On the 28th the mob once more surged through the streets, raised the tricolour, and seized the Hotel de Ville. On the 29th the troops mutinied; the mob burst into the Louvre and the *The Revolution of July* Tuileries, and by nightfall were masters of the capital. Before the next morning the walls of Paris were placarded by Thiers with a proclamation in favour of Philip, Duke of Orleans, the son of Egalité Orleans, who had played an unworthy part in the Revolution of 1789, and the shoddy Revolution of July was virtually achieved. On the 31st, Orleans, on the invitation of the Chambers, assumed the office of lieutenant-general of the kingdom. Meanwhile Charles X. had retired from St. Cloud to Rambouillet; there he announced (2nd August) his abdication in favour of his grandson Henry, Duc de Bordeaux, better known as the Comte de Chambord. At the same time he appointed Orleans lieutenant-general and regent, and bade him proclaim "Henry V." But the concession was too late, or Orleans was too ambitious. The Crown was offered to Orleans on 7th August by the Chambers, and on the 9th he was proclaimed King of the French, under the style of Louis Philippe. A week later Charles X., his family and Court, sailed for England.[1] Such was the issue of the "glorious days of July"; thus did M. Thiers "dispose of the French Crown by a handbill, and overthrow the dynasty by a placard". The discussion of the significance of the "July Revolution," and the character of the "July Monarchy" must be reserved for a later chapter.

It is time to turn to the history of the reaction elsewhere.

In no country was it more violent than in Spain. Of all the Spanish Bourbons Ferdinand VII. was perhaps the most contemptible; a miserable compound of bigotry, sensualism, superstition and cruelty. None the less his restoration in 1814 to the throne of his father was hailed by the Spaniards with limitless enthusiasm. Ferdinand had hardly reached Madrid before he plunged into an "orgy of reaction".[2] In 1812 the Cortes had drawn up a Constitution modelled upon the French Constitution of

Bourbon Restoration in Spain

---

[1] He resided first at Lulworth Castle, afterwards at Holyrood, and died in Austria in 1836.

[2] Phillips.

1791, and based on the principle of the sovereignty of the people. The power of the Crown was reduced to a shadow, and the Legislature was to be supreme. But fantastic and extravagant as was the Constitution of 1812 it might have formed, in the hands of a strong and wise ruler, the starting-point of a constitutional régime. Ferdinand was neither strong nor wise. He revoked the Constitution, dissolved the Cortes, restored the Inquisition, recalled the Jesuits, reinstated the nobles with all their oppressive privileges, gagged the Press, let loose all the forces of disorder, and relentlessly persecuted all the adherents of the Bonapartist régime. For six years the royalist terror reigned supreme. But even for Spain the reaction was too violent. The provinces were soon honeycombed with secret societies, largely recruited from the army. Isolated insurrections were put down with barbarous cruelty, but in 1820 the flag of revolution was unfurled at Cadiz, and Ferdinand, as feeble as he was cruel, made abject surrender. The Constitution of 1812 was restored; a single Chamber Legislature was entrusted with supreme authority; the executive was completely subordinated to it; the authority of the Crown was reduced to nullity; a radical ministry was installed in office; the Holy Office was once more suppressed; the religious houses were dissolved, and from the "orgy of reaction" Spain plunged with characteristic extravagance into an orgy of reform.

But in the years immediately succeeding Waterloo no country could be permitted to regard itself as an isolated unit. The "moral Pentarchy" was watching with anxiety the development of events in Spain, and the more so as the revolutionary contagion spread to Portugal and Italy.

In 1807, as we have seen,[1] the Portuguese royal family **Portugal** had transferred the seat of government to Brazil. After the restoration, the former regent, now John VI., declined to return to Europe. He appointed as regent Lord Beresford, the former commander of the English troops in Portugal, and proclaimed the union of the Portuguese dominions under the title of the "United Kingdom of Portugal, Brazil and the Algarves". Portugal was thus virtually reduced to a position of a dependency of Brazil. The position was not relished at Lisbon, where insurrection, stimulated by Spain, broke out (1820). The regent was deposed, and John VI. was persuaded to return reluctantly to Europe. Dom Pedro, his son, was left as regent in Brazil, and was instructed, at all hazards, to preserve Brazil to the House of Braganza; "and in case of any unforeseen circumstances which should make the union of Portugal and Brazil impracticable . . . to place the crown upon his own head". The unforeseen happened. The Brazilians, in 1822, declined to recognise the orders of the Cortes any longer, declared their country independent, and proclaimed Dom Pedro as Constitutional Emperor. In Portugal itself the political pendulum swang violently from side to side. In 1821 John VI. accepted complacently a liberal Constitution. But in 1823, under pressure from Spain, from his Spanish Queen and his second son Dom Miguel, the King, with equal complacency, accepted a reactionary ministry.

From the Peninsula the revolutionary movement spread **Italy** to Southern Italy. Between Spain and the Two Sicilies there were the closest ties, historical and dynastic, but Ferdinand I. of Naples was a much more indolent reactionary than his Spanish kinsman. There was, how-

[1] P. 89.

ever, quite enough reaction to provoke active discontent, particularly in the army and among the members of an exceedingly powerful and widespread secret society known as the Carbonari (Charcoal burners). In 1820 discontent blazed out into insurrection. The Spanish Constitution of 1812 was proclaimed, and King Ferdinand was compelled to declare his acceptance of the Constitution on oath. But Austria was now supreme in Italy, and Prince Metternich did not permit the puppet princes, whose strings were pulled from Vienna, to act independently of him. King Ferdinand, therefore, having taken the oath to the Constitution with peculiar solemnity, wrote to the Emperor of Austria to protest that he had acted under duress, and that the oath was consequently null and void. Austria was only too glad to get an excuse for direct interference in Southern Italy, more particularly as she was able to act on a mandate from the Powers.

The Troppau Congress

For some time past the Holy Allies had been regarding with growing uneasiness the insurrectionary movements in Southern Europe, and in October, 1820, the three Eastern Powers met in Conference at Troppau in Bohemia, where Lord Stewart (Castlereagh's brother) watched the proceedings on behalf of England. On 19th November, 1820, Russia, Austria and Prussia issued a protocol in which the doctrines of the Holy Alliance were set forth with startling explicitness. "States which have undergone a change of government due to revolution," so it ran, "the results of which threaten other States, *ipso facto*, cease to be members of the European Alliance, and remain excluded from it until their situation gives guarantees for legal order and stability. . . . If, owing to such alterations, immediate danger threatens other States, the Powers bind themselves, by peaceful means, or if

need be by arms, to bring back the guilty State into the
bosom of the Great Alliance."

France expressed, in general terms, adherence to the Great
protocol, but Castlereagh protested that the principle set Britain and
the Holy
forth therein was "in direct repugnance to the funda- Alliance
mental laws of the United Kingdom". From Troppau
the Conference adjourned to Laibach in Carniola (January,
1821), and at Laibach a mandate was given to Austria
to send 80,000 men to Naples. The Austrians marched,
practically without resistance, upon Naples; vengeance
was exacted from all who had taken part in the recent
movement; the principles of legitimacy were triumph-
antly reasserted, and a system of government was
established which was afterwards described (by Mr.
Gladstone) "as an outrage upon religion, upon civilisa-
tion, upon humanity and upon decency".

Against the doctrines proclaimed at Troppau and the
policy sanctioned at Laibach, England, by the mouth of
Castlereagh, entered an emphatic protest:—

"England stands pledged to uphold the territorial arrangements established at the Congress of Vienna. The
invasion of a weaker State by a stronger one for the
purpose of conquest would demand our immediate interference. But with the internal affairs of each separate
State we have nothing to do."

Thus it was Castlereagh alone who prevented the general
acceptance of the doctrine of interference which the Holy
Allies were anxious to maintain.

But while Austria was finding congenial occupation
in Naples and in Piedmont, France, under Villèle, was
itching to go to the assistance of Bourbon absolutism
in Spain. The Congress which in 1822 met at Vienna
and which adjourned to Verona in October was more than

agreeable to the project; but before the formal mandate was given to France an event of European significance had occurred.

Canning .

On the death of Lord Castlereagh (August, 1822) the English Foreign Office passed into the control of George Canning. In principle there was no difference between the policy of Castlereagh and Canning; in the method of asserting the principle there was all the difference in the world. By the mouth of Wellington, who went as England's representative to Verona, Canning bluntly informed the Powers that "while England was no friend to revolution, she did emphatically insist on the right of nations to set up for themselves whatever form of government they thought best, and to be left free to manage their own affairs, so long as they left other nations to manage theirs." France had already seized the excuse of an outbreak of yellow fever in Spain to mass an army of 100,000 men on the frontier for the purpose of establishing a *cordon sanitaire*. Canning's protest was too late to stop the intervention of the French, who in April, 1823, marched an army into Spain under the Duc d'Angoulême, and re-established the absolute authority of King Ferdinand. France remained in military occupation of Spain until 1827.

The Spanish Colonies

But though powerless to avert the French occupation of old Spain, Canning was determined to prevent the extension of French interference to new Spain.

For some years Spain had experienced increasing difficulty in governing her South American colonies. In 1819 she had purchased peace with the United States by the sale of Florida to the States for five million dollars. But the improvement thus effected in her general situation was merely temporary. Meanwhile the trading

interests of Great Britain suffered severely from the prevailing anarchy in South America. For outrages un-
numbered upon British ships no redress could be obtained
from Spain. In 1823 Canning appointed Consuls to the
Spanish colonies for the protection of British trade, and
France was at the same time bluntly informed that
though Spain might subdue her revolted colonies if she
could, no other Power should do it for her. Finally, on
the 1st of January, 1825, the Powers were informed that
Great Britain had recognised the independence of Buenos
Ayres, Colombia and Mexico. The Powers protested, but
nothing came of the protest, and Canning held on his
way, heedless of the Holy Allies, and he found a powerful
ally in the United States. On 2nd December, 1823, President Monroe had declared, on the invitation of Canning
and with his pledge of support, " that any interference on
the part of the Great Powers of Europe for the purpose
of oppressing or controlling the destiny of the Spanish
American States, which had declared their independence
would be dangerous to the peace and safety of the United
States, and would be considered as the manifestation of
an unfriendly disposition towards them ". Such was the
origin of the famous " Monroe doctrine ". The action of
Great Britain and the United States was decisive; by
1830 the Spanish Empire in South America had ceased
to exist, and the following independent republics had
come into being : Mexico, Guatemala, Colombia (= New
Granada and Venezuela), Peru, Chile, Bolivia, Paraguay
and Rio de la Plata or Buenos Ayres.

Not less prompt and decisive was Canning's action in Portugal
regard to Portugal. There, as in Spain, the reactionary
party, led by Dom Miguel, looked for support to France,
the liberal party to Great Britain. At the request of the
latter a British squadron was sent to the Tagus " to con-

firm in the eyes of the Portuguese nation the strict intimacy and goodwill subsisting between the two Crowns" This gave Dom Miguel an excuse, and early in 1824 he effected a *coup d'état* and virtually superseded his father, John VI. The latter escaped on board an English man-of-war, and managed to reassert his authority. In 1825 Canning routed Dom Miguel and his French friends, and at the same time effected a final settlement of the long-standing difficulty between Portugal and Brazil. John VI. was induced to recognise the independence of Brazil under the sovereignty of his son Dom Pedro, though retaining the imperial title for his life-time. But in 1826 John VI. died. Once more factions broke out in Portugal; Spain and France were keen to interfere on behalf of the reactionaries, but they were stopped by the prompt action of Canning, and, thanks to him, the liberal Constitution was saved.

But decisive as was the influence of Canning in Western Europe it was exerted with even more important results in the East. To that quarter the attention of the Powers had been turned since 1821 with ever-increasing anxiety; for the Greek Revolt had opened a new chapter in European history.[1]

---

[1] In this and the following chapter I have made free use of a previous work of my own: *George Canning and his Times* (Murray, 1903).

CHAPTER XIII

THE GREEK WAR OF INDEPENDENCE AND THE EASTERN QUESTION

That shifting, intractable and interwoven tangle of conflicting interests, rival peoples and antagonistic faiths that is veiled under the easy name of the Eastern Question.—JOHN MORLEY.

It offers in detail a chequered picture of patriotism and corruption, desperate valour and weak irresolution, honour and treachery, resistance to the Turk and feud one with another. Its records are stained with many acts of cruelty. And yet who can doubt that it was on the whole a noble stroke, struck for freedom and for justice, by a people who, feeble in numbers and resources, were casting off the vile slough of servitude, who derived their strength from right, and whose worst acts were really in the main due to the masters, who had saddled them not only with a cruel, but with a most demoralising yoke?—W. E. GLADSTONE, on the Greek Revolt.

FOR Europe as a whole the Greek insurrection marks the beginning of that sheaf of problems which we know as "The Eastern Question".

In one sense the Eastern Question dates from the time (1343-1453) when the Ottoman Turks began to "encamp" in the midst of the bundle of races which inhabit the Balkan peninsula. Constantinople fell into their hands in 1453, and thenceforward, for about two centuries, the Turk was the terror and scourge of Christian Europe. Then the problem altered. In the seventeenth century, and still more clearly in the eighteenth, the power of

the Turks exhibited obvious signs of decadence. The
Habsburgs began for the first time to make headway
against them in Hungary and Transylvania, and Russia
pushed down to the Black Sea. These Powers—sometimes singly and sometimes in combination—were constantly at war with Turkey during the eighteenth century.

Treaty of Kainardji, 1774

In 1774 Russia dictated to the Porte the decisive Treaty of
Kutchuk-Kainardji, by which (i) Russia obtained for the first time a
firm grip upon the Black Sea, by the acquisition of Azof, and the
acknowledgment of her right to free commercial navigation ; (ii)
Russia secured a permanent Embassy at Constantinople and certain
rights of protection in regard to the Greek Church in Turkey ;
and (iii) the Principalities of Moldavia and Wallachia, together with
the islands of the Ægean, were handed back to Turkey only on
condition of " better Government ".

Russia's rights under the treaty were not in all cases
distinctly defined, but henceforth the Czar of Russia was,
in his dual capacity as Head of the Slav family and
Head[1] of the Greek Church, recognised as in some sort
the protector of a large proportion of the peoples subject
to the Porte.

Treaty of Bucharest, 1812

In 1783 Catherine II. annexed the Tartars east of the
river Boug, and in 1792 pushed her frontier to the
Dniester. By the Treaty of Tilsit (1807) Alexander I.
stipulated, as we have seen, for the cession to Russia of
Moldavia and Wallachia. This great prize was denied to
him, but by the Peace of Bucharest (1812) he snatched
Bessarabia from the Turks, and secured for his allies, the
Serbians, complete control over the administration of
their domestic concerns.

So far the advance of Russia in South-eastern Europe
had not excited the alarm of the other European Powers.
In 1791 the younger Pitt attempted to convince his

---

[1] The term " Head " is here used in a popular, not a legal sense.

RUSSIA'S WESTERN ADVANCE

NORWAY

SWEDEN

FINLAND 1809

Treaty of Neustadt 1721

St. Petersburg

Esthonia

Treaty of

Livonia

Riga

Courland 1795

I Partition 1773

II Partition 1793

III Partition 1795

Second Partition 1793

Treaty of Bucharest 1812

Treaty of Kainardji 1774

Treaty of Jassy 1792

Ukase of 1783

For settlement of Poland in 1815. see Map p.

English Miles

0   100   200   300

B.V.Y.

Extent at accession of Peter the Great ____

Acquisitions from Sweden 〰 from Poland 〰 from Turkey ‖‖

countrymen that they had a vital interest in the Eastern Question; but Great Britain refused to take alarm, and for the next thirty years other matters claimed her attention.

The Greek Revolt

When, therefore, in 1821 the news of the Greek Revolt reached the Powers assembled in Conference at Laibach, no exceptional significance appeared to attach to it. It was no more—and no less—an international question than the revolutionary movements, apparently similar in character and origin, which had lately broken out in Spain, Portugal and Naples. Castlereagh, for instance, regarded it simply as one more instance of the prevailing "organised spirit of insurrection". As a matter of fact, it was on an altogether different plane of importance. Not only was it destined to add another nation to the European polity; it also came to be recognised, in the after time, as the real opening of a new chapter in European history.

Causes of the Greek Revolt

To all appearance the Greek Revolution was a bolt from the blue. In reality it was far otherwise. The Greeks, though blotted out as a nation by the Turks, had never been crushed as a people. Much of the public administration was in their hands, and a large share of commerce and wealth; they manned the navy, and controlled the finances. In the islands they enjoyed practical autonomy, and in the Morea had a large measure of it; the Greek Church was a strong bond of union; and, in the eighteenth century, there had come an intellectual revival which had recalled the glories of ancient Hellas. Into a soil thus prepared the French Revolution had flung seed broadcast, and in 1815 the Philikè Hetaireia was founded. This secret society quickly enrolled 200,000 members, all of whom looked to the expulsion of the

Moslems and the restoration of the Greek Empire at Constantinople.

The insurrection began in March, 1821, under Prince Alexander Hypsilanti, who raised his standard in Moldavia in the confident expectation that Russia would back him. But the Czar Alexander was not only the ruler of Russia but the founder of the Holy Alliance. He frowned upon the enterprise, and by June, 1821, Hypsilanti's rising had collapsed. *Hypsilanti's Rising in Moldavia*

Far different was the measure of success attained by the movement in the Morea and the islands of the Ægean. The Turks, taken unprepared, were beaten all along the line, and had recourse to cruel reprisals. The Greek Patriarch was murdered in Constantinople, and a wholesale massacre of the Christians was ordered in Macedonia and Asia Minor. On both sides the struggle was conducted with the utmost ferocity, and the serious attention of the Powers was inevitably attracted to it. *Rising in the Morea and the Islands*

Moreover, Russia had her own quarrel with the Turk, and although the Czar always regarded the Greeks as rebels, who ought to be left to their fate, it was difficult to prevent the two quarrels in which the Porte was involved reacting on each other, if not merging into one.

England also became keenly interested in the struggle. Lord Byron aroused immense enthusiasm on behalf of the Greeks, and in 1822 Lord Castlereagh's (Londonderry's) death opened the Foreign Office to George Canning. Canning was a firm friend to the Greeks, but his main cause for anxiety was lest Russia should be allowed to exploit the Greek insurrection for her own purposes. His policy, therefore, was to induce Turkey to come to terms with the Greeks before Russia got a chance of interference

For three years (1822-25) the Greeks, despite internal feuds, more than held their own against the Turks; but in 1824 a fresh complication arose. The Sultan called to his assistance Ibrahim Pasha, the son of his vassal, Mehemet Ali of Egypt. Ibrahim occupied Crete in 1824, and in 1825 crossed to the Morea, where he "harried, slaughtered and devastated in all directions" The rumour ran that he meant to carry off all the Greeks who were spared by his ferocious troops into bondage in Egypt. And while Ibrahim devastated the Morea the Turk himself was steadily gaining ground. Missolonghi, after an heroic defence of a year, to which English volunteers had largely contributed, fell in 1826, and, in 1827, despite the efforts of Lord Cochrane, General Church and others, Athens was compelled to surrender.

Alexander succeeded by Nicholas I. The Greek cause seemed desperate. But in 1825 Alexander of Russia had died and been succeeded by his brother Nicholas. Nicholas had all Alexander's shrewdness and ambition, with none of his mysticism. To him it mattered nothing whether the Greeks were rebels so long as their rebellion subserved Russian interests. In 1826, however, Canning induced the new Czar to combine with England to force an armistice on the Porte and to recognise the autonomy of Greece under Turkish suzerainty. The ferocities of Ibrahim had "staggered humanity," and France joined England and Russia.[1] Turkey, however, obstinate as usual, ruined Canning's policy and played straight into the hands of Russia. In 1827 the allied fleets were sent into the Levant with ambiguous instructions. The Turks fired on an English boat in the harbour of Navarino; a general action ensued, and the Turkish fleet was entirely destroyed. The battle of Navarino secured the liberation of Greece, but apart

The battle of Navarino (20th October, 1827)

[1] Treaty of London, July, 1827.

from this, all the advantages of the joint intervention were reaped exclusively by Russia. Canning died in August, 1827, and the fruits of his firm diplomacy were dissipated by his successors. Wellington deplored Navarino as an "untoward event" and apologised to the Porte for the accident. The Czar, on the contrary, advanced single handed against the Porte. The campaign of 1828 was a failure, but in 1829 Russia put forth her strength; Diebitsch crossed the Balkans, occupied Adrianople and threatened Constantinople; Kars and Erzeroum had already fallen, and on 14th September, 1829, the Porte accepted the Treaty of Adrianople—a treaty second only in importance in the history of the Eastern Question to that of Kainardji.

Russia restored her conquests, except the "Great Islands" of the Danube; but her title to Georgia and the other provinces of the Caucasus was acknowledged; all neutral vessels were to have free navigation in the Black Sea and on the Danube; practical autonomy was granted to the principalities of Moldavia and Wallachia under Russian protection; Russian traders in Turkey were to be under the exclusive jurisdiction of their own Consuls, and in regard to Greece the Porte accepted the Treaty of London, thus virtually acknowledging its independence. *Treaty of Adrianople*

The final settlement of Greece was referred to a Conference in London where the Greek frontier was ultimately fixed at a line extending from the Gulf of Volo on the East to Arta on the West. The form of government was to be a Constitutional Monarchy, and the Crown, having been successively declined by Prince John of Saxony and Prince Leopold of Saxe-Coburg (afterwards King of the Belgians), was eventually accepted in 1832 by Prince Otto of Bavaria. Capodistrias, who had been ruling Greece since 1827, was assassinated in 1831, and the way was clear, therefore, for Prince Otto. But Otto was not a happy choice; he neglected the national feelings, and chafed under the limitations imposed on him by the Constitution. An abortive revolution broke out in 1843, and a more successful one in 1862, when King Otto was expelled. The Greeks were anxious for a king from the English royal family, and the Crown was offered to Prince Alfred. But the protecting Powers, England, France and Russia, had pledged themselves not to allow any of their cadets to accept the throne, and in 1863 England obtained for the Greeks the services of a Danish prince, and at the same time presented him with the Ionian Isles. King George's task was not entirely easy, but under him Greece has made some progress on the path of Constitutional Government, and after many attempts obtained a rectification of her frontier by the acquisition of Thessaly and a strip of Epirus (1884).

The Duke of Wellington declared the Treaty of Adrianople to be the "death-blow to the independence of the Ottoman Porte, and the forerunner of the dissolution and extinction of its power". The Duke underrated the recuperative powers of the "sick man" and the cleverness with which he could make use of the jealousies of European Powers. The Hellenic rising, issuing in a Greek kingdom, has indeed added one more factor to the well-nigh insoluble problem of the "Eastern Question," but the Turk himself, despite loss of provinces and curtailment of jurisdiction, has exhibited unexpected vitality.[1]

[1] Some modification of these statements may now (1926) be called for. Reference should therefore be made to my *Europe and Beyond* (Methuen), chapters iii., xi., xii., and xiv., and to my *Eastern Question* (Clarendon Press), Third Edition (1924), Epilogue II.

CHAPTER XIV

FRANCE AND HER REVOLUTIONS (1830-1852)

> The English have a scornful insular way
> Of calling the French light. The levity
> Is in the judgment only. . . .
> —Mrs. Browning.

The name of Napoleon is in itself a complete programme. It stands for order, authority, religion; national prosperity within; national dignity without.—Louis Napoleon, in 1849.

THE July Revolution, though shoddy in character and limited in its immediate scope, exerted considerable influence beyond the borders of France. It definitely closed for Europe at large the period of reaction inaugurated at Vienna. Italy, Portugal, Switzerland, and several of the German States, testify to the liberalising impulse derived from "the glorious days of July". The more important of these movements will receive attention in due course.[1] The most striking and the most permanent effect was traceable in the kingdom of the Netherlands. *The July Revolution*

The Union of Belgium and Holland under the House of Orange was one of the most characteristic efforts of the Viennese diplomatists. Diplomacy demanded a stout barrier between France and Germany, and cared little how it was constructed. Between Belgians and Dutch- *Belgian independence*

[1] See pp. 177, 197 *seqq.*

men there was little in common, either of race, creed or
tradition, and what little there was was speedily ob-
scured by the stupidity of the Hague Government after
1815.   It soon became obvious that the Belgians, though
numerically predominant, were to be converted into Dutchmen with all possible speed.   Against this fusion strong
opposition manifested itself in Belgium.   The clericals
united with the democrats, and both found encourage-
ment and opportunity in the upheaval of 1830.   Insurrection broke out in Brussels in August, and quickly
spread to Liége, Louvain and other towns in the Southern
Netherlands.   The King offered limited concessions; the
Belgians demanded Home Rule, and both parties appealed
to the Powers.   Russia, Austria and Prussia were
strongly opposed to the destruction of their handiwork,
but Lord Palmerston cordially espoused the Belgian
cause, and secured the assent of the Pentarchy to the independence and neutralisation of Belgium under European
guarantee.   The Belgians themselves created a difficulty
by the election of the Duc de Nemours, second son of
Louis Philippe, as king.   Palmerston refused to permit
such an extension of French influence and Prince Leopold
of Saxe-Coburg, the widowed husband of the English
Princess Charlotte, was elected in his place [1] (June, 1831).
Holland was then coerced into submission (1832) by
England and France.   Thus Belgium, largely through
the determined efforts of Lord Palmerston, came into
being as an independent kingdom.

We must now return to the effects of the July Revolution upon France itself.

The Citizen   From the outset the position of the "Citizen" King
Monarchy

[1] In 1832 King Leopold married Princess Louise, eldest daughter
of Louis Philippe.

was one of great embarrassment. King of the French neither by Divine Right nor by the suffrages of the people his basis of authority was exceedingly narrow. The Legitimists scowled at the man who had treacherously supplanted the Comte de Chambord, and legitimist insurrections broke out at Lyons, Grenoble and in La Vendée. The republicans, men like Lamartine and Barrot, were equally dissatisfied. They accepted Louis Philippe, but only in the hope of surrounding the " Citizen Monarchy " with republican institutions. Among the mass of the people Louis Philippe and his bourgeois ministers, Thiers and Guizot, excited no enthusiasm. The new régime was constitutionally respectable, but unheroic and dull. The actual form of the constitution underwent little alteration from that of 1814. The Chambers obtained, concurrently with the Crown, the right of initiating legislation; the members of the Upper House were nominated only for life, but the supreme question of the ultimate responsibility of ministers was left unsolved. Not to the end was it really decided whether Louis Philippe was to be a " Constitutional " sovereign in the English or in the Bourbon sense. Thiers held that " the King reigns but does not govern"; but Louis Philippe himself was exceedingly tenacious of the control of the executive. "They shall not," he was wont to say, "prevent my driving my own carriage."

Neither the King nor his ministers drove it with much success, either at home or abroad. Nothing indeed did more to dissipate the small measure of popularity enjoyed by the Orleans monarchy than the ineffectiveness of its foreign policy. Starting from a principle of non-intervention Louis Philippe contrived by a combination of weakness and unscrupulousness to alienate sympathy at

Foreign Policy

home and to offend his best friend abroad—Great Britain.

The first rock of offence was in regard to Egypt. France had long regarded herself as having a special interest in the affairs of that country. In 1831 Mehemet Ali, the ambitious adventurer who had become Pasha of Egypt, attacked and conquered Syria, which like Egypt itself was under Turkish suzerainty. The Porte appealed to the Powers for help, but Russia alone was willing to afford it. France and England compelled the Sultan to buy off the hostility of his vassal by the cession of Syria and his confirmation in Candia, which had been granted to him as the price of assistance in the Greek insurrection. Russia reaped her reward in the Treaty of Unkiar Skelessi, which secured to Russian ships of war exclusive rights in the Black Sea and the Dardanelles, and virtually established a Russian protectorate over Turkey.

In 1839 the whole question was once more reopened by the attempt of Turkey to recover Syria from the grasp of her Egyptian vassal. Mehemet Ali, backed by France, was again successful. Constantinople itself was threatened, and again the Porte was compelled to appeal for the protection of the Powers. Lord Palmerston was determined that come what might Unkiar Skelessi should not be repeated. With France dominant in Egypt and Russia supreme at Constantinople, England's position in the Eastern Mediterranean and even in Asia would be very seriously compromised. Consequently, he concluded with Russia, Austria and Prussia the Quadruple Treaty of London (15th July, 1840), by which the Powers agreed to coerce Mehemet Ali into submission and to pacify the Levant. France was now completely isolated, and Louis

Philippe threatened war with England. Palmerston went on his way unheeding. The English fleet captured Beyrout, Sidon and St. Jean D'Acre; France was informed "in the most friendly and inoffensive manner that if she threw down the gauntlet, England would not refuse to pick it up;" Louis Philippe drew back; the fiery Thiers was replaced by the pacific Guizot; Mehemet Ali was deprived of Syria and Candia, and had to content himself with the hereditary pashalik of Egypt; and, finally, by the Treaty of London (13th July, 1841) the Treaty of Dardanelles were closed, under the guarantee of the London, July, 1841 Pentarchy, to the ships of war of all nations. The latter stipulation was specially significant, and marked a real triumph for Palmerston. Unkiar Skelessi was torn up, and the Black Sea was no longer a Russian lake. For twelve years the Eastern Question ceased to threaten the peace of Europe.

In the eyes of Frenchmen the Government of Louis Philippe was seriously discredited by the Egyptian fiasco, nor did it improve its position by its intervention in the affairs of Switzerland or of Spain.

Between 1830 and 1848 Switzerland was in a condition The of perpetual unrest, and in 1847 civil war broke out. In Sonderbund 1845 the Seven Roman Catholic Cantons had formed a Sonderbund or league for mutual defence. The Republic was threatened with disruption; Austria and France backed the Sonderbund, England the Protestant-liberals. The active intervention of France was averted by the tactics of Lord Palmerston; the Sonderbund was dissolved, the Jesuits expelled, and unity re-established (1848). That France should have taken part with Austria on behalf of absolutism and ultramontanism was exceedingly distasteful to French Liberals.

The
Spanish
Marriages

Still more were they disgusted by the treacherous conduct of Louis Philippe in connection with the Spanish marriages.

The question of providing the young Queen Isabella of Spain with a suitable husband had been for some time under discussion between the Courts of England and France. In 1843 and 1844 Queen Victoria and Louis Philippe exchanged visits, and the Queen then agreed to the engagement of the Duc de Montpensier, younger son of Louis Philippe, to Maria Louisa, younger sister of Queen Isabella, provided that the marriage should not take place until after the birth of an heir to the Spanish throne. On 10th October, 1846, the Spanish Queen married her cousin, the Duke Francis—a man notoriously unfit for marriage and therefore acceptable to Louis Philippe. On the same day Montpensier was married to her sister. A more shameless plot, a more flagrant violation of a diplomatic understanding, it would be impossible to conceive. Its authors reaped no advantage. Embarrassments were multiplying around the Citizen Monarchy. Of these two were particularly insistent. On the one side the Liberals were demanding parliamentary reform; an extension of the franchise; a real parliamentary executive, and above all, a purification of the corrupt administration. On the other, the Parisian artisan was clamouring for a recognition of the right to work (*droit au travail*).

The *droit
au travail*

From the outset, as we have seen, the Orleans Monarchy had rested on the support of the bourgeois; nobles, peasants and artisans had held, for the most part, sullenly aloof. Particularly the artisans. In France, as in England, the first half of the nineteenth century was a period of rapid economic change. The application of steam to manufactures revolutionised industry; the hand-worker succumbed before the competition with machinery; the factory superseded domestic work, and even in France the "self-sufficing" household tended to disappear. No great economic revolution can be effected without suffering to the poor; statesmanship may mitigate, it cannot avert it. In England the fiscal reforms of Sir Robert Peel knocked the bottom out of the Chartist movement; in France the Socialists sought to cure economic distress by effecting a political revolution. Socialism had long been fashionable in Paris. For years past the salons had been discussing the theories of Fourier (1772-1837) and St. Simon (1760-1825), and many fantastic but short-lived experiments were the result. But these philosophers preached to a select audience. Louis Blanc preached to the masses, and from him the French artisan learnt of his "right to work" at the hands of the State. It was this doctrine which supplied the driving power of the Revolution of 1848, and which was thus responsible for the overthrow of the Orleans Monarchy.

But other causes, some of them temporary and accidental, contributed to this result.

Causes of the Revolution of 1848

When the French Chambers met in December, 1847, the outlook for the Government was gloomy. Respectability was outraged by the Spanish marriage plot; Liberalism was disgusted by Guizot's gravitation towards Austria and his support of the Sonderbund; and from different quarters there were cries for electoral reform; for the purification of the public service; for the removal of the innumerable "placemen" who gave the Government a permanent majority in the Chamber of Deputies; above all for the provision of State employment. The immediate cause of the outbreak in Paris was the obstinate bungling of the Guizot ministry in regard to a banquet which the Reformers had organised for 22nd February, to advertise and promote their objects. Interdicted by the Government, it was abandoned by the Reformers, but on the same day Barrot rose in the Chamber to propose the impeachment of the ministry.

The Revolution of 1848 In Paris the temper of the mob was rising rapidly. Crowds were beginning to parade the streets; the familiar barricades were erected, only to be demolished by the troops. On the 23rd Guizot's resignation was announced together with an intimation that the formation of a new ministry had been entrusted to Count Molé. Molé failed in his efforts, and Thiers accepted the task on condition that Odilon Barrot, the leader of the Extreme Left, might be associated with him. On the 24th the new ministry was announced and a dissolution promised. But it was too late. Not even Barrot could control the mob. Several collisions had already taken place between the troops and the people; the corpses of fifty victims had been paraded through the streets; the National Guard had mutinied, and on every side Barrot was received with cries of "Vive la République". Before nightfall of the 24th Louis Philippe abdicated in favour of his grandson the Comte de Paris, and appointed as regent the Duchess of Orleans. The abdication was as futile as it was faint-hearted, and sealed the fate of the dynasty. The King and Queen escaped to England; the Duchess of Orleans and her two sons stood their ground courageously in the Chamber. But the Chamber was invaded by an armed mob; the regency and the dynasty were swept aside, and a Provisional Government, consisting of Lamartine, Ledru-Rollin, Garnier-Pagès and others. was appointed. On the same evening Lamartine, speaking from the Hotel de Ville, proclaimed a Republic.

"In France," said Louis Napoleon, "we make revolutions but not reforms." Never was the profound truth of this saying more signally illustrated than in 1848. By the weakness of the executive and the excitability of the Parisian mob a reform movement had been diverted into Revolution. It was, indeed, "less a revolution than a collapse" (Dickinson). Even down to February, 1848, there was nothing in the nature of a settled design to overthrow the bourgeois monarchy, though France was frankly bored by it. "La France s'ennuie." Thus Lamartine summarised the results of the experiment which closed in 1848.

But despite its apparently accidental character the Revolution of 1848 had a real significance. Lamartine might vapour about the old catchwords of "Liberty, Fraternity and Equality"; but it was not to assert these principles that the Parisian artisan took off his coat. To him the hero of the Revolution was not Lamartine but Louis Blanc; he was looking not for a mere political republic but for a socialist millennium. The true significance of 1848 is disclosed in the following decree (25th February). *Significance of the Revolution of 1848*

"The Government of the French Republic engages to guarantee the subsistence of the workman by his labour. It engages to guarantee work to all citizens." The doctrines of the *Organisation du Travail* had indeed come home to roost. To fulfil their pledge the Government established "national workshops," where all might obtain work at fixed wages. Before the end of May there were 115,000 applicants; work could not be found for them, and it was derisively proposed that they should *The National Workshops*

11

be employed to bottle off the Seine. France was threatened with industrial ruin; the Government plucked up courage to end the fantastic experiment; the Socialists revolted; a state of siege was declared in Paris, and for four days (25th-28th June) a sanguinary conflict raged in its streets. The Republic vanquished socialism, but destroyed itself.

At the opportune moment a new actor stepped upon the Parisian stage.

Prince Louis Bonaparte

Prince Louis Bonaparte was the third son of Louis, ex-King of Holland. Born in 1808 he was educated largely in Italy, where he took part in various revolutionary movements. In 1836 and again in 1840 he attempted to excite the French people to revolt against the Citizen King. Condemned in 1840 to perpetual imprisonment at Ham he escaped to England in 1846, and on the fall of the Orleans Monarchy he offered his sword and his services to the Republic. Both were declined and he retired to England. But the days of June had taught France a lesson. In September, 1848, Prince Louis was elected to the National Assembly by five departments. Returning immediately to France he announced himself (1st December) as a candidate for the Presidency. Under the Constitution of 1848 the Government was vested in a President and a single legislative Chamber, each elected on the basis of universal suffrage. This gave Louis Bonaparte his chance. Out of 7,000,000 votes cast in the Presidential election less than 2,000,000 went to the four republican candidates. Lamartine, the republican leader, got 19,900, Bonaparte 5,500,000.

Elected President

"The man of destiny" had arrived. As to his predestined mission he himself entertained no doubt. "I believe," he had declared, "that from time to time men are created whom I will call providential, in whose hands the destinies of their country are placed. I believe myself to be one of those men."

From the moment of his election as President of the Republic Bonaparte looked steadily towards the revival of the Empire. He appealed to all classes, more particularly to the peasants, to the priests and the army. Clericals and soldiers were gratified by the restoration of Pope Pius IX. and the overthrow of the Roman Republic in 1849; the peasants were attracted by the magic of his name. The Assembly also played into his hands. With the fear of February and the terror of June always before their eyes, they disfranchised 3,000,000 voters and muzzled the Press (31st May, 1850). The President could now pose as the champion of democracy against timid reactionaries. Frustrated in an attempt to get a formal revision of the Constitution he effected with consummate adroitness the famous *coup d'état* of 2nd December, 1851. The leading Republicans and Socialists were suddenly arrested; troops were posted to crush resistance in Paris; the Assembly was dissolved, and a draft Constitution was submitted to a national vote. On 20th December over 7,000,000 votes were given in favour of Bonaparte's scheme. His own term of office was prolonged for ten years; ministers were made responsible solely to the President; a Council of State nominated by him was to draft laws on his initiative, and legislation was to be in the hands of a nominated Senate and an elected *Corps Legislatif.*

Coup d'état, 2nd December, 1851

A second plebiscite, in November, pronounced by a similar majority (7,824,129 against 253,149) for the transformation of the Presidency into an hereditary Empire, and on 2nd December, 1852, the new Emperor

The Second Empire

was proclaimed as Napoleon III.   In January, 1853, the Emperor married Eugénie, Comtesse de Teba, a Spanish lady of great beauty, and an heir—the Prince Imperial —was born to them in 1856.   By that time the Second Empire seemed to be firmly established in the affections of Frenchmen and in the regard of Europe.   But already it had belied its initial promise.

L'Empire c'est la Paix.   So Napoleon had declared in 1852.   Even as he spoke the sky was darkening with the clouds of a great war—the first of the series in which the Empire was destined to be involved.

CHAPTER XV

THE CRIMEAN WAR AND AFTER (1852-1878)

Tout contribue à développer entre ces deux pays l'antagonisme et la haine. Les Russes ont reçu leur foi de Byzance, c'est leur métropole, et les Turcs la souillent de leur présence. Les Turcs oppriment les coreligionnaires des Russes, et chaque Russe considère comme une œuvre de foi la délivrance de ses frères. Les passions populaires s'accordent ici avec les conseils de la politique : c'est vers la mer Noire, vers le Danube, vers Constantinople que les souverains Russes sont naturallement portés à s'étendre : délivrer et conquérir deviennent pour eux synonymes. Les tsars ont cette rare fortune que l'instinct national soutient leurs calculs d' ambition, et qu'ils peuvent retourner contre l'empire Ottoman ce fanatisme religieux qui a précipité les Turcs sur l'Europe et rendait naguère leurs invasions si formidables.—SOREL.

FOR twelve years the Eastern Question had been permitted to slumber. In 1852 it was rudely awakened by a quarrel about the Holy Places in Palestine. *The Holy Places*

It had long been the custom for Christians to make pilgrimages to various spots in Palestine hallowed by their association with the life of Christ on earth. By a treaty of 1740 the French had obtained from the Porte the right of guarding several of these Holy Places; but in the latter years of the century the French began to neglect their duties which were assumed by members of the Greek Church. In 1850 Louis Bonaparte, anxious to conciliate the French Clericals, asserted his right to place Latin monks again in possession. The demand, supported by Austria and other Roman Catholic Powers, was in substance conceded by the Porte. But the concession roused the anger of the Czar Nicholas, the champion of the Greek Church, the more so as it was made to the upstart Emperor of the French. A strong protest was lodged at Constantinople, and the Czar prepared to utilise the situation for the realisation of long cherished hopes.

Nicholas I. and England

He was sanguine enough to suppose that he could carry England with him in his schemes. He had visited England in 1844 and had attempted to persuade the Government that the dissolution of the " Sick Man " was imminent, and that Russia and England might jointly provide for the partition of the inheritance. Early in 1853 he pressed the same views upon Sir Hamilton Seymour, the English ambassador at St. Petersburg. England refused to regard the Turk as irremediably sick, and resented the offer of Egypt made to her by the Czar.

Wise or unwise, right or wrong, this refusal to come to terms with Russia for the settlement of the Eastern Question was fraught with momentous consequences. It may be held immediately responsible for the Crimean War and ultimately for the lasting antagonism between England and Russia in the Far and Farther East.

The dispute as to the Holy Places was now virtually settled to the tolerable satisfaction of both France and Russia; but the concessions of the Porte only encouraged Russia to make more extensive demands. Under threat of war the Sultan was suddenly required to grant Russia a formal protectorate over all his Christian subjects.

On the advice of Lord Stratford de Redcliffe the Porte refused, and in June, 1853, the Russians occupied Moldavia and Wallachia. In October the Sultan declared war, and at the end of November the Russian fleet destroyed the Turkish fleet off Sinope.

England and France were watching the conduct of The Crimean War Russia with rising indignation. After the massacre of Sinope their allied fleets were sent into the Black Sea, and, despite the efforts of diplomacy to avert it, war was declared (27th March, 1854).

By the time the Anglo-French army, under Lord Raglan and St. Arnaud, reached Varna the Russians had evacuated the Principalities. The allied army was then sent to the Crimea with orders to take Sebastopol. The brilliant victory of the Alma (20th September) seemed to promise speedy success, but Balaclava (25th October) and Inkermann (5th November) proved such stubborn contests that the hope was dispelled, and Sebastopol, fortified by General Todleben, resisted all attacks. Moreover, on 14th November, a great storm dealt destruction to the English transports outside the harbour of Balaclava. The loss of stores inflicted terrible sufferings upon the troops during the severe Crimean winter of 1854-55. Disease followed in the wake of scarcity. The administration completely collapsed; the commissariat broke down; the wretched hospitals were overcrowded, and cholera did its deadly work upon half-starved soldiers. With the turn of the year things began to improve. Miss Florence Nightingale and her devoted band of ladies reorganised the hospitals; in January, 1855, 18,000 Sardinian troops joined the allies under the command of La Marmora; in England Lord Palmerston succeeded Lord Aberdeen as Prime Minister and infused fresh

vigour into the military administration, and in March
the bellicose Czar Nicholas succumbed to the rigours of
the winter, and was succeeded by his son Alexander II.
In May Marshal Pellissier succeeded Canrobert in the
command of the French troops, and on the 28th of the
following month Lord Raglan, who had stuck manfully
to his post, died from cholera.   An assault upon Sebastopol had been repulsed with great loss on 18th June, but
was repeated at the beginning of September.   The capture
of the Malakoff by the French troops rendered the great
fortress untenable, and on the 10th it was evacuated.
The triumph of French arms satisfied Napoleon who now
became anxious for peace.   The capture of Kars by
Russia (28th November, 1855) inclined the Czar in a
similar direction.   Austria exerted herself to arrange
Treaty of   terms acceptable to all parties, and on 30th March, 1856,
Paris,   the Peace of Paris was signed.
1856

The Sultan was required to confirm the privileges of his Christian
subjects, but the Powers, including Russia, explicitly repudiated
any right of interference, individual or collective, between the Sultan
and his subjects ; the Russian protectorate over the Danubian
Principalities was abolished ; the free navigation of the Danube was
established, and Russia was compelled to retire from its shores, by
ceding a strip of Bessarabia to Roumania ; finally, the Black Sea
was neutralised, no vessels of war were to enter it, and no arsenals
were to be established on its shores.

As to the wisdom of the Crimean War opinion is now
sharply divided ; the expenditure of blood and treasure
was enormous, but to describe it as objectless and fruitless is an exaggeration.   For good or evil Russian advance
towards Constantinople had been at least temporarily
checked ; the Sick Man had been set on his legs again,
and Russia's claim to exclusive control of the Eastern

Question had been definitely repudiated by the Western Powers.

For the next twenty years the Eastern Question did not seriously threaten the peace of Europe. Nevertheless it soon became obvious that the many problems connected with it were still unsolved. Among the various populations subject to the Turk in the Balkan peninsula there was almost perpetual unrest. In 1858 the Powers had decreed that Moldavia and Wallachia should remain separate though virtually independent. The two States ingeniously elected the same ruler, Prince Alexander Couza. Europe wisely bowed to the accomplished fact, and in 1859 recognised the union of the Romanic Principalities under the title of Roumania. The agitation in Greece has been already referred to.[1] Crete was only kept quiet (1866-68) by the intervention of the Powers, and in 1875 the whole Eastern Question was again reopened by the outbreak of insurrection among the peoples of Bosnia and Herzegovina who were supported by volunteers from Servia and Montenegro.

The Eastern Question, 1856-75

Russia was only too glad to have the opportunity of fishing again in troubled waters. For some years after the Crimean War Alexander II., an enlightened ruler, had busied himself with domestic reforms. In 1861 he carried through the Emancipation of the Serfs, converting them into peasant proprietors by methods similar to those of Stein and Hardenberg.[2] In contrast to this humane legislation was the severity with which the insurrection of the Poles was subdued in 1863. It was not long, however, before it became plain that the Czar Alexander did not mean to accept the results of the Crimean War as final. In 1870, taking advantage of the preoccupation

Insurrections in the Balkans, 1875

[1] See p. 152.   [2] See p. 107.

of Europe with the Franco-German War, he denounced the Treaty of Paris, so far as it related to the neutralisation of the Black Sea. To this Europe, after some demur from England, agreed (1871). But the insurrection of 1875 gave him a still larger opportunity.

The Porte had entirely failed in its promises to ameliorate the lot of its Christian subjects. In 1875 the Powers once more agreed in a note, prepared by Count Andrassy of Austria, to urge reform upon the Sultan. The Porte politely agreed, but the insurgents refused to be satisfied with mere assurances. The Berlin Memorandum, drafted early in 1876, proposed a time limit, but Lord Beaconsfield, deeming that famous document unjustifiably dictatorial, refused to make England a party to it, and it fell to the ground.

The Bulgarian Insurrection

This was Russia's opportunity: the whole of the Balkan provinces were now in ferment. The Bulgarians raised the standard of insurrection in May, 1876, and in June Serbia and Montenegro declared war upon the Porte. The Bulgarian insurrection was stamped out in blood, and Serbia and Montenegro, despite some initial victories, were crushed by the Ottoman troops. But the atrocities resorted to by the Turks in quelling the Bulgarian revolt aroused profound indignation in England. Accordingly in December, 1876, the Powers held a Conference in Constantinople in the hope of effecting reform without a European war. The Turk, as usual, was eager in his professions of reforms, but stubborn in his refusal to allow Europe to superintend them. Thereupon the Czar declared war (24th April, 1877), and was joined by Roumania. The Russians crossed the Danube in June, but the Turks held out with splendid courage in Plevna, and not until 10th December, 1877, were the Russians

Russo-Turkish War, 1877

able to capture that great fortress. Before the end of January, 1878, they reached Adrianople, and in February Constantinople itself was threatened. Kars had already fallen, and in March, 1878, Russia dictated to the Porte the Treaty of San Stephano which virtually annihilated the Ottoman Power in Europe. England thereupon intervened, and demanded that the Treaty should be submitted to a European Congress. Russia refused: the English fleet passed the Dardanelles; the reserves were called out, and a large Sepoy force was despatched from India to the Mediterranean. Russia then gave way, and in June, 1878, the Powers met in conference at Berlin. In July a treaty was concluded, by which—

Treaty of Berlin

(i) Serbia, Montenegro and Roumania received small accessions of territory and were declared independent of the Porte ; (ii) Bosnia and Herzegovina were handed over to Austrian occupation—an occupation which has proved to be permanent ; (iii) Russia acquired Batoum and Kars, and recovered the strip between the Pruth and the Danube of which she had been deprived in 1856 ; and (iv) Bulgaria, which by the Treaty of San Stephano had been formed into a large State stretching from the Danube to the Ægean, was divided into two : (*a*) Bulgaria proper, which was to be an independent State under Turkish suzerainty, and (*b*) Eastern Roumelia, which was restored to the Sultan, who agreed to place it under a Christian governor approved by the Powers.

This division was manifestly artificial, and in 1885 Alexander of Battenberg (Prince of Bulgaria) united Eastern Roumelia to Bulgaria. The Powers protested, Russia with special vehemence, but acquiesced, and in 1895 a formal reconciliation was effected between Russia and the new Bulgaria.

Shortly after the conclusion of the Treaty of Berlin it was announced that the good offices of England had been rewarded by the cession of Cyprus.

The settlement of 1878 was regarded at the time as a triumph for Great Britain and a distinct check to Russia, and Lord Beaconsfield, its real author, reached the zenith of a dazzling, though transient, popularity. It has now become the fashion to assume that his work was in part fruitless and in part mischievous. But without entering upon debatable ground it may be stated with confidence that events in the East have developed, for good or evil, on lines widely divergent from those laid down in the Treaty of San Stephano. The check to Russian ambition administered by England at Berlin may have served to intensify Anglo-Russian rivalry in Asia, but it undoubtedly delayed, if it did not avert Russian ascendancy at Constantinople. Between the Czar and the object of his ambition there are now interposed the considerable barriers of Bulgaria and Roumania.

Note.—See note to p. 152.

CHAPTER XVI

REACTION AND REVOLUTION IN ITALY (1815-1849)

Since the fall of the Roman Empire (if even before it) there never has been a time when Italy could be called a nation any more than Europe could be called a ship.—FORSYTH.

WE have already noted the intervention of Sardinia The Rise of in the Crimean War. Remote as was the interest Sardinia of Sardinia in the questions at issue, that intervention proved to be the turning-point in the history of modern Italy. It convinced Europe, despite the recent defeats at Custozza and Novara, that the Sardinians could fight, and it enabled Cavour to claim a place in the Congress of Paris as the representative not of Sardinia but of Italy.

In order to appreciate the significance of these statements a long retrospect is necessary. I have hitherto, of set purpose, omitted all but the barest reference to events in Italy, and in Germany, in order to present a continuous narrative of the two most striking and most characteristic political movements of the nineteenth century.

Napoleon I. clearly foresaw the destiny in store for Reaction Italy. "Italy," he wrote, "is one sole nation; the unity in Italy after 1815 of customs, of language and literature, will in some future, more or less remote, unite all its inhabitants under one Government. . . . Rome is the capital which some day the Italians will select." He not only foresaw it,

173

he did much to achieve it. He created an Italian kingdom; he trampled under foot the prejudices and jealousies of the smaller States; he built bridges and made roads; he unified the law and the administration; he taught the Italians to fight.

The diplomatists of 1815 did what they could to obliterate all traces of his work, and so far as territorial repartition was concerned they succeeded.[1] But they were powerless to erase from the minds of the Italian patriots the lessons which they had learnt from the Napoleonic occupation. As Mazzini himself said: "The intellectual ferment, the increase of national prosperity, the outburst of fraternisation, are facts irrevocably committed to history".

Neapolitan Insurrection, 1820 Nevertheless, the history of the period 1815-30 is one of reaction broken only by sporadic and seemingly fruitless insurrections. Of all the petty despots restored to the Italian thrones in 1815 the most despicable was the Bourbon Ferdinand I., King of the Two Sicilies. In 1815 he pledged himself to respect the liberal Constitution conferred upon Sicily by Lord William Bentinck (1812). In the next year this Constitution was torn up at the bidding of Metternich. In 1820, as we have seen,[2] the revolutionary fever spread from Spain to Italy, and Ferdinand was compelled to make wholesale concessions and establish the "Spanish Constitution". But the Holy Alliance intervened, and Austria was entrusted with the congenial task of restoring absolutism in Southern Italy. In 1821 the work was accomplished; "order" once more reigned in Naples, and for the brief remainder of his reign (ob. 1825) Ferdinand was able to indulge without restraint his insatiate passion for political persecution

[1] See p. 129.   [2] P. 139.

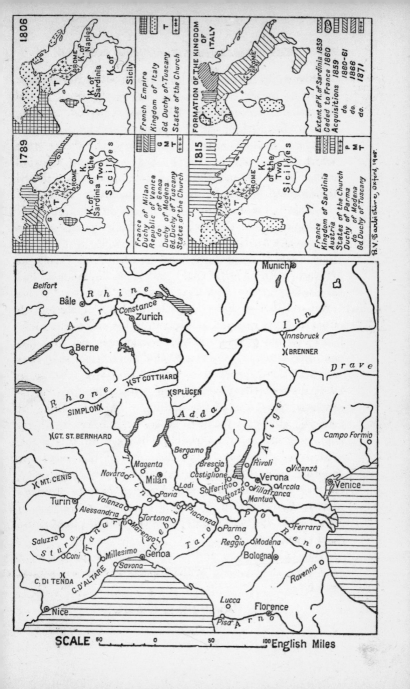

Insurrec-
tion in
North
Italy

Meanwhile insurrection had broken out in North Italy. There, as in the South, it was largely the work of the famous secret society, the Carbonari (Charcoal burners, 1820). But though the Government of Victor Emmanuel I. had proved violently reactionary, the insurrection which broke out in March, 1821, was anti-Austrian rather than anti-monarchical. Joining hands with the malcontents of Lombardy the Piedmontese threatened the Austrian rear as the latter marched to restore order in Naples. But the rising was wholly profitless. As soon as the Austrians had done their work in the South they turned northwards and crushed the revolt at Novara (9th April, 1821). Victor Emmanuel had abdicated, on the first sign of trouble, in favour of his

Charles
Felix of
Sardinia

brother, Charles Felix. With the help of Metternich Charles Felix restored absolutism in his sub-alpine kingdom; for ten years (1821-30) reaction reigned supreme, and the Austrian yoke was riveted more firmly than ever on her Italian provinces. It is, however, a mistake to suppose that the yoke, though bitterly resented by the patriots, was universally galling. The late Duke of Argyll, strongly inclined as he was towards liberal opinions, has left remarkable testimony on this point. "If ever," he wrote, "the dominion of one race over another seemed justified by at least material prosperity, it was the dominion of the Austrian Empire over its Italian provinces at that time . . . the whole face of the people and the country was the face of pleasantness and peace." [1]

But "pleasantness and peace" had to be purchased at the price of complete abandonment of patriotic aspirations.

[1] *Autobiography*, i., p. 211.

> It is death
> To speak the very name of Italy
> To this Italian people.

It was after the fiasco of 1821 that one of the foremost Mazzini of Italian liberators first began to interest himself in Italian politics. Born in Genoa in 1805 Joseph Mazzini resolved while still a youth to dedicate his life to the cause of Italian liberation. He joined the Carbonari soon after he left the University, but from the first he disliked both their aims and methods. "They had no programme, no faith, no lofty ideals," and he determined that it should be his mission to supply the lack. His opportunity came with the Revolutions of 1830.[1]

The "July Revolution" in France fanned into flame the Insurrections of 1830 revolutionary embers in Italy. The conflagration centred in the Papal States, where Bologna, Ancona and other towns attempted to put an end to the Temporal dominion of the Pope. Parma and Modena followed suit, and the Duchess Marie Louise and Duke Francis IV. were compelled to flee. They joined Gregory XVI. (elected to the Papal chair in 1831) in appealing for the help which Prince Metternich was only too anxious to afford. Once more an Austrian army marched South. Modena was restored to Francis, Parma to the ex-Empress, and the Romagna to the Pope. Gregory XVI. promised reforms, but nothing was done, and as soon as the Austrians France and evacuated the Romagna (July, 1831) insurrection broke Austria in Italy out afresh. Once more the Austrians returned, intending to occupy Ancona, but France, growing jealous of Austrian supremacy in Italy, determined to anticipate them. In February, 1832, a French force occupied Ancona and for

[1] In this and the following chapter I make free use of a previous work of my own ; *Makers of Modern Italy* (Macmillan & Co.

six years (1832-38) Austria and France confronted each other in the Papal States.

Young
Italy

Italy derived no advantage from their rivalry, but the patriotic movement was making progress. In 1830 Mazzini was entrapped by a Government spy, arrested, and imprisoned in the fortress of Savona. Brought to trial after six months' imprisonment he was acquitted, but was expelled from Italy. It was while in exile at Marseilles that he founded (1831) the famous *Association of Young Italy*. This association was to take the place of the Carbonari; its programme was definite and ambitious. The Austrians were to be expelled; Italy to be liberated and unified; and a reformed Papacy was to assume the moral leadership of the world. The ultimate form of government was to be determined by the people, though a Republic was to be commended by fair argument. Such was the programme of *Young Italy*, and Mazzini was not without hope of its immediate if partial realisation.

Charles
Albert of
Piedmont

In 1831 Charles Felix of Sardinia died, and was succeeded by his cousin Charles Albert. A Liberal and a Carbonaro, great things were hoped from him. Mazzini at once addressed to the King an eloquent appeal, beseeching him to lead Italy to the goal of liberty and unity. Charles Albert refused to respond except with an order that Mazzini should be arrested if he attempted to return to Italy. But though the Sardinian King frowned upon it, the *Young Italy* movement attracted thousands of ardent spirits, and for ten years the hopes of the patriots in all parts of Italy were focussed upon its programme. The attitude of Charles Albert was a bitter disappointment to his quondam associates, and a plot was formed for his assassination in which Mazzini was unhappily involved.   An unsuccessful raid upon Savoy (1834) further contributed to damage Mazzini's reputation among moderate Liberals, and after many vicissitudes he found—like most political exiles—a home in England (1837).

In Italy the association which he founded did splendid work in keeping the Italian ideal alive during a period of disillusionment and reaction.   Gradually, however, there emerged other parties which, with similar ends in view, sought to attain them by more moderate means.   Of these the most important were the Neo-Guelphs and the Piedmontese Liberals.

The Neo-Guelphs, led by Vincenzo Gioberti,[1] were men who combined devout Catholicism with ardent nationalism.   They looked to the Papacy, purified and reformed, to put itself at the head of the Italian movement.   In 1846 they believed that their chance had come.   In that year Gregory XVI. died and was succeeded in the Papal chair by Pius IX. (Pio Nono).   Pio Nono, a genial, kindly ecclesiastic of Liberal inclinations, began his reign with promises of extensive reforms.   Nowhere in Italy were they more sorely needed.   Corruption was rampant, and abuses of every kind existed in the extremest forms. The Neo-Guelphs acclaimed Pio Nono as the predestined saviour and liberator of his country.   His protest against the Austrian occupation of Ferrara raised enthusiasm to the fever height.   Mazzini hailed his accession as fifteen years ago he had hailed the accession of Charles Albert. Charles Albert himself offered to place his sword at the service of the Papacy, if war with Austria ensued.   But the Pope's zeal for reform soon slackened.   A measure of freedom to the Press and permission for the enrolment of a

The Neo-Guelphs

Pio Nono

---

[1] His work, *Il Primato morale e civile degli Italiani*, was published in 1843.

national militia were conceded, but little more.   Tuscany and Piedmont followed the lead of the Papacy, and Charles Albert wrote: " If Providence sends us a war of Italian independence I will mount my horse with my sons, I will place myself at the head of an army . . . what a glorious day it will be in which we can raise a cry for the independence of Italy."

It is clear, therefore, that in the years preceding 1848 two movements were making progress in Italy : one for domestic reform in its several states ; another towards liberation, if not towards unification.

The Revolution of 1848
In 1848 the storm-cloud burst. A Liberal demonstration in Milan (2nd January) gave the Austrians the opportunity of firing on the mob, and several people were killed.   These " proto-martyrs of Italian independence," as they were somewhat grandiloquently called, undoubtedly set the match to the train already carefully laid.   Insurrections broke out in Palermo and Naples, and Ferdinand II. was compelled to concede a " Constitution " (29th January). Duke Leopold of Tuscany followed his example (February), and in March Charles Albert called a Parliament at Turin, and Pio Nono one at Rome.   But the news of the outbreak of Revolution in Vienna (March) aroused larger hopes in Italy than any which could be satisfied by domestic reforms.   The moment had surely come for striking a blow at the Great Power by whom the petty despotisms in Italy had been so long maintained.   If Austria were driven out of Italy, the people could deal with domestic tyrants.   Metternich was already in exile ; why should not his puppets follow him ?

War against Austria
In the spring of 1848 these hopes seemed likely to be realised.   The Milanese rose, drove out the Austrians and established a Republic.   Venice, under Daniel Manin, did

the same. The rulers of Parma and Modena, scared by the fate of Metternich, took flight. Charles Albert of Sardinia put himself at the head of the national movement and declared war on Austria. The Duke of Tuscany joined him, and the peoples of Parma, Modena and Lombardy (Milan) united themselves by plebiscite with the Sardinian kingdom. Already it seemed as though the dreams of the patriots had been fulfilled; the foreigner was expelled; North Italy was united under the House of Savoy. But the success was too rapid; Austria was too strong. The veteran Radetsky inflicted a crushing defeat on Charles Albert at Custozza (24th July, 1848), and again at Novara (23rd March, 1849). After the battle of Novara, Charles Albert abdicated in favour of his son Victor Emmanuel and a few months later died at Oporto. The victory of Austria in the North emboldened the puppet princes to creep back to their thrones, but not until 25th August did the Venetians, spurred to the most heroic efforts by Daniel Manin, finally surrender. *Charles Albert succeeded by Victor Emmanuel*

Stirring events had, in the meantime, been taking place in Rome.[1] The pace had become too fast for Pio Nono. He had refused to join the movement against Austria, but had put Count Rossi—a reforming minister—in power. In November Rossi was murdered, and the Pope fled to Gaeta. In February, 1849, a Republic was proclaimed, and three triumvirs—among them Mazzini—were appointed to carry on the Government. But the Roman Republic of 1849 was merely a splendid episode. Louis Napoleon, anxious to conciliate the Clericals, sent an army to Rome to restore the Pope. Under Garibaldi the Romans fought bravely but in vain; Garibaldi himself *The Roman Republic*

[1] *Cf.* G. M. Trevelyan's brilliant monograph *Garibaldi's Defence of the Roman Republic.*

had to fly, the Republic collapsed and the Temporal power was restored. With French influence dominant in Rome, with the Austrians re-established in the North and Bomba (Ferdinand II.) in the South, reaction once more reigned supreme. Nevertheless, the "year of Revolution" left permanent results on Italy. From the Alps to Cape Passaro there was not a State which had not felt the breath of liberty; Austrian supremacy, though ultimately restored, had been rudely shaken; the hopes of the Neo-Guelphs had been shattered. Above all, patriots of all parties had learnt to concentrate their hopes upon the House of Savoy and look to the establishment of a Sardinian hegemony. Thus Gioberti himself in the *Rinnovamento* (1851) declared: "Except the young sovereign who rules Piedmont, I see no one in Italy who can undertake our emancipation".

Victor Emmanuel II.

To that object Victor Emmanuel had already consecrated his life. A task, necessarily preliminary, was to set his own house in order. For Piedmont, as for Italy, the outlook was black when on the evening of Novara Victor Emmanuel was called to the throne. Crushed beneath a terrible military disaster; burdened with a heavy war indemnity; frontierless and poor; without place in the Councils of Europe—who could, in 1849, have predicted the future in store for her? In the midst of reaction Victor Emmanuel set himself resolutely to the work of reform, and to aid him in the task he called to his councils one of the most remarkable statesmen of the nineteenth century—Count Camillo di Cavour.

Cavour

By birth a Piedmontese noble, Cavour (1810-61) had travelled much, especially in England, where he made a real study of economic and political questions. In 1847 he started the *Risorgimento*—to educate the Italians in constitutional ideas, and in 1848 he was returned as member for Turin to the first Parliament of Piedmont. Appointed to the Ministry of Commerce and Agriculture (1850) he was able to apply the sound economic and financial principles learnt in England, and the material prosperity of Piedmont advanced by leaps and bounds. In 1851 he became Minister of Finance and in 1852 Prime Minister. He at once announced a large programme of reform—financial, military and ecclesiastical, and at the same time declared that Piedmont must "begin by re-establishing in Europe, as well as in Italy, a position and prestige equal to her ambition".

His opportunity came with the outbreak of the Crimean War. Deserted by all his colleagues and supported only by the King, Cavour determined to send a large Sardinian contingent to join England and France in the Crimea. This resolution was the turning-point in the history of Sardinia and of Italy. The troops fought bravely; the victory of Tchernaia (16th August, 1855) wiped out the stain of Novara; Sardinia recovered her prestige, and when the Conference assembled in Paris, Cavour took his place among the representatives of the Powers. Austria strongly resented both his presence and his mission, but, despite her protest, Cavour brought before the Congress the pitiable condition of Italy, more especially of Naples, and he fearlessly fixed the blame on Austria. England and France cordially supported him, but the former did not go beyond moral support. Napoleon III. had not only a genuine sentiment for Italy, but definite ambitions for himself. Of both Cavour skilfully made use. *Sardinian Intervention in the Crimean War*

"Que peut-on faire pour l'Italie?" was Napoleon's question to Cavour in 1855. In 1856 Cavour answered *Napoleon III. and Italy*

it, and the foundations of the fateful alliance were laid. Interrupted for the moment by the attempt of Orsini, an Italian conspirator, on the life of Napoleon (January, 1858), it was cemented by an interview between Cavour and the Emperor at Plombières (20th July, 1858). Austria was to be expelled, and Northern and Central Italy (including the Papal Legations) were to be united under the House of Savoy. One painful sacrifice Victor Emmanuel had to make at once. He gave his daughter Princess Clothilde in marriage to the Emperor's cousin Prince Jerome Napoleon (Plon-plon). Another sacrifice, hardly less painful, was promised—the cession of Savoy, and possibly Nice, to France.

Cavour would infinitely have preferred an English alliance; but Lord Palmerston, interviewed in 1856, could give him no hope of armed assistance; Cavour was convinced that without foreign help the dead-weight of Austria could never be moved, and he was compelled, therefore, to pin his faith to the restless ambition of Napoleon.

CHAPTER XVII

THE UNIFICATION OF ITALY (1859-1871)

> But, Italy, my Italy !
>   Can it last this gleam ?
> Can she live and be strong ?
>   Or is it another dream
> Like the rest we have dreamed so long ?
>   —MRS. BROWNING.

ON 1st January, 1859, Europe was startled by Napoleon's words to the Austrian ambassador in Paris : " Je regrette que les relations entre nous soient si mauvaises ". Still more suggestive was Victor Emmanuel's memorable speech at the opening of Parliament at Turin (10th January) : " Our country, small in territory, has acquired credit in the Councils of Europe, because she is great in the idea she represents, in the sympathy she inspires. This situation is not free from peril, for while we respect treaties we cannot be insensible to the cry of anguish (grido di dolore) that comes up to us from many parts of Italy." No one could misunderstand the allusion. The speech excited the wildest enthusiasm in Italy, and profound anxiety in Europe. " It fell," said Sir James Hudson, " like a rocket on the treaties of 1815." England did her best to avert the coming war, but on 23rd April Austria sent to Turin an ultimatum demanding disarmament. Cavour confidently accepted the challenge. On 13th May Victor

Franco-Sardinian War against Austria, 1859

185

Emmanuel went to Genoa to meet Napoleon, the "generous ally" who had come "to liberate Italy from the Alps to the Adriatic".

The allies carried everything before them. The victory of Magenta (4th June) drove Austria back behind the Mincio; Milan was occupied in triumph (8th June); and on 24th June the double victory of San Martino and Solferino drove Austria into Venetia. But Napoleon was already alarmed at the fruits of his own handiwork. The Clericals, encouraged by the Empress, were growing restless in France; the Prussians were reported to be mobilising on the Rhine; the outburst of national feeling in Italy might carry things further than he had intended.

Truce of Villafranca

On 11th July, therefore, Napoleon met the Emperor Francis Joseph at Villafranca, and there, without Sardinia, terms were arranged which were ratified in the Treaty of Zurich (November, 1859). Austria was to cede Lombardy to Sardinia, but to retain Venetia and the great fortress of Mantua. The Italians felt themselves betrayed; Cavour resigned; on all sides the treachery of the "vulpine knave" was bitterly denounced. In the midst of growing excitement Victor Emmanuel alone kept his head. The paper conditions, as he well knew, did not represent the real achievements of 1859. An

Union of Central and Northern Italy

enormous step had been taken towards freedom and unity. The peoples of Central Italy were absolutely resolved neither to receive back their old rulers, nor to become parts of an Italian federation under the Pope. In 1860 Modena, Parma, Tuscany and the Romagna united themselves by plebiscite with the new kingdom of North Italy.

Savoy and Nice

Napoleon now claimed his price. Victor Emmanuel was compelled to pay it, and make the bitter sacrifice of

Savoy and Nice. Nice gave France access to Italy; Savoy, though not Italian, was the cradle of his race. Garibaldi, himself a Nizzard, denounced the treachery of Cavour and his "cowardly set" who had made him "an alien in the land of his birth". But Cavour was not less a patriot because he was a diplomatist, and knew that Napoleon dare not return empty handed to Paris. And he was beginning to understand how much had been achieved. On 2nd April, 1860, Victor Emmanuel opened at Turin a Parliament representative of no less than 11,000,000 Italians.

The credit of the next great step towards unification belongs not to Cavour nor to Victor Emmanuel but to Garibaldi:—not to the statesmen but to the "knight errant". The tyranny of the Bourbons in the South had now reached a point which was unendurable. Ferdinand II. ("Bomba") died in 1859 and was succeeded by Francis II. ("Bombino"), but the change was if anything for the worse. In 1860 the Sicilians, encouraged by Mazzini, raised the standard of revolt at Palermo, Messina and Catania. Garibaldi, collecting his famous "thousand" volunteers, took ship from Genoa, flew to their assistance (May, 1860), and within two months was master of Sicily. Thence he crossed to the mainland, and marched without resistance into Naples (7th September). Bombino fled to Gaeta, and Garibaldi was proclaimed dictator of the Two Sicilies. The situation was now exceedingly complicated. The marvellous achievement of Garibaldi had raised him to the position of a popular idol, and he now declared that he would not annex his conquests to the Crown of Italy until he could proclaim Victor Emmanuel in Rome itself. Cavour, though he had secretly abetted Garibaldi's enterprise, realised the extreme danger of his attitude.

Garibaldi's Conquest of the Two Sicilies

Garibaldi in Naples

Pio Nono had lately proclaimed a crusade for the recovery of the Romagna, and Victor Emmanuel had despatched troops for the twofold purpose of defending the Romagna from the Pope and, if necessary, of obstructing Garibaldi's attack on Rome itself. Cavour had to use all his adroitness in this delicate situation. The whole of Europe, except England, was against him; the Pope put the King under the ban of the Church, and Garibaldi, mistrusting the ways of diplomacy, was eager to advance on Rome, where the Pope was under the protection, diplomatic and military, of France. The situation was intensely critical, but it was saved by the genius of Cavour. "If we are not in La Cattolica before Garibaldi we are lost; the revolution would spread all over Italy. We are compelled to act." Thus he wrote on 11th September; exactly a week later (18th September) the Sardinian army met and routed the Papal troops—mostly foreign mercenaries under French officers—at Castel Fidardo, and on the 29th compelled General Lamoricière to

Union of North and South

surrender at Ancona. Meanwhile the Garibaldians and Neapolitans had been engaged on the Volturno (19th September-1st October) without decisive result. In October Victor Emmanuel joined Garibaldi; the Two Sicilies were annexed by plebiscite to the Italian kingdom; and having taken Capua (2nd November), Garibaldi and Victor Emmanuel rode into Naples side by side (7th November). Garibaldi, having introduced the King to his new subjects, refused all reward or decoration and retired to Caprera. Francis held out for some months at Gaeta, but after the departure of the French fleet surrendered to Victor Emmanuel (13th February, 1861). On 18th February a Parliament, representing all Italy save Rome and Venice, met at Turin. The Union of

North and South was formally completed, and Victor
Emmanuel reigned over 23,000,000 Italians.

But without Rome Italy, as Castelar said, was "a head- Death of
less body". Garibaldi was determined to take it; Cavour Cavour
desired it not less ardently, but he knew, as Garibaldi
did not, that the diplomatic difficulties were insuperable.
In this hour of great need Italy lost her greatest statesman (5th June, 1861). Cavour had not Mazzini's pro-
phetic gifts; he could not arouse popular enthusiasm like
Garibaldi; he was perhaps less cool than Victor Emmanuel, but he was an enlightened domestic reformer
and the greatest diplomatist in Europe. He gauged to a
nicety the political situation; he knew the limits of the
possible; to him, therefore, more than to any other
individual, Italy owes her unity and freedom.

One problem he left unsolved. The position of the The Pro-
Papacy in Italy presented indeed a problem perhaps blem of
Church
insoluble. Cavour, like his master, attempted to induce and State
the Pope to accept the principle of "a free Church in a
free State (*libera Chiesa in libero stato*), to surrender the
patrimony of St. Peter—the last remnant of the Papal
States—and to retain simply a spiritual sovereignty. But
the Pope was inflexible. Prayers and threats alike failed
to move him; to nothing but actual force would he
yield.

Garibaldi was determined to apply it. Raising the
cry "Rome or death," he once more crossed from Sicily
to the mainland (July, 1862). The Government was
compelled to interfere, and at Aspromonte (29th August)
his volunteers were scattered, and Garibaldi himself was
wounded and taken prisoner. But in 1864 Victor Emmanuel at last came to terms with Napoleon in regard
to Rome. By the September Convention (1864) France

agreed to evacuate Rome during the next two years, and in 1865 the Italian capital was transferred from Turin to Florence.

Union of Venetia and Italy

But for the moment interest was concentrated on another part of Italy. The long rivalry between Austria and Prussia had now reached the zenith, and in 1865 it was clear that the inevitable conflict would not be much longer postponed.[1] In that year Victor Emmanuel offered his assistance to Austria in return for the cession of Venetia. Though the refusal of Francis Joseph was natural it was none the less fatal. In 1866 Bismarck came to terms with Italy, and in the same year the Austro-Prussian war broke out. Disastrously defeated in Germany, Austria more than held her own in Italy. Both on land and sea the Italian forces were defeated (June-July, 1866). But Bismarck kept his word; Venice was wrested from Austria, and by plebiscite united itself with Italy (October, 1866).

Almost simultaneously the last of the French troops evacuated Rome, and Italy was at last rid of the foreigner.

Rome

But Rome, and Rome only, still remained to mar the unity of Italy. Garibaldi was resolved that it should mar it no longer. Encouraged by the Government he raised a band of volunteers, landed at Leghorn and marched on Rome. Napoleon despatched a French force for its defence; at Mentana (3rd November, 1867) the French routed the Garibaldians, and once more occupied Rome. Garibaldi, still the hero of the populace, was arrested by the Government, and deported to Caprera.

But the final scene in the long drama was at hand. The outbreak of the Franco-German War (1870) neces-

[1] See p. 211.

sitated the withdrawal of the French troops from Rome.
Once again Victor Emmanuel appealed to the Pope "with
the affection of a son, with the faith of a Catholic, with
the soul of an Italian," to accept the inevitable. The
only reply was a *non possumus*. The Italian troops,
therefore, moved on Rome; only formal resistance was
offered, and on 20th September, 1870, the royal troops
occupied the city. A plebiscite yielded 40,788 votes
for the King, 46 for the Pope, and on 2nd June, 1871,
Victor Emmanuel made a triumphal entry into the
city, henceforth to be the capital of Italy. "The work
to which we consecrated our lives is accomplished. After
long trials Italy is restored to herself and to Rome." So
spake "il rè galantuomo" to the first Italian Parliament which met in Rome. The work of unification was
accomplished.

Italy has had to pass through much tribulation since Italy
1871. The art of Parliamentary Government is not 1871
learned in a day. "The worst of chambers," said Cavour,
"is better than the most brilliant of ante-chambers."
Had he lived, the path of Parliamentary Government
might have been smoothed for his country: without
him it has been stony and not always clean. And while
there has been corruption at one end of the scale, there
has been social disorder at the other. In the South
particularly it has been found difficult to eradicate the
habits formed under long years of despotism. Politically,
not less than socially, there is a wide gulf between North
and South, and efforts to bridge it have not entirely succeeded. Moreover, modern Government is expensive
—especially where there is leeway to make up—and
Italians groan under a terrible load of taxation and debt.

But all these things are trivial as compared with the

still unsolved problem of Church and State. The "prisoner of the Vatican," whose infallibility was decreed by an Œcumenical Council (1869) on the eve of the dissolution of his Temporal Power, still maintains the *non-possumus* attitude, still declines all attempts at compromise. Until this problem is solved, good citizenship and loyal Catholicism must, in theory at least, remain divorced in Italy, to the distress and embarrassment of all those to whom both sentiments are precious.

CHAPTER XVIII

GERMANY (1815-1851)

REACTION, REVOLUTION AND REACTION

By the help of God I hope to defeat the German revolution just as I vanquished the conqueror of the world.—METTERNICH.

IT has been said of the Italian *Risorgimento* that it was "the one moment of nineteenth-century history when politics assumed something of the character of poetry" (Lecky). Nor can it be denied that a romantic interest attaches to the story which enshrines the memories of Mazzini and Daniel Manin, of Bettino Ricasoli and the Poerios, of D'Azeglio and Nino Bixio and Garibaldi.

But the unification of Germany was more substantial and imposing, though less romantic and less difficult. Bismarck had far more to work upon than Cavour. Italy knew nothing of unity between the fall of the Roman and the transient existence of the Napoleonic Empire. Germany for a thousand years had never lost the semblance of unity, however little it realised the substance. Nevertheless, the establishment of the Federal Empire under the Hohenzollern must take rank as the largest, if not the most amazing, political achievement of the century in Europe.

To disclose the main steps by which that consumma-

13   193

tion was attained is the purpose of this and the following chapter.

The Settlement of 1815

The leading features of the settlement of Germany in 1815 have been already sketched. Both from the territorial and the constitutional standpoint that settlement was full of significance. By the relaxation of their grip on Poland and the simultaneous acquisition of large provinces in the heart of Germany and upon the Rhine frontier the Hohenzollern were unconsciously laying the foundations of Prussian hegemony and German unity. The gravitation of the Habsburgs towards non-German lands in the South was equally significant. The surrender of the Netherlands and the establishment of a preponderant influence in Italy proved that she was concentrating her energies upon the consolidation of her dynastic interests, to the exclusion of those of Germany.

The constitutional settlement was, as we have seen, a grievous disappointment to the patriotic party. Only in Prussia was there any genuine anxiety for a strong bond of unity, and even there opinion was divided. Austria was equally opposed to a revival of the old Empire and to the substitution of any effective federal union. The smaller States desired the system which would interfere least with their own autocratic government. As to unity they were, for the most part, entirely indifferent.

The "Bund" was the characteristic outcome of these divergent and ambitious interests. It encouraged the autocratic tendencies of the sovereign princes, and at the same time provided the weakest guarantees for national defence and the slenderest basis for national unity.

But no more in Germany than in Italy could the diplomatists efface the effects of the Napoleonic occupa-

[1] See pp. 127 *seqq.*

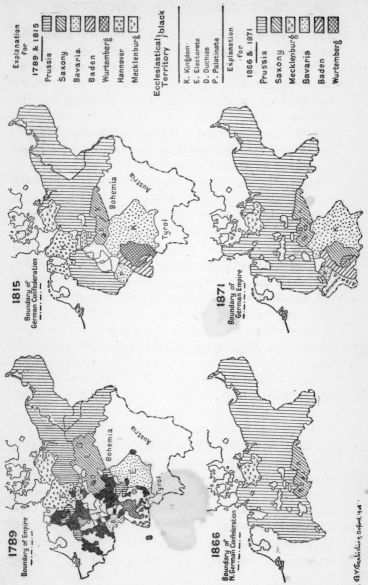

Explanation
for
1789 & 1815

Prussia
Saxony
Bavaria.
Baden
Wurtemberg
Hannover
Mecklenburg

Ecclesiastical } black
Territory }

K. Kingdom.
E. Electorate.
D. Duchies
P. Palatinate

Explanation
for
1866 & 1871

Prussia
Saxony
Mecklenburg
Bavaria
Baden
Wurtemberg

1815
Boundary of
German Confederation

Bohemia
Austria
Tyrol

1871
Boundary of
German Empire

1789
Boundary of Empire

Bohemia
Austria
Tyrol

1866
Boundary of
N.German Confederation

G.Y.Goulistone Oxford 1918

tion.   Napoleon had let light into many dark places; he had reduced the political divisions from 800 to 30; he had imposed taxes which were equal though severe; he had introduced a legal and administrative system which was coherent and effective : above all, he had roused the German people to fight him.   He had no intention of making a united Germany any more than a united Italy, but in both cases he contributed powerfully though unconsciously to that consummation.

Reaction in Germany

The period of German history between 1815 and 1848 is one of almost unrelieved reaction.   In Germany, as in Italy, Metternich's was the dominating influence.   It was, of course, in the Austrian dominions that it was most directly felt, but, to the disgust of the "patriots," the reaction was hardly less marked elsewhere.   The Kings of Bavaria and Würtemberg and the grand Duke of Baden did indeed grant "Charters" on the French model to their respective subjects, but only in the Duchy of Weimar were the stirrings of vigorous political life really discernible.   The centre of the Liberal movement was the University of Jena, where the students organised themselves into a society for the promotion of German unity.   It was this society which arranged a patriotic festival at the Wartburg to commemorate the tercentenary of the Reformation and the fourth anniversary of the battle of Leipzic (17th October, 1817).   The occasion was more than innocent and the incidents were devoid of serious significance, but they excited the alarm of the reactionaries ; the Duke of Weimar was bidden to curtail the liberties of his subjects, and the Universities and the Press were henceforth watched with even greater jealousy. In 1819 further alarm was aroused by the murder of Kotzebue, a dramatist, who was suspected of having

The Wartburg Festival

warned the Czar Alexander against the revolutionary spirit in the German Universities. Hardenberg made it an excuse for refusing to establish representative institutions in Prussia, and Metternich summoned representatives of the leading States to confer with him at Karlsbad. "By the help of God I hope to defeat the German revolution just as I vanquished the conqueror of the world." For the moment it seemed as though Metternich's boast might be justified. The Karlsbad Decrees, subsequently adopted by the Federal Diet at Frankfort, accurately reflect both his methods and aims. They extinguished liberty of the Press; transferred the control of the Universities to Government officials; prohibited the formation of societies and the holding of political meetings; and established at Mainz a central commission which has been truly described as "a sort of inquisition for the discovery and punishment of democratic agitators."

The Karlsbad Decrees (Nov. 1819)

Metternich was once more master in his own German house.

Thus matters went on with little change until the outbreak of the July Revolution in France. Nor did that event seriously disturb the even current of affairs in the larger German States. In some of the smaller States there were faint echoes of the Parisian movement, and the rulers of Hanover, Saxony, Brunswick and Hesse were compelled to make some concessions to the Liberal opinions of their subjects; but the domination of Metternich was still unshaken; to him all concession was "unpardonable error," and in his hands the machinery of the "Bund" was used exclusively to one end—to repress any sign of a revolutionary or even a Liberal agitation in any of the German States. At the Diet of 1832 opportunity was taken to confirm the Karlsbad Decrees. A

Revolutions of 1830

The "Bund"

monster meeting had been held in the Palatinate to celebrate "the dawn of liberty, of German unity and the fraternisation of all free nations". This was enough for Metternich. He declared that "Germany is a prey to frightful disorders," and that "the powers of the Diet must be set in motion to repress it". At his bidding they were. Once more political meetings were forbidden; the Press was censored; all revolutionary songs and symbols were prohibited, and it was announced that the Diet claimed the right to interfere in the individual States in the event of a deadlock between the ruler and his Constitutional Assembly.

The discovery of a conspiracy for blowing up the Diet at Frankfort in 1833 still further stiffened Metternich's back. A conference was held at Münchengrätz in 1833 between the Emperors of Austria and Russia and the Crown Prince of Prussia, who entered into a mutual league not only to suppress Liberal movements in Germany but to resist the democratic tendencies of England and France in Europe at large.

The Zollverein   In all this dreary period between 1815 and 1848 there appeared in Germany only one symptom which gave hope of better things to come. While the federal machinery was employed almost entirely for the repression of popular feeling; while the individual rulers, particularly in the greater States, were consistently reactionary; while the hopes of unity grew fainter, there was in progress one development fraught with tremendous consequences for the future of Germany.

Prussia, with her scattered and heterogeneous provinces, was the first to realise the inconvenience and loss involved in the existing fiscal system. German industry was strangled by the innumerable custom barriers between State and State; transportation was almost impossible; means of communication were non-existent; trade was at a standstill, and the people groaned under the weight of taxation required for the maintenance of a mischievous and antiquated system.

In 1818 the Prussian minister, Maassen, took the first step by the establishment of free commercial intercourse between the several Hohenzollern provinces. Some of the Southern States imitated the arrangement, and between 1819 and 1836 practically all the German States except Austria, associated themselves with Prussia in a vast Customs-Union or *Zollverein*. All commercial barriers between State and State were thrown down; internal custom-houses were destroyed; the vast army of officials was dismissed, and a common external tariff was arranged. Not only was an immense impulse thus given to German trade, but also to the sentiment and fact of German unity. The construction of railways, roads and canals; the improvement of postal arrangements; the promotion of commercial intercourse came in the wake of the *Zollverein* and silently prepared the way for organic political changes in the future. Thus the significance of the *Zollverein* is threefold. It brought the several States into more neighbourly relations, and provided a strong financial guarantee against disruption; it brought them together under the leadership of Prussia, and it accustomed them to the exclusion of Austria. Tardily Austria awoke to the significance of these events, and in 1852 made desperate efforts to obtain admission to the *Zollverein*, but by that time Prussia was strong enough to insist on her exclusion. Thus the extent to which the *Zollverein* contributed to the ultimate Prussianisation of Germany can hardly be over-estimated.

Constitu-
tional Re-
form in
Prussia

Prussia was, meanwhile, taking steps to put her own house in order.   Frederick William III.—one of the few weaklings produced by the virile Hohenzollern race—had fallen more and more under the influence of Metternich. In 1815 he had promised to establish a central represen- tative Assembly elected by the Provincial Estates and to grant to his people a written Constitution.   He was never intentionally faithless to his promise, but excellent reasons for delay were suggested by the reactionaries in Vienna and Berlin, and in 1840, after a reign of forty- three years, the old King died—his promise still unfulfilled. During his last years the Progressives had acquiesced in the postponement of reform, partly out of deference to the prejudices of the King, and partly in acknowledg- ment of the important results secured to Prussia by his enlightened economic and financial administration.

Frederick
William
IV.

All the more eagerly, therefore, did the Prussian Liberals welcome to the throne his successor Frederick William IV. (1840-61).   But the new King, though he was a cultured patron of art and letters, believed no less ardently than his father in the Divine Right of monarchy. Lacking, however, his predecessor's prestige he was unable to resist altogether the demand for some constitu-

United
Provincial
Diet at
Berlin

tional concessions.   In 1847, therefore, he summoned to Berlin representatives from all the Provincial Estates. The Liberals bitterly resented the cumbrous and anti- quated form of the States-general, and also the strict limitations imposed by royal edict upon its functions. While the Diet might advise it must not control.   "The Crown can and must govern according to the laws of God and of the land, not according to the will of majorities." Such a subordinate position the Progressives were not willing to accept: violent language was used, and in four months the Assembly was dissolved and the experiment of a "United Provincial Diet" was at an end. One more effort at reform had failed; one more incentive had been provided to Revolution. Revolution came in 1848.

In Germany, as in Italy, the revolutionary movements of 1848 had a twofold aspect and significance. They were directed, on the one side, to the extension of constitutional liberties in the several and divided States; and on the other, towards the realisation of national unity in some permanent and effective form.

The year of Revolution in Germany

Baden, the most liberally governed State in Germany, was the first to feel the impulse of the February Revolution in Paris. On 3rd March the Grand Duke granted a new Constitution, which formed a model for the other German States. Ministerial responsibility; freedom of the Press; religious equality; trial by jury, and equality of taxation, were among the concessions demanded and made. The rulers of Würtemberg, Nassau, Darmstadt, Hesse-Cassel, Weimar and Brunswick followed suit; in Bavaria, King Lewis, despite the comparative liberality of his rule, was obliged to abdicate in favour of his son Maximilian II. (20th March), and Saxony and Hanover ultimately followed the lead of Baden.

In Berlin disturbances broke out on 18th March, and Frederick William IV. at once conceded the whole Baden programme. An accidental collision between the troops and the people led to some serious street fighting (18th-20th March), and Berlin was only pacified by the removal of the troops from the capital and a promise from the King to assume the leadership "of a free and new-born German nation". The United Diet was to meet immediately, with power to summon a national Constituent

Assembly which should draft a Parliamentary Constitution for the Hohenzollern dominions.

Revolution in Austria

But naturally it was in Vienna, so long the centre of reaction, that the convulsion was most violent: so violent indeed as to shake even Metternich from the pedestal of power. The insurrection of 13th March drove Metternich into exile in England; that of 15th May compelled the Emperor Ferdinand himself to fly to Innsbruck.

But the insurrection in Vienna was the least of the difficulties by which in this critical year the Habsburg Emperor was confronted.

In the spring of 1848 it seemed as if nothing could save from immediate dissolution the heterogeneous mass of races and nationalities which were united under the Austrian Crown. Italy, Hungary and Bohemia blazed simultaneously into revolution. The character and fate of the Italian Revolution have been already indicated.[1]

Insurrection in Hungary and Bohemia

Hungary and Bohemia demanded not separation but constitutional autonomy under the Habsburgs. The Habsburgs were saved only by the racial disunion of the several provinces subject to their rule. Between the Magyars of Hungary, the Slavs of Bohemia and the Italians there was nothing in common save dislike of Austrian rule. "From the charnel house of the cabinet of Vienna a pestilential wind sweeps over us, benumbing our senses and paralysing our national spirit." So spake Kossuth, the leader of the Hungarian revolt; but Hungary itself had to contend with the separatist tendencies of Serbs and Croats to the south of the Drave. In June there met at Prague, a pan-slavist congress representative of Czechs, Moravians, Poles, Slovaks, Serbs and Croats; but riots broke out, and Prince Windischgrätz, who

[1] See p. 180.

commanded the Austrian forces, reduced the city to submission, and by the end of June the Bohemian movement collapsed. In October, Vienna rose for the third time, and the Emperor took refuge in Olmütz, a fortress in Moravia. But against disciplined troops bravely led the Viennese were as powerless as Italians or Czechs, and by 31st October Windischgrätz was master of the capital.

But Hungary was still unsubdued. The task was too much for the Emperor Ferdinand. On 2nd December, 1848, he abdicated in favour of his nephew the Archduke Francis Joseph, who at the age of eighteen assumed the heavy burden of the Imperial Crown. Accession of Francis Joseph

The Hungarians at once refused to acknowledge the new sovereign; war broke out; the Hungarians were badly beaten at Kapolna (2nd February, 1849); the Hungarian Constitution was rescinded, and Hungary was incorporated in the Austrian Empire. In the guerilla warfare that followed the Magyars under Kossuth and Gorgei more than held their own, and on 14th April Kossuth proclaimed the independence of Hungary and the perpetual exclusion of the House of Habsburg from their throne. In the name of legitimacy the Emperor now appealed to the Czar Nicholas. Russia responded with 200,000 men; the rebellion was crushed; Hungary lost all its independent rights and was reduced to a state of simple vassalage. The remnants of rebellion were stamped out with ferocity: hundreds of patriots were sent to the gallows; Kossuth escaped to England.

Victorious over its foes in Italy, in Bohemia and in Hungary the Austrian Government, now in the strong hands of Schwarzenberg, gave short shrift to its German subjects. The "March laws" were repealed, and Metternich's autocratic and centralised system was restored. From Vienna the reaction spread to Berlin and the lesser courts; the revolutionary impulse of 1848 was spent. Absolutism was once more supreme.

It has been shown that as regards the domestic liberties of the several States the revolutionary year left little permanent impress upon Germany. How fared it with the movement towards national unity?

Movement towards National Unity

So far back as October, 1847, representatives from the States belonging to the *Zollverein* had met at Heppenheim near Heidelberg, with the object of enlarging the scope of that union in a political direction; but the agitation which broke out in the spring of 1848 convinced the leaders that the time had come for the realisation of a larger scheme. They determined to call a Convention to meet at Frankfort for the purpose of organising a Constituent Assembly for the whole of Germany and at the same time to obtain the sanction of Prussia and the Federal Diet to such an Assembly. The assent of Frederick William IV. was given on 17th March; that of the Federal Diet on 30th March, and the Preliminary Convention met on the 31st. Arrangements for the Constituent Assembly were rapidly completed, and on the 18th of May, 1848, 586 representatives, elected on the basis of universal suffrage, came together at Frankfort from every State of the Germanic Confederation.

The Frankfort Parliament 1848-49

This historic Assembly was charged with no less a task than the drafting of a Constitution for the whole of Germany. Among many difficulties which confronted it the most serious arose from the question as to the relation of the mosaic Empire of the Habsburgs to the Germanic body. On this point the Frankfort Parliament was sharply divided. The "Great Germans," including not only the Austrian deputies, but also those from Bavaria and most of the South German States, stoutly opposed the exclusion of the non-German Habsburg provinces. The " Little Germans," starting from the idea of a glorified *Zollverein* and looking to the headship of Prussia, insisted that their inclusion would be fatal to the realisation of German unity in an effective form. Again as regards a Federal Executive Austria favoured a Directory of seven Princes, while the Little Germans insisted on an hereditary Empire. On both points the latter eventually carried their point, and in March, 1849, the new Constitution was completed. Under this, Germany was henceforth to be a Federal State under an hereditary Emperor. There was to be a Parliament of two Chambers, one representing the States of Germany, the other the people, and to this Parliament the federal ministers were to be responsible. On 28th March the Imperial Crown was offered to Frederick William IV. of Prussia. But by this time the situation had materially altered. Austria was no longer a negligible quantity. Under the young Emperor and the new minister, Schwarzenberg, she was fast regaining the position she had temporarily lost. Frederick William IV. was hardly less under the influence of Schwarzenberg than his predecessor was under that of Metternich. He had no mind to brave the wrath, possibly the forcible opposition, of Austria; still less to accept the Imperial Crown at the hands of a democratic Assembly and thus proclaim himself " the serf of the Revolution". The offer was, therefore, to the grievous disappointment of the Progressives, definitely declined by him. Prussia was not, in Bismarck's phrase, to be " dissolved in Germany." Germany was to be absorbed ultimately into Prussia; but not until the offer of the Imperial Crown

Offer of Imperial Crown to Frederick William IV. of Prussia

came from the sovereign princes would a Prussian sovereign by Divine Right deign to accept it. The Frankfort Assembly struggled against the acceptance of defeat; but defeat was now inevitable. The States withdrew their delegates, and the radical rump having transferred their deliberations to Stuttgart were eventually dispersed by force (July, 1849).

Restoration of the "Bund"

Two years of confusion followed, but in 1851 the "Bund" was restored and the work of the Unionists seemed utterly effaced. In reality it was not so. The Frankfort Parliament had given a powerful impulse to the movement for unity, though the end was ultimately achieved by very different means.

The years between 1851 and 1861 were in the main years of placid reaction in Germany. Austria recovered from the troubles of 1848 with a rapidity which reflects the highest credit on Schwarzenberg, but her strength was sapped by the disaffection of Hungary. In Prussia important reforms were effected under Von Roon in armaments and military organisation; but for ten years the surface calm was unbroken in Germany. The War of Italian Independence in 1859, dealt as we have seen,[1] a serious blow at the political and military prestige of Austria, but not until after 1860 did things begin to move with any rapidity in Germany. The decade between 1860 and 1870 is the most fateful in her annals and demands a chapter to itself.

[1] P. 186.

CHAPTER XIX

THE PRUSSIANISATION OF GERMANY (1860-1870)

Germany became strong in herself and in the world in the nine-teenth century through Prussia, through Prussian politics and military service, through Prussian sense for actualities and Prussian cult of power.—PROF. ERIC MARCKS.

IN 1861 Frederick William IV. of Prussia died and was succeeded by his brother, who took the title of William I. In 1862 he called to his counsels Count Otto von Bismarck. It was these two men who, with the help of Von Roon and Moltke, made the modern German Empire. William I

The new King had been Regent since 1858 and came to the throne with a clear comprehension of the work before him. The new minister was equally clear both as to end and means, and had already much experience both in German politics and European diplomacy.

Born in 1815, Otto von Bismarck was by descent and temper a typical Prussian Junker (squire). Educated at the Universities of Göttingen and Berlin he entered the Civil Service, but in 1839 was recalled to manage the paternal estates in Pomerania. Known as "mad Bismarck"—a hard rider and a hard drinker—he neverthe-less proved his administrative capacity, and served as Deputy for his Order in the provincial Pomeranian Diet in 1845. Two years later he became a member Bismarck of the United Diet at Berlin. He was at this time a rigid Conservative with a strong religious belief in the divinely appointed monarchy, and used every effort to save Frederick William IV. not merely from the extreme democrats, but from his own transient deference to Liberalism. In 1851 he was sent as Prussian representative to the newly reconstituted Federal Diet at Frankfort. This was the turning-point of his political career. He entered the Diet with feelings of deep reverence for Austria and its policy. He left it eight years later convinced (as he wrote to Von Schleinitz) "that the one constant factor in Austrian policy is its jealousy of Prussia, and that for every minor German State the royal road to Austria's favour is hostility to Prussia" (12th May, 1859). Further, he insisted that "Prussia's connection with the 'Bund' is a weakness which must be cured sooner or later *ferro et igni*, if we do not apply timely remedies". Recalled from the Diet in 1859 he served for three years as ambassador at St. Petersburg, and, in 1862, for a few months, at Paris.

When, therefore, in 1862 Bismarck assumed the reins in Prussia he was intimately acquainted alike with the rottenness of the existing political system in Germany and with the main currents of European diplomacy. In Paris he had taken the measure of Napoleon III., the man with whom he was to cross swords, and whom he regarded as "half dreamer and half trickster".

In 1863 the Emperor Francis Joseph proposed a conference of the sovereign princes of Germany to discuss a revision of the Federal Constitution. Prussia, on Bismarck's suggestion, declined the invitation on the ground that the "Austrian project did not harmonise with the proper position of the Prussian monarchy or with the

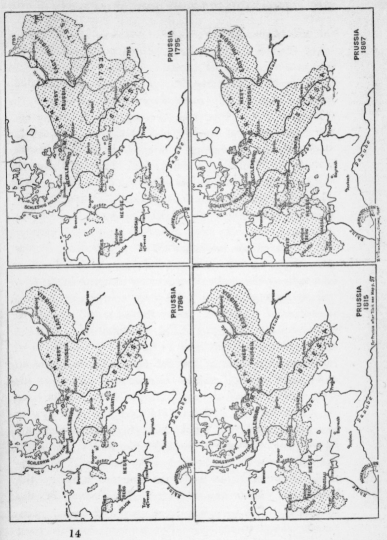

PRUSSIA
1795

PRUSSIA
1867

PRUSSIA
1786

PRUSSIA
1815

For Prussia after Tilsit see Map p. 97

14

interests of the German people". Austria might well have taken up the challenge thus thrown down but for the intervention of another question of grave significance.

The
Schleswig-
Holstein
Question The death of King Frederick VII. of Denmark in 1863 reopened one of the most embarrassing questions in German politics. Frederick was not only King of Denmark but Duke of the German Duchies of Schleswig, Holstein and Lauenburg. His death, without direct male heirs, dissolved a personal union between Denmark and the Duchies which had subsisted since 1460. Holstein was a State of the Germanic Confederation; Schleswig was indissolubly united to Holstein. In both the Salic law survived. Denmark had long been anxious for the complete incorporation of the Duchies in the monarchy; but this was opposed both by the German Diet and by the Duke Frederick of Augustenburg who had strong claims upon the Duchies though none upon the throne of Denmark. Bismarck perceived their enormous importance to the naval development of Prussia and was determined by hook or by crook to acquire them for his master. But he was not yet strong enough to do so by *force majeure*, and he determined therefore to induce Austria to pull the chestnuts out of the fire for him. By the Treaty of London (1852), England and France had guaranteed "the territorial integrity of Denmark," but of their intervention Bismarck had no fear, and upon the rest of the parties he turned the tables with consummate adroitness. In 1864 the Duchies were by the Treaty of Vienna handed over to Austria and Prussia conjointly. But what was to be done with them? Bismarck offered to recognise Frederick of Augustenburg as Duke on terms which would have meant his complete subjection to Prussia. The Duke declined the terms:

Austria protested against them, and things looked like war between the two great German Powers when a temporary compromise was patched up at Gastein (1865). Prussia was to occupy Schleswig; Austria was to occupy Holstein, and to sell Lauenburg to Prussia.

The Convention of Gastein was merely a makeshift. To Bismarck it was valuable only as a means of enabling him to fix a quarrel upon Austria. In January, 1866, he complained that the Austrians were encouraging—as well they might—the "pretensions" of Frederick of Augustenburg, the legitimate heir. Prussian troops were accordingly poured into Holstein, and the Austrians were expelled. To avenge this outrage upon Austria the German Diet ordered a mobilisation of the federal forces against Prussia (14th June, 1866).

Rupture between Austria and Prussia

This was precisely what Bismarck wanted. He had not only been spoiling for the fight, but steadily preparing for it. The Prussian army had been re-armed with the needle-gun and brought up to a high state of efficiency by Von Roon. The diplomatic situation was favourable. Napoleon III. was not only involved in his disastrous Mexican enterprise, but had, in 1865, been won over to approval of Bismarck's plans by a personal interview at Biarritz. Italy had been similarly secured (8th April, 1866) by the promise of Venetia in return for assistance against Austria.[1] Russia was friendly. Bismarck had indeed "counted the cost"; Prussia was the strong man armed, and could plunge into the conflict, confident in her might if not in her right. On the latter point Bismarck was opposed not only by the whole of Germany, but by the Prussian Parliament, and even the Prussian King.

[1] See p. 190.

But his masterful character overbore all scruples and overcame all difficulties.

On 14th June the Diet at Frankfort rejected a scheme proposed by Bismarck for the complete reorganisation of the "Bund" and accepted the Austrian motion for federal execution against Prussia. The Prussian delegate was thereupon withdrawn. The States threw in their lot with Austria. A war, destined to be the most fateful in German history, was the inevitable result.

The Seven Weeks' War

Prussia declared war upon Hanover, Saxony and Hesse on 15th June. By the 18th her troops were in occupation of the three States. On the 18th she declared war upon the other members of the "Bund," including Austria. A battle at Langensalza, in which the Hanoverians had the best of it (27th June), was followed (28th June) by the pusillanimous surrender of the Hanoverian army. The terms of the capitulation involved the extinction of the kingdom of Hanover and its incorporation in Prussia. Meanwhile the main Prussian army had marched to meet the Austrians in Bohemia, and a week's brilliant campaign culminated on 3rd July in the crushing defeat of the Austrians at Sadowa (Königgrätz); before the end of the month the Prussians were within striking distance of Vienna; terms of peace were arranged on the 26th; the brief but decisive war was over.

Treaty of Prague

The definitive treaty was signed at Prague (2nd August, 1866). Bismarck, who had thought out every move in the intricate diplomatic game, had already decided to secure Austria's friendship in the greater struggle still ahead of Prussia. Hence the terms were made as lenient as possible, consistent with the attainments of the essential object of the war.

Austria lost no territory (except Venetia to Italy) and the war indemnity was light, but she was excluded henceforward from Germany. The "Bund" was dissolved after an inglorious existence of half a century; Hanover, Hesse-Cassel, Schleswig-Holstein, Lauenburg, Nassau, and the free city of Frankfort-on-Main were annexed to Prussia, and all the States north of the Main were to form a North German Confederation under the Presidency of Prussia.

Dissolution of the "Bund"

The annexations were of immense significance. For the first time the Hohenzollern were masters of continuous territory stretching from the Rhine to the Baltic; they gained nearly 25,000 square miles of territory and 5,000,000 subjects, and (in Kiel) a magnificent naval base.

But the broad result of the Seven Weeks' War lay in the exclusion of Austria from the Germanic body and the definite acceptance of the Prussian hegemony by the States north of the Main.

In February, 1867, an Assembly met at Berlin representative of all the States of the North German Confederation; Prussia, Saxony, the Grand Duchies of Mecklenburg-Schwerin, Mecklenburg-Strelitz, Oldenburg and Saxe-Weimar, the Duchies of Brunswick, Anhalt, Saxe-Coburg-Gotha, the free cities of Hamburg, Lübeck and Bremen with smaller Duchies and Principalities— twenty-two in all. The new Constitution was there formally approved. The executive was vested in the King of Prussia as hereditary president, assisted by a federal chancellor; the Legislature was to consist of (i) a Federal Council (*Bundesrath*), consisting of plenipotentiaries from the Constituent States, and (ii) a *Reichstag*, elected by universal suffrage. There was to be compulsory military service throughout the Confederation on the Prussian model. The princes retained certain sovereign

North German Confederation

rights; they might still summon local Estates, levy local taxes, and be separately represented at foreign Courts, but the whole conduct of foreign affairs, the raising and control of the army, and the decision of peace and war were vested in the President.

But even this did not represent the full extent of Prussia's dominion over Germany. The chief Southern States, Bavaria, Baden and Würtemberg, concluded a Convention by which their armies were placed at the disposal of Prussia in time of war, and in 1867 they entered into a new commercial union with the Northern Confederation. The affairs of the *Zollverein* were to be settled by a Customs Parliament sitting in Berlin to which the Southern as well as the Northern States were to send deputies.

The Prussianisation of Germany was all but complete. But the final consummation of German unity was to be attained, by a certain dramatic irony, through the intervention of the hereditary enemy, who was even now watching with extreme jealousy the rapid growth of Hohenzollern power. The relations between Napoleon III. and Bismarck must, however, form the subject of a separate chapter.

Austria-Hungary

It remains to notice the reorganisation of the Habsburg dominions after the events of 1866. Excluded from Germany and expelled from Italy, Austria was at last compelled to come to terms with the Hungarian subjects who had been reconquered for her in 1849 by Russian arms. Many experiments had been tried since 1849 but the Magyars refused any settlement which did not recognise the independence of Hungary and the equality of the two Crowns. In 1867 a compromise (*Ausgleich*) was reached by the labours of Count Beust, who had

The Ausgleich

transferred his services from Saxony to Austria, and the Hungarian patriot Francis Deák. By this "dual system" the two Crowns of Austria and Hungary, and the two Legislatures were henceforth to be distinct, while affairs common to them both—foreign policy, war and finance—were to be controlled by common ministers. Each Legislature was, moreover, to appoint a "Delegation"—to meet alternately in Vienna and Pesth—for the discussion of affairs common to the two parts of the "dual Empire".

The system, though terribly complicated, has worked with tolerable success, thanks to the political and personal tact of the Emperor Francis Joseph. But that the problems raised by the racial jealousies of the many peoples united under his rule have been finally solved no observer of contemporary politics would venture to assert.

CHAPTER XX

THE SECOND EMPIRE AND THE FRANCO-GERMAN WAR

L'Empire c'est la paix.—NAPOLEON III.

The title I covet most is that of an honest man.—NAPOLEON III.

The great questions of the time are not to be solved by speeches and parliamentary votes but by blood and iron.—BISMARCK.

The Second Empire

THE circumstances under which the Second French Empire came to the birth have been already described.[1] In a speech delivered at Bordeaux in October, 1852, Napoleon had clearly defined his programme. The revived Napoleonic Empire would stand primarily for peace. "L'Empire," he said emphatically, "c'est la paix." We have already seen how far that promise was fulfilled during the first decade of the new régime. But if the Crimean War and the War of Italian Independence falsified promises, they were not without compensations in military and political prestige. No such compensation attached, as we shall see, to the wars of the second period of the reign.

But the Empire was to stand not only for peace, but for social, economic and moral reform. "I, like the Great Emperor, have many conquests to make. . . . I wish to conquer to religion, to morality, to prosperity, that part of the population, still so numerous, which, in the midst of a country of faith and belief, scarcely knows the pre-

[1] Chap. XIV.

cepts of Christ, which, in the heart of the most fertile country in the world can scarcely enjoy the prime necessities of its produce. We have immense districts of virgin soil to clear, roads to open, harbours to dig, rivers to render navigable, canals to finish, our network of railways to complete. We have, opposite Marseilles, a vast kingdom to assimilate to France. We have all our great ports of the West to bring near to the American Continent, by the rapidity of the communications we have yet to create. . . . Such are the conquests I meditate, and all of you who surround me, who desire like myself the welfare of our country, you are my soldiers." [1]

In this respect promises were not wholly unfulfilled. *Social* The emotions of the strange being who for twenty years *Reform* controlled the destinies of France were genuine though transient. Napoleon III. had a real interest in economic and social development, and during the first ten years of his reign much was done to redeem the pledges given at Bordeaux. The forces of anarchy were repressed; social order was restored; industry was encouraged; the means of communication were vastly improved; railways, canals and harbours were constructed; banks were established, and an impulse thereby given to agriculture and commerce; Paris was rebuilt and rendered more splendid and spacious if not more beautiful; schemes were promoted for workmen's dwellings, for insurance against accidents and old age; labour combinations were legalised; thrift was encouraged by benefit and co-operative societies; industrial exhibitions were organised, and a long step was taken towards freedom of commercial intercourse by the conclusion of the Cobden Treaty with England (1860). France had indeed surrendered political

[1] Quoted by Dickinson.

liberty, but the ensuing despotism was undeniably beneficent.

Consti-
tutional
Reform
Between 1860 and 1870 several steps were taken to liberalise the Constitution. The ministers continued (until 1869) to be responsible only to the Emperor, but the Legislature was permitted to criticise and even, within limits, to interrogate them, to initiate legislation and to publish its debates. The Empire thus ceased to be despotic; unfortunately, it ceased also to be efficient.

Foreign
Policy
The verdict of history may pronounce the Crimean War to have been a blunder, but, in the eyes of contemporaries, it enormously enhanced the prestige of the French Emperor. France undoubtedly occupied at the Peace of Paris (1856) a position to which she had been a stranger since the fall of the first Napoleon. History again can perceive that the War of Italian Independence gravely accentuated the difficulties of Napoleon. The annexation of the Romagna to the Italian kingdom alienated the French Clericals; the expulsion of the Bourbons from the Two Sicilies further estranged the legitimists; while the absorption of Savoy and Nice into France aroused the distrust of Europe. But contemporaries were dazzled by the military achievements of Magenta and Solferino, and by the territorial aggrandisement of France.

It needed no historical research to detect and expose the ruinous folly of the foreign policy of the second decade of the reign.

The
Mexican
Adventure
Anything more fatuous than Napoleon's policy in regard to Mexico it would be difficult to conceive.

The Mexican Republic had for some years been in a state of chronic disorder, intensified by civil war between the two parties into which its politicians were divided. In 1861 the republican leader Benito Juarez overthrew Miramon who represented the Clericals and Monarchists. Miramon appealed for support to the great Catholic Powers in Europe, and in this appeal Napoleon's vivid and fantastic imagination saw an opportunity for killing several birds with one stone. He determined to place on the throne of Mexico the Archduke Maximilian, brother of the Emperor Francis Joseph of Austria. In the choice of a candidate he displayed acumen. Maximilian was not only a member of a leading Catholic House, but was the husband of the Princess Charlotte, daughter of King Leopold of Belgium, and had won personal reputation as the ruler of Lombardy and Venice. His promotion to an Imperial throne might therefore be expected to gratify Habsburgs, Saxe-Coburgs and Orleanists, and thus soothe susceptibilities roused by recent French diplomacy. French Catholics would welcome an adventure which had something of the crusading spirit about it; the Empress Eugénie and her countrymen would rejoice in a monarchical triumph in Mexico; English, French and Spanish commercial interests would be served by the restoration of order and the payment of debts.

Juarez gave Napoleon a pretext for interference by the repudiation of the Mexican debt. England, Spain and France agreed to enforce payment, and a joint expedition was despatched for that purpose (January, 1862). But as soon as they discovered Napoleon's ulterior designs England and Spain withdrew, and France was left alone with an awkward job on her hands. Forty thousand French troops were poured into Mexico; opposition was crushed; an assembly of Mexican notables was induced to elect Maximilian as Emperor (July, 1863), and in May, *The Emperor Maximilian*

1864, that unfortunate prince arrived to take possession of his throne.

It soon became obvious that his throne and even his person was safe only so long as French bayonets surrounded him. In 1865 the bayonets were withdrawn. Napoleon had been tempted to the Mexican adventure partly by the præ-occupation of the United States of America (1861-65). But the American Civil War ended in 1865, and one of the first fruits of restored unity was an order to Napoleon to evacuate Mexico and a refusal to recognise Maximilian. Napoleon obeyed the order in 1867, and Maximilian, deserted by his patron, was left to confront his subjects. After a short but brave struggle he was taken prisoner and shot.

The Mexican tragedy was a terrible blow to the prestige of Napoleon, and contributed largely to his downfall. But a political gambler cannot withdraw from play after a ruinous loss. The Mexican disaster compelled Napoleon to stake all upon a last desperate throw. The Franco-Prussian War was the inevitable result.

Luxemburg

"The French Empire," says Lord Acton, "was imperilled as much as the Austrian by the war of 1866." "It is France which has been conquered at Sadowa," said Marshal Randon. These statements point to an important truth. The rapidity and completeness of the Prussian victories in 1866 entirely upset the calculations of Napoleon. He had watched with some uneasiness the growth of Hohenzollern power. But in 1865 Bismarck met Napoleon at Biarritz and secured his benevolent neutrality by the promise of compensation—perhaps a Rhine Province, or Luxemburg, or even Belgium. Napoleon swallowed the bait and allowed Prussia to make her plans for the overthrow of Austria. But he was dumbfounded by the event. Instead of coming in as a well-compensated arbiter at the close of a long conflict he found himself a humble suitor to Bismarck for an unconsidered trifle. The Rhenish Palatinate was his first suggestion. Bismarck laughed in his face and showed his letter to Bavaria, to whom the Palatinate belonged. The request served only to cement a Prusso-Bavarian Alliance. A demand for Belgium, probably stimulated by Bismarck himself, had no better result for Napoleon, but served Bismarck's purposes admirably. Published to the world in 1870 the proposal alienated English sympathies from France. Luxemburg remained.

The Grand Duchy of Luxemburg was peculiarly situated. It was included in the German Confederation, ruled by the King of Holland, and garrisoned by Prussia. Foiled elsewhere Napoleon negotiated with the King of the Netherlands for the purchase of Luxemburg. The King was willing, but Bismarck demurred. Neither France nor Prussia, however, was quite ready for war, and the question was settled by a Conference of the Powers in London (May, 1867). By the Treaty of London the Grand Duchy was neutralised under European guarantee; the King of Holland retained the sovereignty; the fortifications of Luxemburg itself were demolished and the Prussian garrison was withdrawn. Napoleon's last chance of a " compensation " disappeared.

He now tried to persuade himself and his friends that no " compensation " was really necessary ; that Germany was weakened rather than strengthened by the events of 1866. But the military and commercial rapprochement between Prussia and the Southern States proved the hollowness of such professions.

Meanwhile things were going badly elsewhere for

Napoleon. From the Italian dilemma no escape was possible. To abandon Rome meant a rupture with the French Clericals; to retain it meant the forfeiture of Italian support in the impending struggle with Prussia. At home the outlook was gloomy. The finances, already embarrassed by profusion and corruption, became further involved by the Mexican fiasco; constitutional concessions earned little gratitude; worst of all, Napoleon's own health was failing. Prestige must at all costs be recovered in the interests of the dynasty. Would anything avail but a brilliantly successful war?

The Hohenzollern Candidature in Spain

A pretext for war was found in the Hohenzollern candidature for the throne of Spain. Having got rid of their Queen Isabella, the Spaniards in 1869 declared for a Constitutional Monarchy, and offered their throne to Prince Leopold of Hohenzollern-Sigmaringen. Prince Leopold hung back; but Bismarck procured a renewal of the offer, and on 4th July, 1870, it was accepted by the Prince.

Napoleon immediately (6th July) intimated to Prussia that France would regard the accession of a Hohenzollern to the throne of Spain as a *casus belli*, and on 12th July Prince Leopold, at his own instance, revoked his acceptance of the Crown. Once more war seemed to have been averted, but, with almost incredible fatuity, Napoleon now demanded that the King of Prussia should not merely express formal approval of Prince Leopold's revocation, but should also promise "that he would not again authorise this candidature". This rather insolent demand was presented to the King at Ems by Benedetti, the French ambassador (13th July). The King declined to go beyond his approval of the revocation.

Bismarck's chance had come. He had been patiently

waiting for it since 1866. "That a war with France would succeed that with Austria lay," in his judgment, "in the logic of history". That such a war was the one thing needful to complete and consolidate German unity was also part of his conviction. That it might restore to Germany Alsace and Lorraine, unrightfully withheld in 1815, was his hope.

Authorised by his master to inform the ambassadors and the Press of the events which had passed at Ems, Bismarck, after consultation with Moltke and Roon, did so in terms which were designed to inflame passions both in Paris and Berlin[1] (14th July). It certainly fulfilled its object. The Parisian populace demanded war, and the Empress Eugénie and the Duc de Gramont pressed it upon the Emperor and the Cabinet. Napoleon was not ready, and he knew it. Bismarck also knew it, and precipitated the conflict while craftily making France appear as the aggressor.

The French declaration of war reached Berlin on 19th July. The Prussian preparations were complete. Within three weeks Roon poured 500,000 men into France, and had a second 500,000 ready to replace them if they fell. On 20th July Bavaria threw in her lot with Prussia, and on 2nd August the war began.

France was without allies. There had been much negotiation between Napoleon and the Emperor of Austria, but no actual treaty had been concluded. Napoleon imagined that he would be able to march into South Germany as a liberator and that Austria would

The Franco-German War

---

[1] Bismarck's part in precipitating the outbreak of war has been endlessly discussed: *cf. e.g.,* Acton, *Historical Essays;* Rose, *European Nations;* Bismarck, *Reminiscences;* Ollivier, *L'Empire libéral.*

then join him.   In both expectations he was disappointed.
Bismarck had squared Alexander of Russia by the hint
that it would be a convenient opportunity to tear up the
Treaty of Paris (1856).   Russia in return kept Austria
quiet.   France had no friends.   Germany rose as one
man.

The war itself was short and sharp.   The French
soldiers displayed splendid courage and dash, but they
were badly led and hopelessly outnumbered; there
was no organisation, no strategy, no supplies.   Mac-
Mahon was defeated at Weissenburg (4th August) by the
Crown Prince of Prussia; still more seriously in the
bloody encounter at Wörth (6th August), and was driven
back on Chalons.   On the same day Prince Frederick
Charles (the "Red Prince") and Steinmetz drove back
the French under General Frossard from Spicheren (6th
August).   On the 18th the Germans won the battle of
Gravelotte, and Marshal Bazaine, who commanded the
French, shut himself up in Metz.   Leaving Prince
Frederick Charles to blockade Metz the Germans advanced, under the Crown Prince, on Paris.   MacMahon,
ordered to advance from Chalons to the rescue of Bazaine
at Metz, was caught with his fine army of 130,000 men
by the Germans at Sedan (1st September).   The French
fought with splendid but fruitless gallantry; they were
completely outnumbered and outmanœuvred, and on 2nd
September Napoleon surrendered to the King of Prussia.
The Emperor himself and more than 80,000 Frenchmen
became prisoners of war.   The first phase of the war was
over; it had lasted exactly a month.

The Third
Republic

The military disaster at Sedan was immediately
followed by political revolution in Paris.   The Empire
collapsed; the Empress fled to England, and a Republic

was proclaimed (4th September, 1870). A "Government of National Defence" was hastily formed under General Trochu, Governor of Paris, Jules Favre and Gambetta. Thiers declined office, but set off on a tour to the European Courts to try to persuade them to mediate on behalf of France. Towards the end of the year Bismarck was seriously afraid that intervention might rob Germany of some of the fruits of the war; but his plans had been laid too well, and Thiers's efforts, though heroic, were unavailing.

It was hoped that Sedan might end the war; but Bismarck's determination to have Alsace and Lorraine, coupled with Favre's note to the Powers declaring that he would not "yield an inch of French soil, nor a stone of French fortresses," rendered its prolongation inevitable. On 20th September Paris was besieged by the Crown Prince, and the Republic established a supplementary seat of Government at Tours. Gambetta escaped from Paris in a balloon (7th October), assumed a virtual dictatorship and set himself with immense energy and skill to organise the national defence. The first necessity was to succour the beleaguered capital. But on 11th October the Germans defeated the army of the Loire and occupied Orleans. Meanwhile two crushing blows befel the French arms on the Eastern frontier. Strassburg, after a fine resistance, surrendered on 28th September, and a month later Bazaine, with shameful pusillanimity if not positive treachery, delivered the great fortress of Metz, together with 150,000 men and immense stores into the hands of the enemy (28th October). France reeled under the shock of Bazaine's treason, but Gambetta's spirit was unquenchable. He ordered a *levée en masse* (2nd November), and a vigorous campaign on the Loire created

The Siege of Paris

Surrender of Metz

15

in November and December some diversion. Orleans was recaptured (9th November) and a desperate attempt was made to relieve Paris. But both on the South and on the North the Germans repelled all attacks and gradually closed in upon the capital; a final sortie failed on 21st January, 1871, and on the 28th Paris capitulated. An armistice was granted to permit the election of a National Assembly which met at Bordeaux (12th February) and elected Thiers Head of the State. Preliminaries of peace were signed on 26th February and finally ratified at Frankfort on 10th May.

Peace of Frankfort   France ceded to Germany the whole of Alsace (except Belfort), and Eastern Lorraine, together with the great fortresses of Metz and Strassburg, and agreed to pay an indemnity of five milliards of francs within three years. German troops were to be left in occupation until the indemnity was paid.

The Paris Commune   Thanks to the astonishing recuperative power displayed by France and to the patriotism of her thrifty citizens the indemnity was paid before the stipulated day, and her soil was freed from the foreigner. But political did not keep pace with financial recovery. Even while the Germans were at the gates an attempt had been made in Paris to overthrow the Government of National Defence (31st October, 1870). Hardly were the preliminaries of peace signed before the revolutionary forces, always near the surface in Paris, broke loose, and the Hotel de Ville was seized (18th March) by a mob consisting partly of fanatics but chiefly of the ordinary Parisian canaille. The National Guard had been permitted to retain their arms when the rest of the garrison surrendered; the troops fraternised with them and shot their commanders; Thiers and the Chamber withdrew to Versailles, and Paris was handed over to an insurrectionary Commune elected on

26th March. The situation was curious. The German flag still waved over St. Denis: the tricolour over Versailles: the red flag of the Commune over Paris itself. The Government were now compelled to reconquer the capital if France was not to be dissolved in anarchy. Between 2nd April and 21st May, 1871, Paris suffered a second siege far more horrible and destructive than the first. Terrible atrocities were committed on both sides, and when, after six weeks' siege, the Government were again masters of Paris, they found the city in ruins and in flames. The insurgents were ruthlessly shot down; 10,000 persons were exiled or imprisoned, and gradually public order was restored; but not for four years was the Republic definitely established. Thiers was elected President on 31st August, 1871, and held office until 1873. To him France owes the restoration of her credit, financial and political; the reorganisation of her military system on the basis of universal service, and the establishment of the Third Republic.

The Third Republic

In 1873 Thiers was succeeded by Marshal MacMahon —a pronounced monarchist; but the anti-republicans, though in a majority in the Chamber, were hopelessly divided among themselves. Napoleon III. died in England in 1873, and six years later his dynasty ended with the death of the young Prince Imperial in South Africa (1879). Between the legitimists and the Orleanists there was perpetual discord. The Comte de Chambord, as representing the legitimists, refused to abate one jot of his pretensions, or to part with one of his prejudices, even though the price of obstinacy were to be the perpetual exclusion of his house from the throne of France. Under these circumstances the moderates of all parties agreed to the establishment of a Conservative Republic in 1875.

There was to be a President elected by a National Assembly for a term of seven years, and advised by a Cabinet of ministers responsible to the Chambers. Thus the French at last abandoned their old prejudices in favour of a division between the executive and Legislature and adopted the Cabinet system of England. The Legislature was vested in two Chambers: a Senate of 300 members elected for nine years by a process of double election; and a Chamber of Deputies elected by universal suffrage for four years. Admittedly provisional in many of its details the Constitution of 1875 has already had a longer life than any Constitution of the nineteenth century in France; and under it, despite periodic unrest, France has settled down at home and regained a great position abroad.

German Unity

But the destruction of the Second Empire and the establishment of the Third Republic were not the most significant results of the Franco-German War. That must be found in the fact that it placed the coping-stone upon the edifice of German unity, and hardly less directly upon that of Italy.

Napoleon's primary purpose in plunging into war was to arrest the progress of Prussia and to prevent the unification of Germany. Bismarck welcomed and precipitated war in the conviction that only war with France was needed to crown his life-work. And Bismarck calculated while Napoleon guessed. Had the Southern States been disposed to hang back, the revelation of Napoleon's negotiations for the Palatinate would have convinced them of the hollowness of his friendship. There was no hanging back in 1870. The whole Teutonic folk were united against the foe who had laboured for three centuries to keep Germany divided and impotent.

With dramatic irony the Hall of Mirrors in the palace The German Empire of Versailles was selected for the scene of the formal proclamation of German unity. The terms of union had been already settled between Prussia and the Southern States—Baden, Würtemberg, Hesse[1] and Bavaria—and had been ratified by the Diet of the North German Confederation. On 18th January, 1871, King William of Prussia was formally proclaimed first German Emperor at Versailles. The old King accepted the Imperial Crown as the gift not of the German people, but of his fellow princes. Three months later the new Constitution was promulgated (16th April, 1871). The North German Confederation was enlarged to include all the German States south of the Main (except German Austria), and was transformed into a Federal Empire under the hereditary presidency of the Prussian King. The Emperor, assisted by an Imperial Chancellor, responsible only to himself, controls the executive, while the Legislature is vested in a Federal Council (*Bundesrath*) representing the sovereign princes, and a *Reichstag* elected for five years by universal suffrage to represent the people. Thus was Bismarck's great task accomplished : the Prussianisation of Germany was complete.

Doubts have been expressed whether the German Empire will endure. It has even been suggested that in 1860 the Second Empire seemed as firmly established in France as the Hohenzollern Empire in Germany to-day. There is no parallel between them. The Bonapartist Empire was born in dishonour, cradled in corruption and perished in political penury. The modern German

---

[1] *i.e.*, Hesse, south of the Main. In respect of his territory north of the Main the Grand Duke of Hesse was a member of the North German Confederation

Empire represents the long-delayed consummation of an historical evolution ; its institutions correspond to a genuine national necessity.   It is the Prussian monarchy which has made Germany, and Germany gratefully realises the fact.   The constituent States have lost something of their dignity and importance, but much less than is commonly supposed; and if they sometimes resent Prussia's overbearing methods, they are forced to acknowledge the solid advantages they derive from the union.   That union is founded upon community of interest, of language, of race and of historical tradition. Resting on such solid foundations it is not likely to be shaken.

CHAPTER XXI

AFTERWORD

THE year 1870-71 is the culminating point of the political history of the nineteenth century. It witnessed in France the collapse of the last of the monarchical experiments and the establishment of the Republic on foundations which have weathered many storms and have endured for thirty-five years. It witnessed the transference of the Italian capital from Florence to Rome and the consummation of the nationality movement in Italy. It witnessed the transformation of the North German Confederation into the German Empire and the consequent completion of German unity. It saw Russia reopen the Eastern Question by the abrogation of the Treaty of Paris, and heard the promulgation of the doctrine of Papal infallibility by the Vatican Council (18th July, 1870). To carry the narrative beyond that point would be to confuse the issue and to court the dangers of an anti-climax.

The nineteenth century had accomplished, in Europe, its characteristic work. The last thirty years have witnessed steady development and consolidation. But the development has taken place on lines clearly defined in 1870; there has been no fresh departure, no breach of continuity, no great territorial readjustment. The

231

modifications in the frontiers of Turkey[1] and Greece; the cession of Cyprus by Turkey to England (1878) and of Heligoland by England to Germany (1890), and the severance of Norway from Sweden (1905)—these represent the chief changes in the map of Europe between 1870 and the present time.

The really significant changes are to be looked for beyond the boundaries of Europe, and in the relation of the European Powers to questions of world-politics.

In the last thirty years Science has done much to annihilate space and time. The marvellous improvement in the means of communication and of transportation has caused a real shrinkage in the size of the world. London and Vancouver are now for all practical purposes as near each other as were London and Edinburgh in 1815. Calcutta is hardly further from the capital of the Empire than was Dublin at the time of the Union. As a result, the centre of political gravity has shifted; Africa, America Asia and Australia have begun to react upon Europe; the Chancelleries have to take account of extra-European States, and the mutual relations of the Powers themselves have been sensibly modified.

No country has been so much affected by this revolution in the conditions of world-politics as Great Britain. The scope of this volume forbids any detailed reference either to the foreign or the colonial policy of Great Britain, but no survey, however summary, would be complete which failed to notice the expansion of Britain in the nineteenth century.

The British Empire, 1800-1900   At the opening of the century the British Crown ruled over less than half as many subjects (20,000,000) as are now contained in the British Isles alone. It now rules

[1] See Chap. xiii.

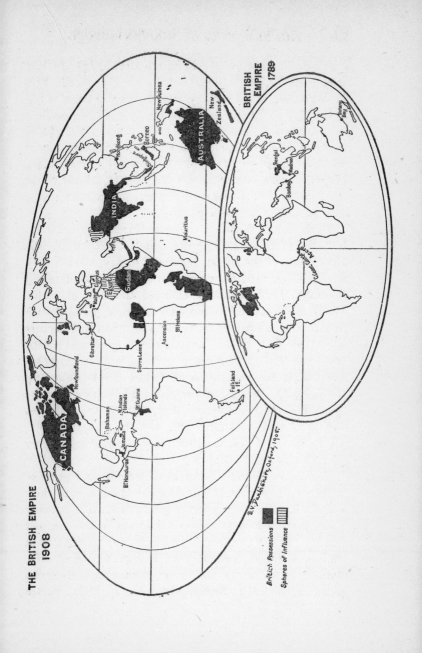

THE BRITISH EMPIRE
1908

BRITISH EMPIRE
1789

CANADA

Newfoundland

Gibraltar

Bahamas

Jamaica

Bʳ Honduras

W Indian
Islands

Bʳ Guiana

Sierra Leone

Ascension

St Helena

Falkland
Is

Malta

Cyprus

Egypt

Sudan

Mauritius

INDIA

Hong Kong

Singapore

Borneo

New Guinea

AUSTRALIA

New
Zealand

Bengal

Bombay

Madras

Botany
Bay

Cape Colony

British Possessions

Spheres of Influence

B.V. Darbishire, Oxford, 1906.

over nine times as many. (Empire = 394,553,581 : British Isles = 42,372,556.) In point of size the Empire which at the beginning of the century was only twelve times as big as the United Kingdom is now ninety-one times as big: in other words, His Majesty King Edward VII. rules over one United Kingdom in Europe and ninety others scattered over the face of the globe. (Area: U.K., 121,027 square miles: British Empire, 11,516,821.) Of the details of this marvellous transformation only a bare summary can be attempted.

India

When Lord Wellesley became Governor-general of India in 1798, we had hardly done more than lay the foundations of the Indian Empire of to-day, though they were laid secure in the possession of Bengal, Madras and Bombay. Lord Wellesley changed the map of India. The North-Western Provinces were brought under British rule by the campaigns of Lord Lake; the third Mysore war (1799) gave us the Carnatic and Tanjore, and constituted the Madras Presidency practically as it exists to-day; while the acquisition of Orissa (1804) linked up Madras with Bengal. Since Lord Wellesley's day we have added the Himalayan districts (1815), the Mahratta territories (1818), Sindh (1843), and the Punjab (1849), not to speak of Assam (1826), and Lower and Upper Burmah (1852 and 1886).

Canada

Canada, in 1800, consisted to all intents and purpose of the two provinces of Ontario and Quebec, with their western frontier resting on the great lakes. The opening out of the North-West has been the work of the last half century. When the Federal Dominion was constituted in 1867 it was composed only of four provinces, Quebec, Ontario, Nova Scotia and New Brunswick. Manitoba joined it in 1870, British Columbia in 1871, Prince

Edward Island in 1873 and the North-West Provinces in
1897, the latter having since been organised into the two
provinces of Alberta and Saskatchewan (1905). To bind
the East and West together in commercial no less than
political bonds the project of a trans-continental railway
was inaugurated in 1881. The work was pushed on with
remarkable vigour and rapidity, and the Canadian Pacific
Railway was opened in 1886. The great railway, running The C.P.R
from Montreal to Vancouver—a distance of 2,909 miles—
is perhaps the most important imperial enterprise of our
time. On strategic as well as commercial and political
grounds it is likely to prove of the highest value. Thanks
to the existence of the Canadian Pacific Railway it is
now possible to reinforce with supplies and men a
squadron at Vancouver from Great Britain in fourteen
days, and a squadron on the China Station in twenty-
five.

Passing from the Northern to the Southern hemisphere Australasia
a not less remarkable development is witnessed. In
1800 the only British subjects in Australasia were the
members of a convict settlement on the coast of New
South Wales. In 1821 New South Wales was opened to
free immigrants, and from that moment steady though
slow progress was made. Van Diemen's Land (now Tas-
mania) was separated from New South Wales in 1825,
and settlements were effected in Queeensland in 1826, in
Western Australia (1829), in Victoria (1836), and in New
Zealand (1840). In 1900 the five Australian Colonies
united into a Federal Commonwealth. Such was the
transformation witnessed in the course of the century in
the Southern Seas.

From Australasia we pass to South Africa. Occupied South
in the name of the Stadtholder of Holland in 1795 Africa

Cape Colony was, as we have seen,[1] handed back in 1802, reconquered in 1806, and finally purchased from the Dutch in 1814. But though transferred to the British flag the population of Cape Colony was still exclusively Dutch. Not until 1820 did British immigration make a start. Almost from the first there were difficulties between the British and the Dutch settlers. The emancipation of the slaves (1833) brought things to a crisis, and between 1836 and 1840 some 10,000 Boer farmers shook the dust of British control off their feet and "trekked" into the great regions beyond the Orange and Vaal rivers. Meanwhile a handful of British settlers established themselves at Port Natal (1824), and after some hesitation on the part of the Home Government Natal was declared a British colony in 1843. In regard to the Boers who had trekked to the North-East the British Government pursued a policy of lamentable inconsistency. In 1848 the sovereignty of the Queen was proclaimed over the whole district between the Orange and Vaal rivers. In 1852 the Government recognised, by the Sand River Convention, the independence of the Boers to the north of the Vaal, and in 1854, by the Bloemfontein Convention, that of the Boers to the south of it. Thus the Orange Free State was added to the Transvaal. In 1877 the Transvaal was annexed; re-ceded in 1881, and conquered and re-annexed, together with the Orange Free State, in 1902.

Meanwhile the sovereignty of Great Britain was being rapidly extended over other portions of Africa. East Africa, ruled by a Chartered Company from 1888, was taken over by the Crown in 1895, and Nigeria—a great

[1] P. 130.

district on the West Coast—after similar apprenticeship, was taken over in 1900.

But while British supremacy was steadily extending throughout Southern, Eastern, Western and Central Africa, events of even greater significance were taking place on its Northern shores.

For the last four hundred years the Eastern Mediter- Egypt and ranean—once the great waterway of commerce—had the Sudan sunk into the position of a mere backwater. Trade had deserted its shores for those of the Atlantic. The Ottoman conquest of Constantinople (1453) and Egypt (1516) had effectually blocked the old commercial routes, and the discovery of the new route to India by the Cape of Good Hope (1498) completed the ruin which Turkish conquest had begun. The decline of Turkish power in the eighteenth century and the contest between England and France for supremacy in India again recalled attention to the importance of the Eastern Mediterranean. Napoleon's attack on Egypt[1] was a significant hint that he appreciated its importance in relation to European supremacy in Asia. Nicholas I. was, as we have seen,[2] equally alive to England's interest in Egypt. In 1869 the Suez Canal was opened, and immediately the Mediterranean regained much of the importance it had lost. Disraeli showed his shrewd appreciation of the new situation when in 1875 he purchased the shares of the Khedive in the Suez Canal, and, in 1878, acquired Cyprus. The purchase of the Canal shares marked the beginning of a new policy. In 1876 England and France established in Egypt a joint financial control which quickly developed into political control. But in 1882 France declined to join England in repressing the rebellion of Arabi Pasha;

[1] See p. 64.   [2] p. 166.

England undertook the work single-handed, and in 1883 she established a "veiled protectorate" which has practically developed into a permanent occupation of Egypt. In the same year troubles broke out in the Sudan which led, after many sacrifices and vicissitudes, to the conquest of the Sudan (1898). Thus Great Britain is now in all but continuous occupation of Africa from Cairo to Cape Town, the continuity being broken only by German East Africa.

This summary treatment of India, Australia, North America and Africa by no means exhausts the tale of British expansion in the nineteenth century, expansion which has brought one-fifth of the whole area of the world under British rule.

Colonial Self-government

But not less important than territorial expansion has been the constitutional evolution of the British Colonial Empire. The two Canadas acquired in 1791 representative Legislatures, but without executives responsible to them. On the advice of Lord Durham, whose famous *Report* of 1839 is a landmark in colonial history, Responsible Government was granted to Canada in 1840, and at the same time the two Canadas (Ontario and Quebec) were united. Self-government worked well, but union did not, and in 1867 by the *British North America Act* the four provinces of Ontario, Quebec, Nova Scotia and New Brunswick were formed into a Federal Dominion. Other provinces have since joined it.[1]

The example of Canada fired the Australasian Colonies. Between 1850 and 1890 the several Colonies of Australia and New Zealand were admitted to the privileges of Self-government, and in 1900 the Australian Colonies united

[1] See p. 234.

in a *Federal Commonwealth* on the Canadian model. Similarly in South Africa : Responsible Government was granted to Cape Colony in 1872, to Natal in 1893 and to the recently annexed Transvaal and Orange River Colonies in 1906 and 1907 respectively. It can hardly be doubted that the South African Colonies will, before long, follow the example of the North American and Australian Colonies and unite in some form of federation.[1]

The extraordinary growth of the British Empire has been the chief factor in the shrinkage of the world. It has also excited, not unnaturally, similar aspirations on the part of other European Powers.

Down to 1870 Germany and Italy were too fully occupied with the task of internal unification to give heed to world-politics. France also was busy throughout the century with domestic revolutions. But the completion of German and Italian unity, and the secure establishment of the French Republic have been followed by excursions into world-politics. Thus in 1881 France established a "protectorate" over Tunis, and subsequently annexed that country. In 1884 the same power compelled China to recognise her protectorate over Anam and Tonkin, and in 1893, taking advantage of the Russian Alliance, France enlarged the boundaries of her Indo-Chinese provinces until they met our own to the north of Siam. Russia had, of course, long been active not only in Persia, but in the "farther East," and in 1898 obtained a "lease" of Port Arthur from China. Germany at the same time obtained a "lease" of Kiao-chau, France of Kwang-chau-wan, and Great Britain of Wei-hai-wei. Germany, meanwhile, had in 1884 de-

World-politics

---

[1] This prediction has already (1910) been fulfilled, though the new South African Constitution is technically not federal but unitary.

finitely embarked upon a policy of colonial expansion in Africa, and in 1890 concluded a treaty with Great Britain delimiting the boundaries of the German Colonies in East and South-West Africa.

U.S.A.

These bare facts are sufficiently indicative of the change coming over world-politics ; but more significant still was the war between the United States and Spain and the results following thereon (1898). Hitherto the United States, while warning off the European Powers from interference on the American Continent, had carefully abstained from anything which might involve them in the complications of a foreign policy. The occupation of Cuba and the annexation of the Philippines announced to the world a new departure. Henceforward the United States was to be reckoned among the " Powers," a fact further emphasised by their participation in the Hague Conferences and in the international expedition organised for the suppression of the Boxer insurrection in China in 1900. It is noticeable that in the mixed contingent which in that year marched to Pekin, Japanese troops also were to be found side by side with the forces of the European Powers.

The Nationality Principle

It would be out of place to do more than hint at these significant events. They obviously herald the approach of a new era in world history. They mark not so much the close of the nineteenth century as the dawn of the twentieth. The period with which this book is concerned historically ended with the great events of 1870-71. Passing reference has been made to some subsequent events simply for the purpose of throwing into bolder relief the characteristic work of the nineteenth century. That work consisted in the revelation of the potent force of nationality as a principle of unification and a principle of disruption. Liberated by the French Revolution and emphasised by the Napoleonic wars, that principle found its most conspicuous illustration in the unification of Germany and Italy; in the quickening of dead bones in the provinces subject to the rule of the Turk; and above all, perhaps, in the movement towards the political unification of the British race scattered in a hundred homes throughout the world.

That is the principle which gives unity and coherence to the myriad phenomena of the period under review. At first sight diverse, unrelated, and even contradictory, they are seen to obey a definite political law. In obedience to that law, during the last hundred years, modern Europe has been remade.

Note.—For amplification of the statements in these concluding paragraphs reference may be made to my *Europe and Beyond* (Methuen, 2nd Edition, 1925), which was written as a sequel to the present volume.

16

HOUSE OF BONAPARTE

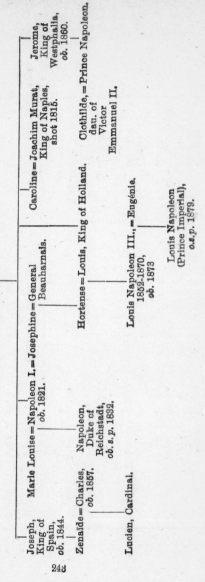

Charles Buonaparte = Letitia Ramolino.

Joseph, King of Spain, *ob.* 1844.

Zenaïde = Charles, *ob.* 1857.

Lucien, Cardinal.

Marie Louise = Napoleon I. = Josephine = General Beauharnais. *ob.* 1821.

Napoleon, Duke of Reichstadt, *ob. s. p.* 1832.

Hortense = Louis, King of Holland.

Louis Napoleon III., = Eugénie. 1852-1870, *ob.* 1873

Louis Napoleon (Prince Imperial), *o.s.p.* 1879.

Caroline = Joachim Murat, King of Naples, shot 1815.

Clothilde = Prince Napoleon, dau. of Victor Emmanuel II.

Jerome, King of Westphalia, *ob.* 1860.

BOURBON KINGS OF FRANCE, SHOWING ORLEANS BRANCH

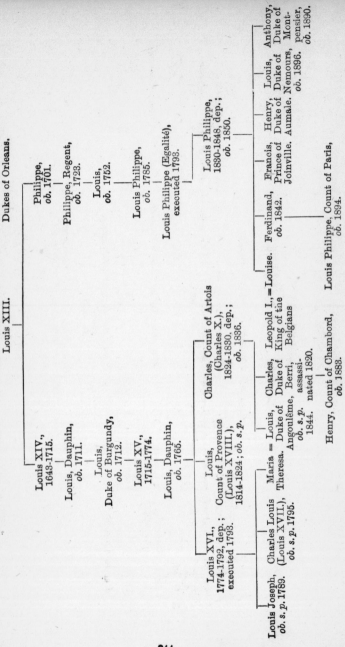

Louis XIII.

Dukes of Orleans.

Philippe, *ob.* 1701.

Philippe, Regent, *ob.* 1723.

Louis, *ob.* 1752.

Louis Philippe, *ob.* 1785.

Louis Philippe (Egalité), executed 1793.

Louis Philippe, 1830-1848, dep.; *ob.* 1850.

Ferdinand, *ob.* 1842.—Louise.

Francis, Prince of Joinville.

Henry, Duke of Aumale. *ob.* 1896.

Louis, Duke of Nemours, *ob.* 1896.

Anthony, Duke of Montpensier, *ob.* 1890.

Louis Philippe, Count of Paris, *ob.* 1894.

Louis XIV., 1643-1715.

Louis, Dauphin, *ob.* 1711.

Louis, Duke of Burgundy, *ob.* 1712.

Louis XV., 1715-1774.

Louis, Dauphin, *ob.* 1766.

Louis, Count of Provence (Louis XVIII.), 1814-1824; *ob. s. p.*

Charles, Count of Artois (Charles X.), 1824-1830, dep.; *ob.* 1836.

Maria = Louis, Duke of Theresa. Angoulême, *ob. s. p.* 1844.

Charles, Duke of Berri, assassinated 1820.

Leopold I., = Louise. King of the Belgians

Henry, Count of Chambord, *ob.* 1883.

Louis XVI., 1774-1792, dep.; executed 1793.

Louis Joseph, *ob. s. p.* 1789.

Charles Louis (Louis XVII.), *ob. s. p.* 1795.

HOUSE OF HABSBURG-LORRAINE

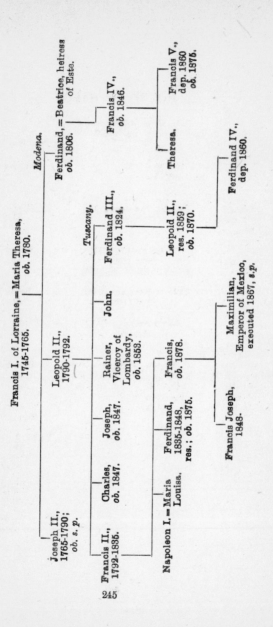

Francis I. of Lorraine, = Maria Theresa, 1745-1765. *ob.* 1780.

Modena.

Ferdinand, = Beatrice, heiress *ob.* 1806. of Este.

Francis IV., *ob.* 1846.

Francis V., dep. 1860 *ob.* 1875.

Theresa.

Tuscany.

Leopold II., 1790-1792.

Ferdinand III., *ob.* 1824.

Leopold II., res. 1859; *ob.* 1870.

Ferdinand IV., dep. 1860.

Joseph II., 1765-1790; *ob. s. p.*

John.

Rainer, Viceroy of Lombardy, *ob.* 1853.

Francis, *ob.* 1878.

Maximilian, Emperor of Mexico, executed 1867, *s. p.*

Joseph, *ob.* 1847.

Ferdinand, 1835-1848, res.; *ob.* 1875.

Francis Joseph, 1848-

Charles, *ob.* 1847.

Francis II., 1792-1835.

Napoleon I. = Maria Louisa.

245

HOUSE OF SAVOY

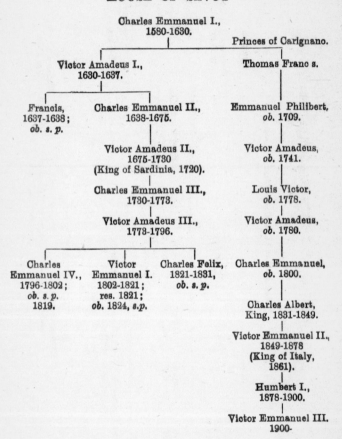

Charles Emmanuel I.,
1580-1630.

Princes of Carignano.

Victor Amadeus I.,
1630-1637.

Thomas Franc s.

Francis,
1637-1638;
ob. s. p.

Charles Emmanuel II.,
1638-1675.

Emmanuel Philibert,
ob. 1709.

Victor Amadeus II.,
1675-1730
(King of Sardinia, 1720).

Victor Amadeus,
ob. 1741.

Charles Emmanuel III.,
1730-1773.

Louis Victor,
ob. 1778.

Victor Amadeus III.,
1773-1796.

Victor Amadeus,
ob. 1780.

Charles
Emmanuel IV.,
1796-1802;
ob. s. p.
1819.

Victor
Emmanuel I.
1802-1821;
res. 1821;
ob. 1824, *s.p.*

Charles Felix,
1821-1831,
ob. s. p.

Charles Emmanuel,
ob. 1800.

Charles Albert,
King, 1831-1849.

Victor Emmanuel II.,
1849-1878
(King of Italy,
1861).

Humbert I.,
1878-1900.

Victor Emmanuel III.
1900-

246

HOUSE OF BRANDENBURG

Frederick I., first King of Prussia, **1701,**
1688-1713.
|
Frederick William I.,
1713-1740.
|

Frederick II., the Great,   Augustus William,
1740-1786 ;   *ob.* 1758.
ob. s. p.

Frederick William II.,
1786-1797.

Frederick William III.,
1797-1840.

Frederick William IV.,   William I.,
1840-1861 ;   succ. 1861 ;
ob. s. p.   " German Emperor,"
1871.

Frederick (III. of Prussia),
March-June, 1888.

William II.,
1888-

APPENDIX II

SHORT LIST OF BOOKS ON THE PERIOD
1789-1878

The following list is in no sense exhaustive, but is merely intended for those who wish to fill in the sketch presented in the foregoing pages. For an elaborate bibliography reference may be made to *Cambridge Modern History*, vols. viii.-x.

A. FOR BEGINNERS

The general history of Europe (1792-1880) may be studied in C. H. Fyffe's *History of Modern Europe*, or more briefly in Lodge's *Modern Europe*, together with a good atlas. *e.g.*, Putzger's or Rothert's, iv. v. b, or Ramsay Muir's.

Among special books on particular chapters, I have included some historical novels.

Chaps. II.-V. :—

> Mallet : *French Revolution.*
> Mahan : *Influence of Sea Power upon the French Revolution and Empire.* (Vol. I., chaps. i., ii.; II., pp. 361-380, and chaps. xvi., xviii., xix.)
> Willert : *Mirabeau* ("Foreign Statesmen").
> Belloc : *Danton.*
> Morley : *Robespierre.*
> Arthur Young : *Travels in France.*

Novels :—

> Dumas : *Ange Pitou; La Comtesse de Charny*, and *Chevalier de Maison Rouge.*
> Erckmann-Chatrian : *Histoire d'un paysan* and *Madame Thérèse.*

Victor Hugo : *L'an '93.*
Stanley Weyman : *Red Cockade.*
Dickens : *Tale of Two Cities.*

Chaps. VI.-XI. :—

Rose : *Life of Napoleon.*
Seeley : *Napoleon.*

Novels :—

Gilbert Parker : *Battle of the Strong.*
Merriman : *Barlasch of the Guard.*
Balzac : *Les Chouans.*
Charles Lever : *Charles O'Malley.*

Chaps. XII., XIV. :—

Jervis and Hassall : *Student's France.*

Chaps. XIII., XV. :—

Alison Phillips : *Greek War of Independence.*
Holland : *Treaty Relations between Russia and Turkey.*

Novels :—

Jokai : *Lion of Janina.*
E. F. Benson : *Vintage.*
Tolstoy : *Sevastopol.*

Chaps. XVI., XVII. :—

Countess Cesaresco : *Liberation of Italy.*
Marriott : *Makers of Modern Italy.*
Bolton King : *Mazzini.*

Novel :—

George Meredith : *Vittoria.*

Chaps. XVIII.-XX. :—

Malleson : *Refounding of German Empire.*
Headlam : *Bismarck.*
Bismarck : *The Man and the Statesman* (trans. A. J. Butler).

Novel :—

Zola : *La Débâcle.*

B. FOR MORE ADVANCED STUDENTS

I.—*General.*

Heeren: *Political System of Europe.*
Rose: *Revolutionary and Napoleonic Era.*
Morse Stephens: *Revolutionary Europe* (1789-1815).
Alison Phillips: *Modern Europe* (1815-1880).
Lavisse et Rambaud: *Histoire Générale.* Vols. viii.-xii.
Seignobos: *Histoire Politique de l'Europe Contemporaine.*
C. M. Andrews: *The Historical Development of Modern Europe* (from 1815).
Kirkpatrick (ed.): *Lectures on the History of the Nineteenth Century.*
Rose: *The Development of the European Nations* (1870-1900).

For the Geography :—

Poole: *Historical Atlas* (Maps, which can be bought separately, Nos. 11, 12, 13, 14, 42, 43, 59, 70, 82, 89).
Himly: *La Formation Territoriale.*

II.—*On Particular Chapters.*

Chaps. II.-V. :—

De Tocqueville: *France before* 1789 (*L'Ancien Régime*).
Sorel: *L'Europe et la Revolution Française.*
Morse Stephens: *French Revolution.*
Cherest: *La Chute de l'Ancien Régime.*
Cambridge Modern History, vol. viii.
Carlyle's *French Revolution* (edited by Rose or Fletcher).
Lord Acton: *Lectures on French Revolution.*
Aulard: *French Revolution.*

Chaps. VI.-XII. :—

Rose: *Napoleonic Studies.*
Fisher: *Napoleonic Studies.*
Fournier: *Napoleon I.*
Oman: *Peninsular War.*
Sorel: *Le Traité de Paris.*
Cambridge Modern History, vol. ix.

Chap. XII., XIV. :—

Dickinson: *Revolution and Reaction in Modern France.*
Marriott: *George Canning and his Times.*

Malleson: *Metternich.*
Hassall: *Castlereagh.*
Pierre de la Gorce: *Histoire du Second Empire.*
H. A. L. Fisher: *Bonapartism.*
Hanotaux: *La France Contemporaine.*
Cambridge Modern History, vol. x. (The Restoration).

Chaps. XIII., XV. :—

Rambaud: *Russia.*
Odysseus; *Turkey in Europe.*
Finlay: *History of the Greek Revolution.*
Driault: *La Question d'Orient.*
Kinglake: *Invasion of the Crimea.*
Holland: *The European Concert in the Eastern Question.*

Chaps. XVI., XVII. :—

Johnston: *Napoleonic Empire in Southern Italy.*
Bolton King: *History of Italian Unity.*
Stillman: *Union of Italy.*
Thayer: *Life and Times of Cavour.*
Trevelyan: *Garibaldi's Defence of the Roman Republic.*
Trevelyan: *Garibaldi and his Thousand.*
Trevelyan: *Garibaldi and the making of Italy.*
Cambridge Modern History, vols. xi. and xii.

Chaps., XVIII., XIX. :—

Sybel: *Die Begründung des Deutschen Reichs* (translated).
Denys: *La Foundation de l'Empire Allemand.*
Fisher: *Studies in Napoleonic Statesmanship* (Germany).
Metternich: *Memoirs.*
Asseline: *Histoire de l'Autriche depuis Marie Thérèse.*
Auerbach: *Les Races et Nationalités en Autriche-Hongrie.*
Busch: Various works on *Bismarck.*

Chap. XX. :—

Sorel: *Histoire Diplomatique de la Guerre Franco-Allemande.*
Chuquet: *Precis de la Guerre Franco-Allemande.*
Lord Acton: *Historical Essays.*

INDEX

Abo, Treaty of, 106, 120.
Abercromby, Sir Ralph, 68.
Aberdeen, Lord, 167.
Aboukir, battle of, 65.
Acre, siege of, 65.
Adrianople, Treaty of, 151.
Africa, 236.
Aix-la-Chapelle, Congress of, 133.
Ajaccio, 57.
Albuera, battle of, 99.
Alexander I., Czar, 68, 111, 119, 121, 132, 149, 150.
Alexander II., Czar, 168, 169, 224.
Alexander Couza, Prince, 169.
Alexander of Battenberg, Prince, 171.
Alexandria, battle of, 68.
Algiers, 136.
Alma, battle of, 167.
Almeida, 99.
Alsace, 46.
Alsace-Lorraine, 43, 125, 126, 225.
Amberg, battle of, 59.
Amiens, Treaty of, 43, 68.
Ancona, 177, 188.
Andrassy, Count, 170.
Angoulême, Duc d', 142.
Anhalt, 213.
Anselme, General, 38.
Arabi Pasha, 237.
Arcola, battle of, 60.
Argyll, 8th Duke of, 176.
Armed Neutrality League, 68.
Artois, Count of (see Charles X.), 31, 73, 122.
Aspern-Essling, battle of, 95.
Aspromonte, battle of, 189.
Assembly, the Constituent, 28.
— the Legislative, 29.
Association of Young Italy, 178.

Athens, 150.
Auerstadt, battle of, 85.
Augereau, 61.
Austerlitz, battle of, 80, 83.
Australia, 8, 235, 239.
Austria, 34, 54, 62, 77, 80, 83, 94, 95, 106, 127, 128, 177, 180, 181, 182, 183, 184, 185, 186, 190, 210, 213.
Austrian Netherlands, 5, 33, 37, 214.

Badajos, 99.
Baden, 77, 128, 201, 214, 229.
Bagration, General, 110.
Bailly, 49.
Balkan Peninsula, 6.
Barclay de Tolly, General, 110.
Barras, 56, 61.
Barrot, Odillon, 155, 160.
Basle, Treaties of, 52.
Bastille, the, 13, 21.
Batavian Republic (see Holland), 54, 63, 68, 76.
Bautzen, battle of, 113.
Bavaria, 77, 201, 214, 223, 229.
Baylen, capitulation of, 92.
Bazaine, Marshal, 224, 225.
Beaconsfield, Lord, 170, 172.
Belgium, 7, 46.
Benedetti, Count, 222.
Bentinck, Lord William, 174.
Beresford, Lord, 139.
Berg, Duchy of, 98.
Berlin, 201; decree of, 85; memorandum of 170.
— Treaty of, 171.
Bernadotte, 84, 105, 114, 117.
Berri, Duc de, 135.
Beust, Count, 214.

Bismarck, 190, 193, 207, 208, 210, 211, 220, 221, 222, 223, 224, 225, 228.
Blanc, Louis, 159, 161.
Bloemfontein, Convention of, 236.
Blücher, General, 114, 115, 116, 123.
Boers, the, 236.
Bohemia, 202.
Bologna, 177.
Bonaparte, Jerome, 82, 115, 184.
— Joseph, 81, 91, 100.
— Louis, 81, 98.
Borodino, battle of, 110.
Bosnia, 169.
Boulogne, 78.
Bourbons, the, 71, 73, 91, 117, 122, 123.
Bourmont, 135.
Boxer Insurrection, the, 240.
Braganza, House of, 89.
Brazil, 144.
Bremen, 213.
Brissot, 30, 46, 48.
British Empire, 8, 231, 239.
Brumaire, *coup d'état* of 18th, 65, 71.
Brunswick, Duke of, 35, 36, 95.
Brunswick, 19, 201, 213.
Bucharest, peace of, 6, 105, 146.
Bulgaria, 171, 172.
Bund, the Germanic, 128, 194, 197, 208, 213.
Burgos, 93.
Burke, 42, 43, 71.
Burrard, Sir Harry, 93.
Busaco, battle of, 99.
Byron, Lord, 149.

CADOUDAL, GEORGES, 73.
Calder, Sir Robert, 79.
Camperdown, battle of, 63.
Campo-Formio, Treaty of, 60, 62, 64.
Canada, 234, 238.
Canning, George, 88, 92, 132, 142, 149, 151.
Canrobert, 168.
Cape Colony, 8, 63, 130, 236.
Cape Finisterre, battle of, 79.
Cape St. Vincent, battle of, 63.
Capodistrias, 151.

Carbonari, the, 176, 177, 178.
Carlyle, Thomas, 27, 48.
Carnot, 46, 56, 61.
Castel Fidardo, battle of, 188.
Castlereagh, 119, 132, 141, 142, 148
Caulaincourt, 116.
Cavour, 182, 184, 185, 186, 187, 188, 189, 191.
Ceylon, 8, 130.
Chambord, Comte de, 127, 137, 155.
Champ de Mars, 28.
Charleroi, 123.
Charles Albert of Sardinia, 178, 179, 180, 181.
Charles Felix, 176.
Charles, Archduke, 94, 95.
Charles IV. of Spain, 90, 91.
Charles X. of France (see Artois) 133, 135.
Châtillon, Congress of, 116.
Chaumette, 49.
Chaumont, Treaty of, 116, 123.
Chauvelin, 44.
China, 239.
Church property, 25.
Church, General, 150.
Cintra, Convention of, 93.
Cisalpine Republic, 60.
Cispadane Republic, 60.
Ciudad Rodrigo, 99.
Clootz, Anarcharsis, 50
Clotilde, Princess, 184.
Coalition, First, 54.
— Second, 66.
— Third, 77.
Coblentz, 35.
Cochrane, Lord, 150.
Code Napoléon, 75.
Collingwood, Admiral, 78.
Committee of Public Safety, 46.
Commune, the, 36, 226.
Concordat of 1801, 75.
Condorcet, 30.
Confederation of the Rhine, 81, 103.
—*North German, 213.
Constantinople, 145, 151, 156, 171, 237.
— Conference of, 170.
Constitution of the Year VIII., 71, 74.
Continental System, the, 85, 98, 104.

Convention, National, 38.
Copenhagen, 88.
— battle of, 68.
Cornwallis, Admiral, 78.
Corsica, 57.
Council of Ancients, 55.
— — Cinq-Cent, 55.
Couthon, 50.
Cuba, 240.
Custine, 37.
Custozza, battle of, 181.
Crete, 169.
Crimean War, 166, 183, 216.
Cyprus, 171, 232.

Danton, 28, 36, 37, 50.
Danzic, 115.
Darmstadt, 201.
Déak, Francis, 215.
Decazès, 135.
Decree of December 15th, 1792, 40.
Denmark, 210.
Desmoulins, Camille, 29, 49, 50.
Diebitsch, General, 151.
Directory, the, 55.
Dresden, 113, 114, 115.
Droit au Travail, 158.
Ducos, 70.
Dumouriez, 34, 36, 46.
Dunkirk, 46.
Dupont, 92.
Durham, Lord, 238.

Eastern Question, 145, 165, 169.
Egypt, 63, 64, 68, 150, 166, 237, 238.
Emancipation, edict of, 107.
Emigrés, the, 33, 48, 55.
Empire, the Second, 162.
Enghien, Duc d', 73.
England, 34, 40, 54, 63, 76, 77, 85, 86, 166, 168, 237.
Erfurt, Treaty of, 103.
Erzeroum, 151.
Eugénie, Empress, 164, 219, 223, 224.
Eylau, battle of, 87.

Favre, Jules, 225.
Ferdinand of Austria, 95, 202.

Ferdinand I. of Naples, 129, 139, 140, 174.
Ferdinand II. (Bomba) of the Two Sicilies, 180, 182, 187.
Ferdinand VII. of Spain, 117, 134, 137.
Ferdinand, Prince of the Asturias, 91.
Feuillants, the, 29.
Fichte, 94.
Finland, 5, 88, 103, 127, 130.
Fleurus, 54.
Fontainebleau, Decree of, 86.
— Treaty of, 91, 116.
Fouché, 73, 134.
Fourier, 159.
Fox, Charles James, 39, 41, 83.
France, 2, 7, 10, 43, 44, 53, 223, 224, 228, 231, 237, 239.
Francis II. of Austria, 81, 116.
Francis II. (Bombino) of the Two Sicilies, 187.
Francis Joseph of Austria, 190, 203, 205, 208, 215, 223.
Franco-Prussian War, the, 190, 220, 228.
Frankfort-on-Main, 5, 128.
Frankfort Parliament, the, 204.
— peace of, 226.
Frederick of Augustenburg, 210.
Frederick VII. of Denmark, 210.
Frederick Charles of Prussia, 224.
Frederick William II. of Prussia, 33.
Frederick William III. of Prussia, 77, 84, 95, 107, 109, 112, 113, 200, 201, 204, 205, 207, 208.
Frossard, General, 224.
Fructidor, coup d'état of, 61.
Fuentes de Onoro, battle of, 99.

Gambetta, Leon, 225.
Gantheaume, 78.
Garibaldi, 181, 187, 188, 189, 190.
Garnier-Pagès, 160.
Gastein, Convention of, 211.
Gaudet, 30.
Genoa, 7, 58.
Gensonné, 30.
George, King of Greece, 152.
Germany, 4, 81, 128, 193, 194, 196, 198, 201, 205, 224, 225, 239.

German Empire, the, 229, 231.
German Liberation, war of, 112, 114, 129.
Ghent, peace of, 130.
Gioberti, Vincenzo, 179, 182.
Girondins, the, 29, 30, 32.
Gneisenau, 108.
Godoy, 90, 91.
Gramont, Duc de, 223.
Gravelotte, battle of, 224.
Great Britain, 2, 130, 232, 238, 239.
Greece, 151, 169, 232.
Greek Revolt, the, 148.
Gregory XVI., Pope, 174, 179.
Grouchy, General, 124.
Guadet, 30.
Guiana, 77.
Guizot, 155, 157, 159, 160.
Gustavus IV., King of Sweden, 77.

HABSBURGS, the, 194, 202, 204.
Hamburg, 213.
Hanover, 5, 77, 84, 128, 197, 201, 212.
Hanse Towns, the, 98.
Hardenberg, 94, 107, 125, 197.
Haugwitz, 77, 84.
Hébert, 49.
Heligoland, 232.
Herzegovina, 169.
Hesse, 5, 229.
Hesse-Cassel, 197, 201, 212.
Hoche, 55, 63.
Hohenlinden, battle of, 67.
Hohenzollern, the, 194, 213, 220, 222, 229.
Holland, 7, 98.
— King of, 221.
Holy Alliance, the, 132, 174.
Hondschoote, battle of, 46.
Hood, Admiral, 46.
Hostages, Law of, 74.
Howe, Admiral, 53, 54.
Hudson, Sir James, 185.
Huguenots, the, 14.
Humboldt, 94, 108, 119.
Hundred Days, the, 126.
Hungary, 127, 202, 203.
Hypsilanti, Prince Alexander, 149.

IBRAHIM PASHA, 150.
Imperial, the Prince, 227.

India, 130, 234.
Inkermann, battle of, 167.
Ireland, 63.
Isabella, Queen of Spain, 158.
Italian War of Independence, 216.
— Republic, 76.
Italy, 6, 57, 58, 127, 129, 139, 174, 178, 183, 190, 191, 202, 231.

JACOBINISM, 42.
Jacobins, the, 27, 29, 47, 49, 52.
Jaffa, 65.
Jassy, Treaty of, 6.
Jemappes, battle of, 37.
Jena, battle of, 85.
John, Archduke, 95.
John, Prince of Saxony, 151.
John VI. of Portugal, 139, 144.
Josephine, Empress, 57, 98.
Jourdan, 53, 58.
Juarez, Benito, 219.
Junot, 89.
Juntas, the, 100.

KAINARDJI, Treaty of, 6, 146, 151.
Kalisch, Treaty of, 112, 120, 127.
Kapolna, battle of, 203.
Karlsbad Decrees, 197.
Kars, 151, 168.
Kossuth, 202, 203.
Kotzebue, 196.

LABOURDONNAIE, Count, 135.
Lafayette, 28, 29, 35.
Laibach, Congress of, 133, 141.
Lamartine, 155, 160, 161.
La Marmora, General, 167.
Langensalza, battle of, 212.
Laon, battle of, 116.
La Rothière, battle of, 116.
Lauenberg, Duchy of, 5.
Ledru-Rollin, 160.
Legion of Honour, 76.
Leipzic, battle of, 114.
Leopold, Emperor, 33, 34.
Leopold of Hohenzollern Sigmaringen, 222.
Leopold of Saxe-Coburg (King of the Belgians), 151, 154.
Leopold of Tuscany, 180.
Lewis of Bavaria, 201.

Liancourt, Duc de, 13.
Ligny, battle of, 123, 124.
Ligurian Republic, the, 60, 76.
Lisbon, 89.
Lombardy, 6, 58, 181, 186.
London, Treaties of, 156, 157, 210, 221.
Longwy, 36.
Louisa, Queen of Prussia, 85.
Louis XIV., 14.
Louis XV., 14.
Louis XVI., 10, 24, 27, 34, 35, 37, 38, 40, 133.
Louis XVII., 55.
Louis XVIII., 117, 122, 125, 133, 135.
Louis Philippe (see Duc d'Orleans), 136, 155, 157, 158, 160.
Louisiana, 68.
Lübeck, 213.
Lunéville, peace of, 67.
Luxemburg, Duchy of, 221.

Maassen, 199.
Mack, General, 80.
MacMahon, Marshal, 224, 227.
Madrid, 100.
Magenta, battle of, 186, 218.
Magnano, battle of, 66.
Malakoff, the, 168.
Malta, 64, 76.
Mandat, 36.
Manin, Daniel, 180.
Mantua, siege of, 60, 186.
Marengo, battle of, 67.
Marie Antoinette, Queen, 34, 35, 48.
Marie Louise, Empress, 98, 104, 129, 177.
Marmont, Marshal, 99, 136.
Maro-Jaroslavitz, battle of, 111.
Martignac, 135.
Martinique, 78.
Masséna, 99.
Maximilian, Archduke, 219.
Maximilian II. of Bavaria, 201.
Mazzini, 174, 177, 178, 179, 181, 187.
Mecklenburg-Schwerin, 213.
Mecklenburg-Strelitz, 213.
Mediterranean, the, 237.

Mehemet Ali, 150, 156.
Mentana, battle of, 190.
Metternich, 105, 113, 119, 128, 132, 140, 174, 176, 177, 180, 196, 197, 198, 200, 202, 204.
Metz, siege of, 224, 225.
Mexico, 218, 219, 220.
Miguel of Portugal, Dom, 139, 143.
Milan, 59, 180, 186.
— decree of, 86.
Mirabeau, 12, 23, 26, 27, 84.
Miramon, 219.
Missiessy, 78.
Missolonghi, 150.
Modena, 181, 186.
Modena, Duke Francis of, 177.
Moldavia, 88, 103, 169.
Molé, Count, 160.
Mollien, 109.
Moltke, 207, 223.
Monroe Doctrine, the, 143.
Montenegro, 169, 170.
Montesquieu, 26.
Montesquieu, General, 37.
Montpensier, Duc de, 158.
Moore, Sir John, 93.
Moreau, 58, 73.
Moscow, 110.
Mount Tabor, 65.
Münchengrätz, Conference of, 198.
Murat, Joachim, 91, 125.
Mysore War, 234.

Naples, 6, 77, 174, 180, 188.
Napoleon I,, Bonaparte, 2, 18, 44, 56, 57, 60, 61, 64, 69, 70, 72, 73, 76, 81, 85, 86, 91, 92, 93, 95, 96, 98, 105, 109, 110, 113, 114, 116, 121, 122, 123, 173, 196, 237.
Napoleon III., 161, 162, 163, 165, 181, 183, 185, 186, 211, 214, 216, 217, 220, 221, 223, 224, 227.
Nassau, 5, 201.
National Assembly, the, 12, 21, 24, 42.
— workshops, the, 161.
Navarino, battle of, 150.
Necker, 13, 17, 25.
Neerwinden, battle of, 46.

Nelson, 64, 68, 78.
Nemours, Duc de, 154.
Neo-Guelphs, the, 179, 182.
Nesselrode, Count, 119.
Netherlands, the Belgian, 127, 130, 153, 154.
— the Spanish, 5, 7.
New Zealand, 8.
Ney, Marshal, 123, 134.
Nice, 38, 184, 187, 218.
Nicholas I., Czar, 150, 166, 168, 203, 237.
Nightingale, Florence, 167.
Nile, battle of, 64.
Norway, 130, 232.
Novara, battle of, 176, 181, 182.

OLDENBURG, 98, 104, 213.
Orders in Council, 86.
Orebro, Treaty of, 106
Orleans, Duc d' (see Louis Philippe), 136.
Orsini, 184.
Otto of Bavaria, 151, 152.

PALAFOX, 92.
Palermo, 180, 187.
Palestine, 165.
Palm, 85.
Palmerston, 154, 156, 157, 167, 184.
Pampeluna, 100.
Papal infallibility, 192, 231.
— States, the, 98.
Paris, Comte de, 160.
Paris, Peace of, 168.
— First Treaty of, 117.
— 20, 21, 46, 61, 65, 121, 124, 225, 226, 227.
Parma, 181, 186.
Paul, Czar, 68.
Pedro of Portugal, Dom, 139.
Pekin, 240.
Pellisser, Marshal, 168.
Peninsula, the, 99.
Peninsular War, 44.
Pentarchy, the, 154, 157.
Philippe Egalité, 49.
Philippines, the, 240.
Pichegru, 61, 73.
Piedmont, 6, 58, 76, 180, 182.

Pilnitz, declaration of, 34.
Pitt, William, 42, 43, 44, 64, 65, 77, 82, 146.
Pius VII., Pope, 98, 117.
Pius IX., Pope, 163, 179, 180, 181, 188.
Plevna, siege of, 170.
Plombières, 184.
Poland, 5, 54, 121.
Polignac, Count Paul de, 135, 136.
Port Arthur, 239.
Portugal, 88, 89, 93, 139, 143.
Prague, Treaty of, 212.
Prairial, law of 22nd, 50, 52.
Pressburg, Treaty of, 80.
Provence, Count of, 31.
Prussia, 4, 35, 54, 77, 80, 83, 84, 85, 106, 107, 127, 128, 190, 194, 198, 199, 208, 211, 212, 213, 214, 222.
Prussian Crown Prince, 224.
Pyramids, battle of, 64.

QUATRE BRAS, battle of, 123.
Quadruple Treaty, 132.
Quiberon Bay, battle of, 55.

RADETSKY, 181.
Raglan, Lord, 167, 168.
Ranke, 15.
Reason, the Feast of, 49.
Reichenbach, Treaty of, 113, 120.
Reichstag, the, 213.
Republic, the Third, 227.
Revolution, French, 13, 240.
— of 1830, 177.
— of 1848, 160, 161.
Richelieu, Duc de, 14, 134.
Ried, Treaty of, 120.
Rivoli, battle of, 60.
Robespierre, 28, 34, 39, 47, 50, 51.
Roland, Madame, 30, 48.
Romagna, the, 168, 218.
Rome, 64, 181, 190, 191.
— King of, 98, 124.
Roon, General, 206, 207, 211, 223.
Rossi, Count, 181.
Roumania, 169, 172.
Rousseau, 18, 19.
Russia, 5, 77, 87, 105, 127, 130, 131, 146, 169, 170, 229, 239.

SADOWA (Koniggrätz), battle of, 212.
St. Arnaud, 167.
St. Cloud, ordinances of, 136.
St. Helena, 125.
St. Just, 50.
St. Lucia, 77, 130.
St. Simon, 159.
Salamanca, battle of, 100.
Sambre, the, 123.
Sand River Convention, the, 236.
San Martino, 186.
San Sebastian, 100.
San Stephano, Treaty of, 171.
Santerre, 29.
Saragossa, 92.
Sardinia, 6, 54, 173, 186.
Savoy, 37, 184, 187, 218.
Saxe-Coburg-Gotha, 213.
Saxe-Weimar, 213.
Saxony, 85, 95, 121, 197, 201, 212, 213.
Scandinavia, 7.
Scharnhorst, 94, 108.
Scheldt, the, 40, 41, 96.
Schiller, 94.
Schleswig-Holstein, 5, 210.
Schönbrünn, Treaty of, 80, 84.
Schwarzenberg, 203, 205, 206, 214, 215.
Sebastopol, battle of, 167.
Sedan, battle of, 224, 225.
Servia, 169, 170.
Seymour, Sir Hamilton, 166.
Sicilies, the Two, 218.
Sicily, 6.
Sierra Morena, the, 99.
Siéyès, Abbé, 29, 70, 72.
Sinope, battle of, 167.
Smith, Adam, 17, 18.
Smolensko, 110.
Solferino, battle of, 186, 218.
Sonderbund, the, 157, 159.
Soult, Marshal, 99, 100.
Spain, 54, 63, 90, 92, 240.
Spanish Colonies, the, 142, 143.
— marriages, the, 158.
Stadion, Count, 94.
States-General, the, 10, 11, 19.
States, United, the, 130, 240.
Stein, 94, 107, 109, 112, 113, 128.
Steinmetz, 224.

Stewart, Lord, 140.
Stockach, battle of, 66.
Strassburg, 225.
Stratford de Redcliffe, Lord, 167.
Sudan, the, 238.
Suez Canal, the, 237.
Sultan of Turkey, 103, 105.
Suspects, law of, 48.
Sweden, 88, 103, 106, 130, 232.
Switzerland, 64, 76, 129, 157.

TALAVERA, battle of, 93, 96, 99.
Talleyrand, 116, 119, 134.
Tauroggen, Convention of, 112.
Tchernaia, battle of, 183.
Terror, the, 48, 49.
Thiers, 136, 155, 157, 160, 225 227.
Tilsit, Treaty of, 87, 89, 103, 127 146.
Tobago, 77, 130.
Tocqueville, Alexis de, 14.
Todleben, General, 167.
Tolentino, peace of, 59.
Töplitz, Treaty of, 120.
Torres Vedras, lines of, 99.
Toulon, 46, 47.
Trafalgar, battle of, 79, 86.
Transpadane Republic, 60.
Trinidad, 130.
Trochu, General, 225.
Troppau, Congress of, 133, 146.
Tunis, 239.
Turgot, 17, 18.
Turin, 187, 188.
Turkey, 65, 150, 232.
Turks, the Ottoman, 145, 171, 237.
Tuscany, Grand Duke of, 54, 81.
Tuscany, 6, 58, 180, 186.

ULM, capitulation of, 80.
United Provinces, the, 33.
Unkiar Skelessi, Treaty of, 156.

VARENNES, 28.
Valmy, cannonade of, 37.
Vendée, la, 46, 49.
Vendémiaire, coup d'état of 13th, 56.
Venetia, 186, 190, 211.
Venice, 7, 58, 70.
Verdun, 35.

Vergniaud, 30, 35, 46, 48.
Verona, 133, 141.
Versailles, 24, 229.
Victoria, Queen, 158.
Victor Emmanuel I., 117, 129, 176.
Victor Emmanuel II., 181, 182, 184, 185, 186, 189, 190, 191.
Vienna, 180, 202, 203, 212.
— Congress of, 119, 131.
— Treaty of, 96, 210.
Vieux Cordelier, le, 49.
Villafranca, truce of, 186.
Villèle, 135, 141.
Villeneuve, Admiral, 78.
Vimiero, battle of, 92.
Vittoria, battle of, 100.
Voltaire, 15, 19.

Wagram, battle of, 96.
Walcheren, 96.
Wallachia, 88, 103, 169.
Warsaw, decree of, 86.
Waterloo, battle of, 1, 124.
Wattignies, battle of, 46.

Wavre, 124.
Weimar, 201.
Wellesley, Lord, 234.
Wellesley, Sir Arthur (see Wellington), 92, 93.
Wellington, Duke of, 114, 119, 122, 126, 142, 151, 152.
Weissenburg, battle of, 224.
William I. of Prussia, 207, 229.
William of Orange, 115.
Windischgrätz, Prince, 202.
Wörth, battle of, 224.
Wurmser, 60.
Würtemberg, 77, 128, 201, 214, 229.
Würzburg, 59.

Yorck, General, 112, 113.
York, Duke of, 46.
Young, Arthur, 17, 22.

Znaim, armistice of, 96.
Zollverein, the, 199, 204, 205, 214.
Zürich, Treaty of, 186.

PRINTED IN GREAT BRITAIN AT THE UNIVERSITY PRESS, ABERDEEN